*To Sula and Miriam*

# THE LAST CRUSADE

# THE LAST CRUSADE

## The Palestine Campaign in the First World War

Anthony Bruce

JOHN MURRAY
*Albemarle Street, London*

First published in 2002
by John Murray (Publishers) Ltd,
50 Albemarle Street, London W1S 4BD

The moral right of the author has been asserted

A catalogue record for this book is available from the British Library

ISBN 0-7195-5432 2

Typeset in Monotype Bembo 12/13.5
by Servis Filmsetting Ltd, Manchester

Printed and bound in Great Britain by
Creative Print and Design (Wales),
Ebbw Vale, Gwent

# Contents

# Illustrations

The author and publishers would like to thank the following for permission to reproduce illustrations: Plates 1, 6 and 9, © Hulton Archive; 2, 3, 4, 5, 8, 10, 11, 12, 13, 14, 15, 16, 17, 18, 19, 20, 21, 22, 23, 24, 25, 26, 27, 28, 29, 30 and 31, Imperial War Museum, London.

# Preface

THE HISTORY OF the protracted struggle between the Ottoman empire and the British and their Arab allies for control of Palestine and Syria during the First World War has been dominated by the presence of T.E. Lawrence. The unresolved controversies surrounding Lawrence's role as a leader of the Arab revolt have ensured that there is a continuing interest in this aspect of the conflict and a stream of publications to support it. But this represents only one dimension of a complex campaign which raises a host of interesting issues about how Britain was drawn into the area, how the war was conducted and what effect it had on imperial interests in the post-war period.

This book provides the first full account in recent times of the whole Palestine campaign and how British and Arab forces worked together eventually to bring about the final collapse of Ottoman authority throughout the Middle East. The starting point for any understanding of these operations and how they were conducted is to examine their relationship to the wider wartime strategy of Turkey and Britain. The changing military priorities of both sides affected their commitment to this theatre, and whether troops were withdrawn or allocated to the Palestine front depended on the course of military events in other areas to which they chose to give greater priority.

This review of grand strategy provides the context for a complete narrative account of the campaign from the first enemy incursions into Egyptian territory in late 1914 to the final Allied dash to Aleppo in the closing stages of the war. The war is examined from the perspective of the opposing commanders and the choices they were faced with. This includes the decision to forge close links between the Allied armies and the leaders of the Arab revolt. The need for effective leadership was clearly an important element in determining the outcome of the campaign but it was not the only one. The

British formed the largest desert column in history as they set out across Sinai in 1916 but its effectiveness would depend on the capacity of the rank and file to fight in conditions of extreme heat, widespread disease and serious supply shortages. Extracts from soldiers' unpublished letters and diaries held in British archives give a clear insight into local conditions and how they affected troops with no experience of the desert. These same sources confirm that the Turks could still be formidable opponents despite the fact that they were fighting for an empire in terminal decline.

Such archival material provided a major source for this book but other sources were equally important in reconstructing the course of events. The three-volume British official history produced by Sir George MacMunn and Cyril Falls, both distinguished military historians, provides a detailed account of the progress of Allied forces that cannot be found elsewhere. Lord Wavell, who served on Allenby's staff in Palestine in 1917–18, produced the only other notable account of the campaign. The Arab revolt has been even less well served by historians although the many Lawrence biographies provide more or less detail of the course of military events in the Hejaz and further north. One notable exception is Jeremy Wilson's substantial authorized biography of Lawrence. It is the most detailed account of his life available. More importantly, it gives access to a wide range of archival and documentary material that could not otherwise be easily obtained. Few historians can match the power of T. E. Lawrence's prose in the *Seven Pillars of Wisdom* and his wartime correspondence which record vividly and in great detail how the uprising unfolded. Allenby has until recently been less well served by biographers but the recent study by Matthew Hughes sets new standards. Like Lawrence, Allenby was an outstanding leader whose reputation has largely survived criticism by revisionist historians.

I would particularly like to acknowledge the efforts of archive staff at the Centre for Military Archives, King's College, London, the Imperial War Museum and the National Army Museum in retrieving a wide range of unpublished material that forms the basis of this study. The British Library and the London Library provided ready access to most of the printed sources. The idea for this book was developed in conjunction with Andrew Lownie, my agent, and it was through his efforts that it became a reality. I have valued the support and commitment of Grant McIntyre, editorial director of John Murray, who has shown great forbearance throughout the long gestation period of this book. His colleagues have played an important role in turning my original typescript into a publishable text, among them Howard Davies as a result of whose efforts many errors and inconsistencies have been removed. This book has been produced entirely outside normal working hours and could not have been completed without the active support of my wife and daughter. I have dedicated it to them.

# Maps

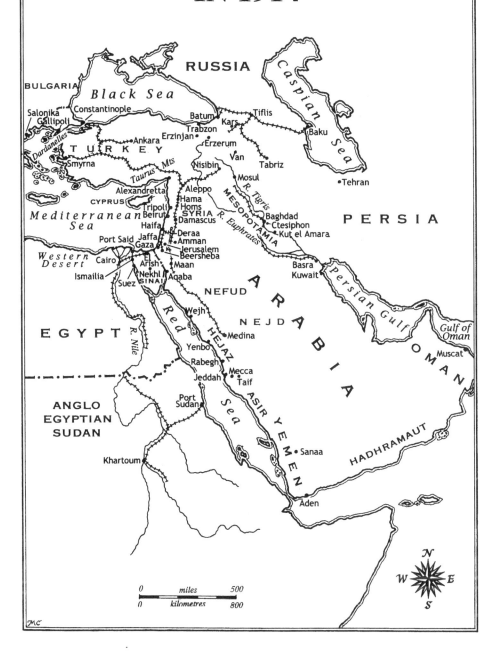

# THE
# TURKISH EMPIRE
# IN 1914

RUSSIA

BULGARIA

Black Sea

Caspian Sea

Salonika
Gallipoli
Constantinople
Dardanelles
Batum
Kars
Tiflis
Trabzon
Baku
Ankara
Erzinjan
Erzerum
TURKEY
Smyrna
Taurus Mts
Van
Nisibin
Tabriz
Mosul
Tehran
Alexandretta
Aleppo
R. Tigris
CYPRUS
Hama
Homs
MESOPOTAMIA
Tripoli
Beirut
SYRIA
Baghdad
PERSIA
Mediterranean
Sea
Damascus
R. Euphrates
Ctesiphon
Haifa
Kut el Amara
Port Said
Jaffa
Gaza
Deraa
Amman
Western
Desert
Cairo
El
Arish
Jerusalem
Beersheba
Maan
Basra
Kuwait
Ismailia
Nekhl
Aqaba
Suez
SINAI
NEFUD
A
Persian Gulf
Gulf of
Oman
EGYPT
R. Nile
Red
Wejh
NEJD
R
OMAN
Muscat
Sea
HEJAZ
Medina
B
Yenbo
Rabegh
Jeddah
Mecca
Taif
I
ANGLO
EGYPTIAN
SUDAN
Port
Sudan
ASIR
YEMEN
A
HADHRAMAUT
Khartoum
Sanaa
Aden

N
W        E
S

0        miles        500
0        kilometres        800

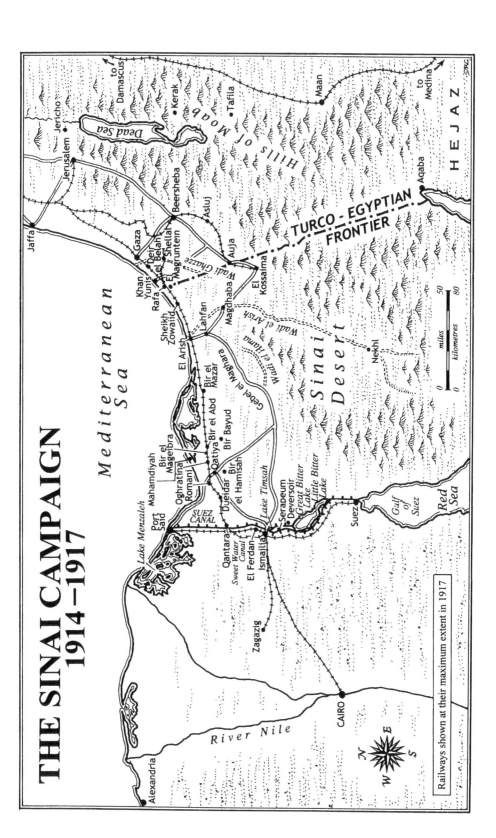

# THE SINAI CAMPAIGN 1914–1917

*Mediterranean Sea*

Alexandria

Port Said
Lake Menzaleh

CAIRO

*River Nile*

Zagazig

Qantara
Sweet Water Canal
El Ferdan
Ismailia
SUEZ CANAL

Romani
Oghratina
Mahamdiyah
Bir el Mageibra
Bir el
Magein...

Djeidar
Bir el Hamisah
Qatiya

Lake Timsah
Serapeum
Deversoir
Great Bitter Lake
Little Bitter Lake
Suez

*Gulf of Suez*

*Red Sea*

Bir el Abd
Bir Bayud
Gebel el Maghara

Bir el Mazar

El Arish
Sheikh Zowaiid
Lahfan

Magdhaba

Wadi el Hama
Wadi el Arish

*Sinai Desert*

Nekhl

Khan Yunis
Rafa

Gaza
Deir el Belah
El Magruntein
Shellat

El Kossaima
Auja

*Wadi Ghazze*

Jaffa

Jerusalem
Beersheba
Asluj

Jericho
to Damascus
*Dead Sea*

Kerak
Tafila

*Hills of Moab*

Maan

TURCO - EGYPTIAN FRONTIER

Aqaba

HEJAZ

to Medina

miles 0 50
kilometres 0 80

N
W E
S

Railways shown at their maximum extent in 1917

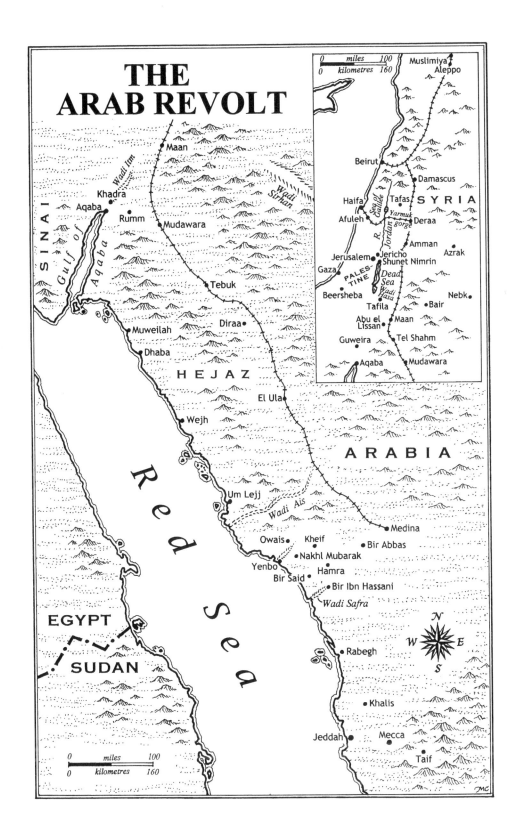

# THE ARAB REVOLT

**Inset map:**

miles 0 — 100
kilometres 0 — 160

Muslimiya
Aleppo

Beirut
Damascus

Haifa · Tafas · SYRIA
Sea of Galilee
Afuleh · Yarmuk gorge · Deraa
R. Jordan

Amman
Azrak

Jerusalem · Jericho
Shunet Nimrin
Gaza

PALES-TINE
Dead Sea
Wadi Hasa

Beersheba
Nebk

Tafila
Bair

Abu el Lissan · Maan

Guweira · Tel Shahm

Aqaba · Mudawara

**Main map:**

Maan

Wadi Itm

Khadra
SINAI
Aqaba
Rumm
Mudawara

Gulf of Aqaba

Wadi Sirhan

Tebuk

Muweilah
Diraa

Dhaba

HEJAZ

El Ula

Wejh

ARABIA

Um Lejj

Wadi Ais

Owais · Kheif
Medina
Nakhl Mubarak
Bir Abbas

Yenbo
Hamra
Bir Said
Bir Ibn Hassani

Wadi Safra

Red Sea

EGYPT

N
W · E
S

SUDAN

Rabegh

Khalis

Jeddah · Mecca

Taif

miles 0 — 100
kilometres 0 — 160

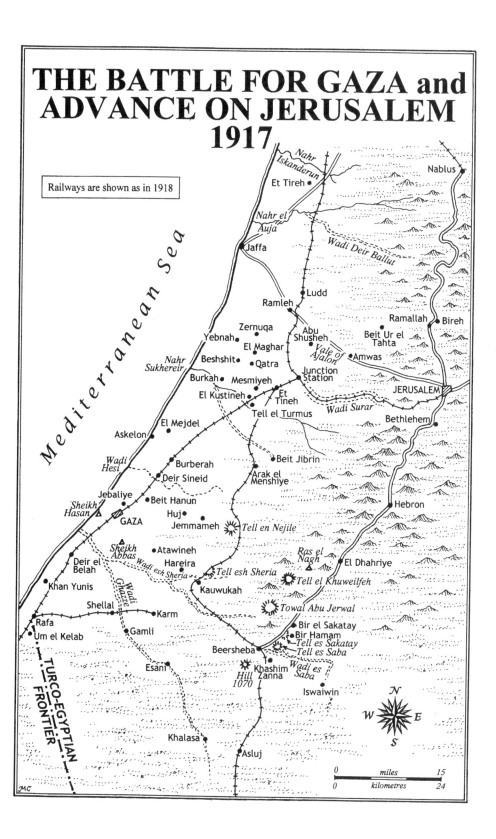

# THE BATTLE FOR GAZA and ADVANCE ON JERUSALEM 1917

Railways are shown as in 1918

*Mediterranean Sea*

*Nahr Iskanderun*

Et Tireh

Nablus

*Nahr el Auja*

Jaffa

*Wadi Deir Ballut*

Ludd

Ramleh

Ramallah • Bireh

Zernuqa

Abu Shusheh

Beit Ur el Tahta

Yebnah

El Maghar

*Vale of Ajalon*

Amwas

*Nahr Sukhereir*

Beshshit • Qatra

Burkah • Mesmiyeh

Junction Station

JERUSALEM

El Kustineh • Et Tineh

Tell el Turmus

*Wadi Surar*

Bethlehem

El Mejdel

Askelon

Beit Jibrin

*Wadi Hesi*

Burberah

Deir Sineid

Arak el Menshiye

Jebaliye

Beit Hanun

Hebron

*Sheikh Hasan* △

GAZA

Huj •

Jemmameh ☀ *Tell en Nejile*

*Ras el Nagh* △

*Sheikh Abbas* △

• Atawineh

Hareira

El Dhahriye

Deir el Belah

*Wadi esh Sheria*

Tell esh Sheria ☀ *Tell el Khuweilfeh*

Khan Yunis

*Wadi Ghuzze*

Kauwukah

Shellal

Karm

☀ *Towal Abu Jerwal*

Rafa

• Bir el Sakatay

Um el Kelab

Gamli

• Bir Hamam

Tell es Sakatay

Beersheba

Tell es Saba

Esani

Khashim Zanna *Wadi es Saba*

☀ *Hill 1070*

Iswaiwin

*N*

*W* ☀ *E*

*S*

TURCO-EGYPTIAN FRONTIER

Khalasa

Asluj

| 0 | | miles | | 15 |
| 0 | | kilometres | | 24 |

JMC

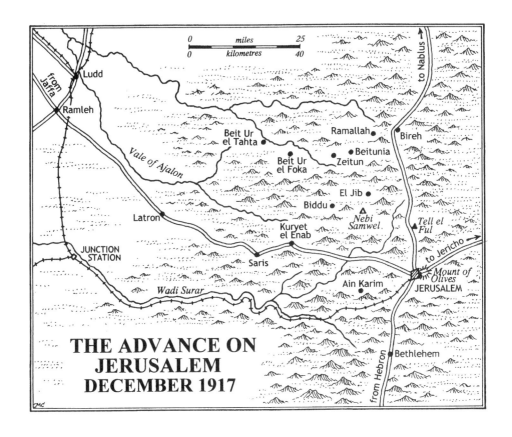

## THE ADVANCE ON
## JERUSALEM
## DECEMBER 1917

# THE PUSH NORTH, 1918

## THE BATTLE OF MEGIDDO
### 18 SEPTEMBER 1918

Haifa
Mt Carmel
Tiberius
Nazareth
Samakh
Abu Shusheh
Jisr el Mejamie
El Afule
El Lejjun (Megiddo)
Beisan
Jenin
*Plain of Sharon*
Iskanderum
Tul Keram
Messudieh
*Wadi el Fara*
*River Jordan*
Arsuf
*Hills of Samaria*
Nablus
Jisr ed Damieh
Ludd
Ramleh
Ramallah
Jericho

miles 25
kilometres 40

JERUSALEM

Gulf of Iskanderun
Alexandretta
Antioch
Aleppo
*R. Orontes*
Seraqab
Hama
Homs
Tripoli
Baalbek
Rayak
Beirut
*Anti-Lebanon*
Sidon
*R. Litani*
*R. Barada*
Damascus
*Mt Hermon*
Kaukab
*R. Barbar*
Tyre
Sasa
Kiswe
Kuneitra
*Lake Huleh*
Jisr Benat Yakub
Haifa
Acre
Tiberias
*Sea of Galilee*
Nazareth
Semakh
Deraa
El Afule
Irbid
Jenin
Beisan
Tul Keram
*Nahr ez Zerka*
Nablus
Ludd
Jericho
Es Salt
Amman
Jerusalem
*Dead Sea*
*Jordan*

*Mediterranean Sea*

N
W      E
S

miles
kilometres      80

# I

# *Imperial War Aims*

GENERAL ALLENBY'S ARRIVAL at the gates of Jerusalem on 11 December 1917 and his ceremonial victory march through the streets of the walled city, accompanied by fighter aircraft circling overhead and volleys of machine-gun fire in the streets, was a great symbolic occasion. The British defeat of the Turks and the capture of the city – one of the holy centres of the Ottoman empire – was a rare Allied victory, achieved after three years of wasteful conflict by a short war of movement with relatively few casualties. It represented a refreshing change from the stalemate that afflicted hostilities elsewhere. On the Western, Eastern and Italian fronts, the First World War was characterized by long and inconclusive battles, seemingly with no clear beginning or ending, that caused massive loss of life but little change in the relative positions of the opposing forces, which remained strongly entrenched.[1] The military conditions that favoured defensive action in France and elsewhere did not apply in the Middle East and the result was a more conventional war of movement in which the cavalry, both British and Arab, played a prominent role.

British politicians, who had become increasingly concerned about the impact at home of the costly war of attrition in France, welcomed the prospect of success that an Allied victory in Palestine seemed to offer under General Allenby's leadership. The fall of Jerusalem and the possible rout of the centuries-old Ottoman empire – the 'sick man of Europe' – would reinvigorate civilian morale, which had been sapped by the continuing slaughter on the Western Front and by the U-boat campaign in the Atlantic, with its disruption of food supplies across the country.[2] Some British politicians moreover saw in the Middle East theatre a way out of the impasse in France. They believed that the occupation of Palestine and the consequent collapse of Germany's principal ally could eventually open up a new front in Europe and lead to a more rapid end to the war. It would also lay the foundations of a more influential role for Britain in the area in the post-war period. In time these arguments imposed themselves on the military authorities in London and policy was modified accordingly.

The dramatic events that unfolded in Palestine in the course of 1917 were directed towards securing the specific aim of taking Jerusalem by Christmas – a deadline that was symbolic rather than of military significance. They were not, however, part of a grand strategy for the region adopted by Britain at the start of the war. Indeed, the opposite was the case: no such strategy existed; British pragmatism and caution were left to rule the day. There were continuing uncertainties about the size of the forces available to the Allies in Egypt and the strength of the Turkish military commitment to Palestine, as well as serious supply bottlenecks. As a result, military policy was developed piecemeal as opportunities presented themselves and a supply infrastructure was created.

At first the main priority of Allied troops in Egypt had been purely defensive – to keep open the lines of communication from the east to Europe, enabling forces from India, Australia and New Zealand to travel to France without interruption. When the war of movement in Europe – both in France and in the East – turned to stalemate, some British politicians looked for a solution elsewhere. Apart from the war at sea, where the Royal Navy scored some early successes, the British and French sought to weaken the Germans by opening up other fronts with the aim of increasing pressure on Germany's military allies. With Italy's entry into the war on the Allied side in 1915, the fortunes of Austria-Hungary deteriorated and the Austrians were forced to fight on two main fronts. Turkey also became the focus of Allied action in the Dardanelles, on the Gallipoli peninsula and on the Salonika front. The ebb and flow of battle against the Turks in these areas helped to determine the resources that could be devoted by the Allies to the Palestine and Mesopotamian fronts.

As Allied failures accumulated on these secondary fronts, some British politicians became convinced that military success in Palestine could offer them a way out. By 1917, the British army was at the gates of Palestine and in a position to advance, having reoccupied the

Sinai desert as part of operations to provide more effective protection for the Suez Canal. In a sudden reversal of policy, the British government ordered General Allenby to advance through Palestine as quickly as possible. As his successes mounted, Allenby remained under continuous political pressure to take more territory. He was ordered on to Damascus and eventually to Aleppo, some 500 miles from Egypt. In the end these later successes did no more than mirror Allied progress on other fronts since Allenby's advance had been stalled in the first half of 1918 by a major German onslaught in France, which had the effect of draining Palestine of his best troops.

The supply of reinforcements to Ottoman Palestine was also affected by developments on other fronts, the demands of Turkey's German ally for military support and her own wish to give priority to the war against the Russians in the Caucasus, where there was a prospect of achieving significant territorial gains. Turkish war aims in Palestine were more stable than those of her opponent. Once she had abandoned her aim of restoring Ottoman rule over Egypt, her objectives were defensive, and focused on maintaining control of the imperial provinces of Palestine and Syria as an integral part of the empire.

★

Had the capture and occupation of Palestine and Syria been one of Britain's original war aims, it is likely that greater reliance would have been placed on naval power and on a series of amphibious operations in northern Syria and Turkey that might have obviated the need for a protracted land campaign. In 1914, however, few policy-makers in Whitehall envisaged the need for such extended ground operations. Even fewer thought them feasible. The Sinai peninsula was a formidable barrier, particularly for a Western European army that had no experience of desert warfare. The area was devoid of proper roads, railways or the reliable water supplies essential to an army on the move. Conditions in southern Palestine – the gateway to Jerusalem and Damascus – were little better and the limited availability of water in particular would be a real constraint on the flexible deployment of military forces.

Initially, British objectives in the region focused almost exclusively on the security of Egypt and the international waterway running through it. Opened in 1869, the Suez Canal had become a vital artery of the British empire and an essential link between London and the Far East.[3] Referred to in the pre-war German press as

Britain's 'jugular', the canal was at the heart of British imperial communications and defence arrangements. The need to ensure that it
remained open in all circumstances had caused Britain to take an
increasing interest in the internal affairs of Egypt. Although that
country had been formally part of the Ottoman empire since 1517
(and remained so until 1914), imperial rule had been exercised, from
1805, by the office of khedive or governor, based in Cairo. In practice
this gave Egypt a degree of autonomy from Constantinople that was
unknown in other parts of the empire. In 1879, having attempted to
serve as a rallying point for opposition to foreign influence in Egypt,
the khedive was overthrown by the Sultan, with Anglo-French
support. In response to a nationalist revolt that ensued in September
1881, the British occupied Egypt later the following year with the
aim of securing the free passage of the canal and protecting the finan-
cial interests of Egypt's European creditors.[4]

Although the office of khedive was maintained after 1881, de facto
power passed to the British consul-general who now ruled the
country, with responsibility for foreign policy and defence as well as
internal affairs. For much of the pre-war period (1883–1907) this
office was held by Lord Cromer. Despite the new political and military realities, Egypt remained a political anomaly. Constitutionally it
continued to be part of the Turkish empire (with the Sultan of
Turkey still nominally head of state) until it was made a British protectorate at the beginning of the 1914–18 war. The British were to
remain on Egyptian soil without interruption until June 1956, just
before Nasser nationalized the canal, when they left under an agreement reached in 1954 following anti-British rioting and strong pressure from the Egyptian government.

The seizure of a province of the Ottoman empire, even if only
nominally under the control of Constantinople, represented a
marked change of direction in nineteenth-century British foreign
policy. Hitherto Britain had been largely consistent in supporting the
physical integrity of the Ottoman empire, which it saw as a useful
barrier between Egypt and potential threats from the east. When
assuming control of Ottoman Egypt in 1882 Britain had been forced
to make an exception to its own policy. But apart from this single act
of annexation, Britain avoided armed intervention in the region and
directed its imperial ambitions elsewhere.

During the nineteenth century relations between Britain and the
Ottoman empire veered between long periods of friendship and

sudden bouts of hostility, with the relationship being conditioned by rivalries among the European powers. It was not until 1906 that relations between British-controlled Egypt and Turkey deteriorated seriously for the first time. During this period, the course of a boundary between the Sinai region of Egypt and Ottoman Palestine, a previously unmapped area, was identified and became the subject of an acrimonious international dispute. Known as the Taba affair after the southernmost point of the line at the Gulf of Aqaba, it raised the prospect of armed aggression on Egypt's eastern border. With no British or Egyptian military presence in the area, the Sinai desert was certainly vulnerable to enemy attack. Having no way of knowing whether Ottoman forces were gathering at the border Britain was compelled to recruit a network of Bedouin agents.[5] Intensive diplomatic efforts eventually resolved the crisis but the fear of possible Turkish aggression remained and was to become a serious factor in Egyptian defence policy. Early steps were taken to establish regular border patrols and to survey the desert (about which little was then known). The Sinai desert was regarded as a buffer zone, with the Suez Canal as the main line of Egyptian defence. But a wider area – covering Palestine and Syria as well as the Sinai desert – was now seen as a potential battleground.

A War Office review of Egyptian security policy undertaken early in 1914 concluded that in the event of war the Germans would encourage the Turks to launch an attack on Egypt across the Sinai desert even though such an attempt was unlikely to be successful. Given the transport and supply problems they would encounter in the early stages of hostilities they would only be able to muster a relatively small force. With this in view the War Office proposed that the defence of Egypt should be static and be based on the deployment of troops along the whole length of the canal. Despite these preparations a contemporary Turkish army plan of attack made no reference to Palestine or Egypt and concentrated on strategy in relation to Russia and the Balkan states, its traditional enemies. When Turkey entered the war and found Britain an adversary this was to change: Egypt was incorporated into Turkish war plans as a potential military target and contingency arrangements were made.

Yet the Ottoman empire was increasingly ill-equipped to deal with another potential enemy. The creative and expansionist period of the empire was long gone. Its economy remained predominantly agricultural and it had not shared in the new wealth generated by the industrial revolution that transformed Western Europe during the nineteenth century. Turkey's problems were compounded by a growing realization of internal malaise. As its subject peoples developed a greater sense of national identity, opposition to the continuation of Ottoman rule grew and demands for self-government or even independence began to emerge, supported by new forms of political organization, often secret in origin.

The empire's decline could be measured by further encroachments on her territory in the period immediately before the First World War. In September 1911, Italy attacked Turkish forces at various points along the North African coast with the aim of capturing Ottoman Libya, an objective that was achieved in part within weeks. In a later phase of this conflict, the Italians failed in their attempt to force the Dardanelles but in April 1912 seized control of the Dodecanese islands.[6] Worse was to follow when Turkey lost her remaining territory in the Balkans during the First Balkan War of 1912–13. Concerted action by Greece, Serbia, Bulgaria and Montenegro led to the expulsion of Turkey from the area and the creation of the state of Albania.

Diplomatic moves in Europe added to the pressures on a weakened Ottoman empire. In 1907 Turkey's long-standing traditional enemy – the Russian empire – had joined forces with Britain and France in the Triple Alliance. Germany and her main ally Austria-Hungary formed a rival alliance and actively sought Turkey's involvement in it, with the aim of maximizing its strength and scope as an effective counter-weight. Germany had been exploring the possibility of an alliance with Turkey since the 1880s and as early as 1882 a German military mission, led by General Colmar von der Goltz, had arrived in Constantinople. He was to be attached to the Turkish general staff for a period of twelve years and, though his role was only advisory, he was engaged in concerted efforts to modernize the armed forces. German state visits and, more importantly, German money and expertise followed. The Berlin to Baghdad railway and other major projects were started. A primary aim of all this activity was to support German foreign policy objectives: strengthening her influence in a strategically important area where Turkey was potentially in a position to damage both Russian and British interests. In Britain's case, Turkey had a dual weapon: apart from the use – or the threat of the use – of force against the Suez Canal she could call in aid her spiritual leadership of Islam. By declaring a holy war ( *jihad* ), particularly if it were endorsed by local Arab leaders, she might be able to undermine the administration of British colonial territories where there was a significant Muslim population – including India.

If Turkey were to be an effective military ally of Germany, however, the process of modernizing the country – and its armed forces – needed to be extended beyond the completion of a few major construction projects. The end of the old regime in 1908 provided the political will to initiate change that had hitherto been lacking. The 'Young Turk' revolution of that year led to the removal of Sultan Abdul Hamid by the Party of Union and Progress and the establishment of the Committee of Union and Progress. Consisting of four senior cabinet ministers, the committee was the driving force of the new administration and soon transformed itself into a dictatorship. Apart from the dominant voice of Enver Pasha, the other members of the committee were Djemal, Minister of Marine, Djavid, Minister of Finance, and Talaat, Minister of the Interior. The new order was strongly nationalistic and intent on reversing years of imperial decline. A period of upheaval ensued as major political and social reforms were introduced, and Enver, who had served as a military attaché in Berlin, was determined to enlist his German allies in support of his modernization programme.

Turkey's defeat in the First Balkan War provided further evidence, if any were needed, of the poor condition of the Turkish army and the need for thoroughgoing reform. This process was led by the Germans who from 1913 effectively established a permanent military presence in the country. At this point a German military mission, headed by General Otto Liman von Sanders, which consisted of some seventy officers, arrived in Constantinople. To enable Liman to work more effectively he was given the local rank of field marshal and the position of Inspector-General of the Turkish army – an appointment which gave him the executive power that his predecessor, Colmar von der Goltz, had lacked. It was his responsibility to identify areas of weakness in military organization and suggest how they might be remedied, although his influence seems to have been confined to corps operating on the European front. Among other problems, it was found that the common soldier was badly equipped and trained, and often forced to live in unsanitary conditions; that the cavalry arm was small in comparison with those of other European armies and many of the surviving horses were in poor condition after their experiences in the First Balkan War. However, helping to modernize the military was only part of Liman von Sanders' function; his real role was to promote the 'Germanization of the Turkish army', a policy which, in assigning well-qualified German officers to important commands, led to continuing tensions between German and Turkish officers. Despite this friction German influence, though strong, was never dominant.[7]

For all its handicaps, the mobilized Turkish army was still potentially large and powerful. Its peacetime strength of 210,000 (including 10,000 officers) could be rapidly expanded. Recruitment was based on a system of conscription that required young men, in peacetime, to serve for two years in the active army (or *nizam*) and then for sixteen years in the reserve. On the outbreak of war in 1914, about a million men were liable for military service. During the course of the war a total of some 2,700,000 men were conscripted, although the maximum strength of the army at any one time never exceeded 650,000 men.

By 1914 the army was divided into four fronts or inspectorates – European, Caucasian, Mesopotamian and Palestine/Arabian – with local headquarters at Constantinople, Erzinjan, Baghdad and Damascus respectively. General headquarters, which was based in Constantinople, coordinated and managed this structure which was maintained throughout the war.

At the beginning of the war the army consisted of 36 divisions, although few were up to strength. Another 34 divisions were mobilized during the course of the war, making a total of 70. In practice, however, death and desertion meant that a maximum of 43 divisions was in action at any one time. Each corps of the Turkish army normally consisted of three divisions. A typical *nizam* division was based on three regiments, each containing three battalions, and a regiment of field artillery. The latter also consisted of three battalions, each battalion having three batteries of three field guns each.

By late 1914, there were two army corps on the Palestine and Syrian fronts, consisting of about 65,000 men and 100 guns. The numerical strength of the Turkish army fluctuated during the war and by 1918 there may only have been about 35,000 men in Palestine, opposing a much larger number of Allied troops. The distribution of forces between the different Turkish fronts varied according to changing political and military priorities throughout the course of the war. It was one of the key features of the Palestine campaign that both the opposing sides were willing to withdraw units – or deny the theatre reinforcements – whenever priorities on other fronts so required. For much of the war Palestine was not viewed as a high priority by either side.

The fluctuating ration strength of the Turkish army, however, revealed little about its real capabilities in the field. Its effectiveness rested largely on the fighting qualities of its rank and file. 'Johnny Turk', as he was known to his enemies, was noted for his courage, powers of endurance and ability to survive in a wide range of adverse conditions. These characteristics reflected the fact that large numbers of recruits came from the rural areas of Anatolia and Armenia, where working life prepared them for the hardships of war. In Wavell's words,

> The Anatolian Turk was the backbone of the empire. He is a fine soldier of the rough-and-ready type, with extraordinary powers of endurance, great patience under hardships and privations, a certain inherited aptitude for warfare, and stolid courage in battle.[8]

But in other respects, they were at a disadvantage. The further they were based from the capital, the less well armed, equipped and trained the rank and file were likely to be. Standards of education were much lower than they were in Western Europe and many soldiers who were promoted from the ranks were still likely to be illiterate. This in turn affected their ability to operate successfully as officers, although by the time of the First World War they were outnumbered by colleagues who had been through a military training course and were closer to Western standards of competence.

★

In the summer of 1914 Turkey remained outside the opposing alliances and in theory its leaders faced a clear choice as the major powers mobilized and fighting across Europe began. For a brief period they seem to have considered each of the major powers as a potential ally. Even the possibility of closer links with Russia was discussed. Britain and France – Turkey's major trading partners – appeared for a short while to enjoy improved relations with Constantinople. A British naval mission had contributed to the modernization of the Turkish navy in the immediate pre-war period and encouraged the government to order two dreadnought battleships from British shipyards, which were funded by public subscription in the wake of a well-organized government publicity campaign.

Enver himself, however, was strongly in favour of entering the war on the German side. German influence in Turkey was powerful enough to help condition the attitudes of other members of the elite. Although the risks were substantial, German military prestige was high and there seemed to be a good chance that Turkey was joining the winning side. The foundation of her wartime role was laid on 2 August when Enver signed a secret treaty of armed cooperation with Germany, although this did not commit him to declaring war immediately on Germany's enemies. A series of unconnected events was to bring public opinion into line by the time the government's decision to abandon its policy of neutrality in favour of an alliance with Germany was announced later in the year.

Early in August, as war was declared between Britain and Germany, the British decided not to honour the contract with Turkey to deliver the two dreadnought battleships then nearing completion. There was a public outcry in Turkey. Relations between Britain and Turkey were irretrievably damaged. Little more than a week later, the German battlecruiser *Goeben*, together with the cruiser *Breslau*, both under the command of Admiral Wilhelm Souchon, arrived in Constantinople, having escaped their British pursuers in an extended chase through the Mediterranean. Shortly afterwards they were transferred to the Ottoman navy, becoming the battlecruiser *Sultan Selim Yavuz* and the cruiser *Midilli*; Souchon was appointed supreme naval commander. In response the British declared that any warships venturing into the Aegean would be regarded as hostile; as a result, their naval mission to Turkey was forced to leave Constantinople.

Despite these unfavourable developments, on 18 August Britain, France and Russia declared their readiness to guarantee Turkish security provided she observed a position of strict neutrality. Uncertainty about the effectiveness of her military forces and the fragile condition of the empire induced Turkey for a short while to remain publicly neutral. The government's public statements, however, did not reflect the true position: in reality Turkey spent the next two months preparing for war as an ally of Germany. The process of mobilizing the army was initiated. The declaration of war was now simply a matter of timing, as the government took advantage of the breathing space to address some of its military weaknesses.

In the forefront of Turkey's war aims were the return of former territory in the Balkans, the reconquest of Egypt and the seizure of the Suez Canal. To the north-east and east she hoped to dominate Persia and Caucasia, recovering long-lost Ottoman territories and establishing pro-Turkish states in those areas. Once in control of Persia, Turkey would be in a position to threaten India through her access to Afghanistan. In view of these wide-ranging objectives, Turkish military leaders resisted the temptation to concentrate all their resources in the Balkans and the Caucasus. As the Middle East assumed increasing strategic importance, there was a gradual build-up of Turkish troops in the area from August 1914. It was also decided not to transfer elsewhere the three infantry divisions based in Palestine. Similarly two divisions in transit through northern Syria were held there in case of an Arab rising or an Allied landing on the Turkish coast. Turkish forces in Palestine were supplemented by locally recruited Bedouin tribesmen, who were deployed on intelligence duties in the Sinai desert. During the autumn, when Turkey had still given no public indication that she was about to end her neutrality, she was secretly concentrating her forces in southern Palestine with the aim of launching an assault on the canal.

Finally, on 29 October, an attack on the Russian navy, inspired by Enver, brought Turkey irrevocably into the war. Supported by pro-war elements in the Ottoman government, Enver ordered Admiral Souchon to launch an assault on the Russian fleet in the Black Sea. Using the *Sultan Selim Yavuz*, the *Midilli* and other Ottoman warships, the Turks attacked several Russian naval installations without warning, following a false claim that a Russian ship had been caught trying to mine the entrance to the Bosphorus. Diplomatic relations with Russia were severed on 30 October and on 2 November the two countries were at war. Britain and France, which had treaty obligations with Russia, entered the war with Turkey on 5 November. A Turkish minister who resigned in protest at his country's declaration of war predicted that 'it will be our ruin – even if we win'.[9]

The declaration of war against Turkey forced Britain to make moves to protect her vital interests in the Middle East. These interests included not only the oil fields of southern Persia but the Suez Canal and Egypt itself, which was to prove invaluable as a staging post, base and training ground for troops moving from Asia, Australia and New Zealand to Europe. Intelligence reports indicated that the canal was already highly vulnerable to a Turkish land attack. Indeed, as early as 23 September, during a period when Turkey was still ostensibly neutral, a group of armed Bedouin was discovered to have crossed the Sinai frontier. The only response at the time was the dispatch of a small column of Egyptian coastguards to destroy water wells at Nekhl, some 70 miles east of Suez.

A major Turkish offensive, however, could only be launched once sufficient regular forces had been concentrated in Ottoman Palestine. These forces would need to cross the Sinai desert, a region traversed by ancient trade routes connecting Africa to Asia. Inhospitable and sparsely populated, with limited water supplies, it had no effective defences against enemy attack. The northern route across the desert, which ran alongside the Mediterranean, had witnessed the passage of several historic armies, including those of Alexander and Napoleon. The British would soon follow.

This was not the only problem that threatened Egypt in the autumn of 1914. Some 70,000 Turkish nationals lived permanently in the country and it was not certain whether they would remain quiescent under British rule. To the south, moreover, the Sudan had only recently been pacified; to the west were the Senussi, currently preoccupied with the Italian presence in North Africa, but soon to turn their guns on the British. The priorities of the War Office in London, however, lay elsewhere and as the dangers to Egypt mounted, the most experienced defending troops were being returned to Europe.

# 2

# *The Defence of the Suez Canal*

BEFORE WAR WITH Turkey had been formally declared, the British had planned to transfer its small peacetime garrison of regular troops in Egypt to France and replace it with a territorial (reserve) division – the 42nd (East Lancashire) – from England. This division arrived in Egypt at the end of September but needed further training to equip it for combat. With the growing inevitability of serious hostilities between Britain and the Ottoman empire, it became apparent that the defence of an important strategic asset would require a more formidable fighting force than could be provided by untrained reserves.

In mid-September, in an attempt to augment the defensive capability of Egypt, an infantry brigade and supporting mountain artillery were retained from the Third Indian Division as it passed through Egypt on its way to France. These troops were themselves subsequently released for service on the Western Front when further replacements arrived from India in mid-November. Indian troops were to play a prominent role in defending the Suez Canal during the first year of the war, as were forces from Australia and New Zealand temporarily based in Egypt while undergoing training in preparation for future service in Europe. By January 1915, the total number of British and imperial troops in Egypt had increased to 70,000 from a very small base. The Egyptian army, which was a separate, locally recruited force under the command of Sir Reginald Wingate, Governor-General of the Anglo-Egyptian Sudan, played virtually no role in protecting the canal. It was fully occupied with its principal task of maintaining internal security and ensuring the defence of the Sudan.

Egyptian defence capabilities were further strengthened by the appointment of Major-General Sir John Maxwell as commander-in-chief in succession to Sir Julian Byng, who left for France in August 1914. Maxwell had spent much of his military career in Egypt and the Sudan, first arriving there in 1882. A veteran of the Battle of Tel el Kebir that same year, he had served under Wolseley and later under Kitchener in the Gordon relief expedition (1885), in the reconquest of the Sudan (1898), and the South African war (1899–1902). Subsequently appointed commander-in-chief in Egypt (1908–12), he knew the country as well if not better than any of his army contemporaries.

The onset of war rapidly changed the political context within which Maxwell had to work. Formally, Egypt still acknowledged the suzerainty of the Sultan of Turkey and an annual tribute was paid to him. However, the nominal ruler of Egypt, the khedive, Abbas Hilmi Pasha, was actively opposed to British rule and wished to maintain his links with Turkey. For the British the security of the canal was their main consideration and these long-established but anomalous governance arrangements could no longer be sustained. Several steps were taken to ensure that Egypt's position more closely reflected political reality. On 5 August, the country was stated to be at war with Britain's enemies. On 2 November, just before Turkey's formal declaration of war, martial law was instituted throughout Egypt. This was followed, on 11 November, by a *fatwa* (decree), issued by the Sheikh ul Islam, the chief religious official in Constantinople, proclaiming holy war (*jihad*) against the Allies. Three days later the Sultan proclaimed a *jihad* on all Turkey's enemies, a call intended to rally Muslims across the world to the defence of the empire. On 18 December, Britain announced the establishment of a protectorate over Egypt. The khedive was deposed and replaced by his uncle, Prince Hussein, who was appointed nominal ruler of Egypt and was given the title of sultan.

In practice, of course, the levers of power were now firmly in the hands of British officials, headed by the first permanent High Commissioner, Sir Henry McMahon, who took office in January 1915 and was to play a major role in bringing the Arabs into the war on the Allied side. Britain's success in maintaining internal security depended in part on the acquiescence of the Egyptians, and a decision was made not to involve the local population in the defence of the country against Turkish attack – an undertaking confirmed in the formal declaration of war against Turkey. In practice, however, the preparation of the canal defences, the construction of the Sinai railway and the subsequent expulsion of Turkish troops from Egyptian soil could only be achieved with the active cooperation and support of the Egyptians.

Although the canal was a formidable barrier to an invading army, its sheer size made it difficult to defend with any degree of confidence.[1] Connecting the Mediterranean and the Red Sea, the canal extends for 101 miles, from Port Said in the north to Suez in the south, through the Sinai desert. Situated some 30 miles from the fertile Nile delta, it is a combination of canal and natural lakes, with the latter determining its course and constituting about a third of the total route. The northern section of the canal extends from Port Said to Qantara and is 25 miles in length. At this end, the canal is virtually dead straight, its banks are low and for part of its length it touches the eastern bank of Lake Menzaleh. The canal continues in a straight line until it reaches Ismailia, at the northern end of Lake Timsah. From this point the route to the Red Sea makes use of Lake Timsah and then the Great Bitter Lake. The final section links the lake to the town of Suez on the Red Sea. The canal's minimum depth is 33 feet; its width 148 feet.

Running parallel to the canal on its western side are the northern and southern branches of the Sweet Water Canal which meet at Ismailia and from there run to the Nile at Cairo. This canal supplies fresh water to the whole area and is a lifeline to the main canal towns of Port Said, Ismailia and Suez. It was to be the source of the piped water that supplied British troops as they advanced across Sinai and into Palestine in 1916–17. The controls to the whole system were located at Ismailia so the occupants of that town could readily deny water to an enemy force holding another part of the canal.

At an early stage, the decision was made to protect the whole length of the canal and Major-General Alex Wilson, commander of the 10th Indian Division, was placed in charge of its defences. The canal zone was divided into three military sectors: the first running from the town of Suez to Deversoir; the second running northwards to El Ferdan; and the third covering the northern segment to Port Said. By the end of 1914, some 30,000 troops were directly involved in the defence of the canal, including twenty-four regiments of the 10th and 11th Indian Divisions, the Indian Imperial Service Cavalry Brigade, the Bikanir Camel Corps and some units of Indian mountain artillery, as well as units of Egyptian artillery drawn from the Egyptian army which was deployed elsewhere. These ground troops were supported by air and sea forces, including British and French warships and reconnaissance aircraft. Warships served as floating batteries and provided a firm basis for the artillery defence of the canal.

These forces could be supplemented by other troops based elsewhere in Egypt and those passing through the country on their way to France. With the arrival in December 1914 of the first Australian and New Zealand troops – including an infantry division, a light horse brigade, mounted rifles and field artillery – some 40,000 additional men were available in reserve if the canal were suddenly to come under serious Turkish threat. This unplanned influx of large numbers of troops forced the army to use facilities that had long since been mothballed. The difficulties were described by Harry Hopwood, an NCO in the Manchester Regiment, in a letter to his mother written early in 1915:

> There are a big lot of troops here mostly Australians, and barracks almost like Aldershot. It is quite an eye opener in this respect. The barracks are very big ones, but very dirty, in fact filthy. They were built by Napoleon about 100 years ago and have been condemned some years back, but I suppose it has been necessary to use them again. They are invested with bugs but we had a full day cleaning them down.[2]

The defending forces had a dual role: to halt an invading force and prevent it moving down the road towards Cairo, as well as keeping the canal open and ensuring that it did not sustain serious damage. In the first phase of the war, the canal itself was seen as the main bulwark of the British defensive system. This reflected a long-established and soundly based tenet of pre-war defence policy, which had envisaged the use of warships in support of the defending ground forces. There was, however, a real risk that canal traffic could be disrupted if the waterway was used as the barrier between Sinai and the rest of Egypt.

The main British defences were located on the west bank of the canal, where trenches were dug between a series of fortified posts; these were supplemented by a series of posts and trenches on the east bank, protected by barbed wire. The two systems were linked by bridge and ferry. These defensive works could only be supplied by the railway which ran from Cairo to Ismailia and then parallel with the Sweet Water Canal to the north and south. There were no sur- faced roads in the canal zone in 1914 and water transport was in short supply. In order to reduce the formidable task of guarding more than 70 miles of canal, a large area east of the canal between Port Said and Qantara (and opposite Lake Menzaleh) was flooded, thus making direct access to the canal impossible in this area. A further cut was made in the eastern bank to the north of Qantara, which provided protection to the flank of a fortified area.

The plan to base Egypt's eastern defences on the Suez Canal fol- lowed a decision to abandon the Sinai desert to the enemy in the event of war with Turkey. The decision, which was implemented in November 1914, reflected the fact that Egyptian authority in the region was then represented by no more than a few contingents of local police who maintained frontier controls and were present at other key points. It was clear to the British that the peninsula was not immediately defensible and the frontier posts were quickly evacuated. In the remaining weeks of 1914, the Turkish army stepped into the vacuum and its forces advanced into Egyptian ter- ritory, occupying the Sinai settlements of El Arish and Nekhl. The first hostilities of the war in this theatre took place in this period when, on 20 November, a small unit of the Bikanir Camel Corps was attacked by 200 Bedouin (in Turkish pay) while on patrol some 20 miles east of Qantara and was forced to withdraw with heavy losses.[3]

While the main British objective was to prepare the canal defences and organize the troops to face an expected invasion, the War Office also investigated the possibility of launching a pre-emptive strike against Turkey with the aim of causing major disruption to its extended supply lines. During December 1914, Lord Kitchener, the Secretary of State for War, raised with General Maxwell the idea of launching a combined assault on Alexandretta in the Gulf of Iskanderun, where British troops could be landed near a vulnerable point of rail communications between Turkey and Syria. Railway track and rolling stock would be the prime targets for destruction. However, the size of the forces required and the risks involved quickly ruled out the project, although it was to be resurrected peri- odically during the course of the Middle East campaign, particularly when progress elsewhere seemed to have stalled. The area did not

entirely escape Allied naval action as British light cruisers were soon
ordered into action against the main Syrian ports in order to disrupt
the unloading of Turkish military supplies. British warships shelled
Alexandretta and Haifa and appeared off Beirut. Elsewhere, the
Turkish-occupied Red Sea port of Aqaba was also attacked.

On some occasions, landing parties were sent ashore to destroy
specific facilities. During an incident at Alexandretta, according to
the British official history of the war, the Royal Navy forced the
Turks to blow up two railway engines, 'lending them gun cotton for
the purpose'. The British naval officer supervising the operation was
'solemnly given Turkish rank for that day to preserve Turkish
dignity. The end of the comedy is said to have been a claim by the
Baghdad Railway Company against the Turkish government for
wanton and malicious damage to the former's property by a *Turkish*
officer.'[4] Such raids had little more than symbolic effect and were
abruptly discontinued when the Turkish authorities threatened
reprisals against individual Allied subjects still resident in Ottoman
territories. Kitchener had no great enthusiasm for such ventures. He
was 'convinced that the passive defence of the canal itself, on the line
of the canal, was the only possible method of protecting Egypt from
attack by land'.[5]

★

While these initial moves were being made, plans for a major Turkish
invasion of Egypt were under development. At this time, Turkey had
about 65,000 troops and 100 guns in Syria and Palestine. Originally
organized into two corps (VI and VIII Corps), these troops, in
September 1914, were formed into the Turkish Fourth Army. Its first
commander, Zekki Pasha, had already been instructed in August to
make plans for an attack on the canal, whose vital importance to
British interests was fully recognized by the Turkish general staff.
Thus some three months before she entered the war the Turkish
army was already being mobilized. But Zekki's plans for the Egyptian
front were not sufficiently ambitious to meet with the approval of
Djemal Pasha 'the Elder', one of the leaders of the Young Turk revolution and Minister of Marine, who in November 1914 was
appointed governor and commander-in-chief in Syria and Palestine,
a position he held virtually until the end of the war.

With Djemal's direct involvement in Palestine, greater emphasis
was given to the wider political objectives of an invasion, including

the need to foment a domestic revolt within Egypt. If this campaign was successful, Djemal's ultimate aim of conquering the whole country might be achieved. Zekki was duly replaced by Mohammed Djemal Bey (known as Djemal Kuchuk, 'the Lesser'), the commander of VIII Corps, an able soldier who was to fight in Palestine throughout the war. He was assisted by another influential member of VIII Corps – General Friedrich Kress von Kressenstein, a Bavarian officer who served as chief of staff and played a key role in determining Turkish strategy in Palestine over the next three years. Important advisory roles were taken by other German officers, including Colonel von Frankenberg-Proschlitz who served as chief of staff of the Turkish Fourth Army under Djemal Pasha.

Planning the expedition and massing troops on the Egyptian border took several weeks and it was not until mid-January 1915 that the Turkish invasion force was ready to move. Some 20,000 men with one howitzer and nine field batteries had been assembled in the Beersheba area in readiness for the attack. These troops were to be supplied by about 10,000 camels, which would carry water, food and ammunition. Teams of oxen would pull guns and pontoon wagons across the desert. The units represented at the front included the 10th Division, a regiment of the 23rd Division, the 25th Division and various cavalry and camel companies. The 27th (Arab) Division was to remain in reserve in Beersheba.

The size of the Turkish invasion force, however, was modest compared with the objectives it had been set and the strength of the defending forces. The successful invasion of Egypt with inferior forces was only likely to succeed if it triggered a major internal revolt against British rule as Turkish forces approached the canal. Without this support, the expedition was doomed to failure.

The ambitious aims of the expedition helped to determine where the main force should cross the desert in order to maximize the success of any attack across the canal. Three alternative routes were available. The most accessible route was the northern coastal track that ran from El Arish to Qantara, passing through Bir el Abd and Qatiya. This route normally had the easiest access to water – there were occasional oases with brackish wells – but it was also in range of British warships operating in the Mediterranean which could cause serious disruption to the progress of the expedition. The southern route, which ran from El Kossaima to Suez, was the least accessible and had few positive advantages, except for Nekhl, which had a good water supply. The central route across the desert pointed in the direction of Ismailia on the canal and went from a starting point at Beersheba towards Hassana and the Wadi Muksheib. If the invasion force could occupy the Ismailia area, it would control the Sweet Water Canal and would be in a position to deny the British elsewhere on the canal access to fresh water. This action would be essential if the Turks intended to advance westwards beyond the canal in the direction of Cairo. These tracks had a sufficiently firm surface to carry several thousand troops and, more important, they offered easy access to large quantities of water. Unusually, after several years of drought, there were several heavy storms during the winter of 1914–15 and water had collected in stone cisterns placed at strategic points along the central route. The other two routes, however, could not entirely be ignored as Djemal needed to secure his flanks and confuse the British about the real direction of his attack on the canal. He would, therefore, need to allocate some troops to each of the three routes.

The invasion force left Beersheba in mid-January 1915. The main force, which was split into two, was sent down the central route, with a day's gap between the two groups. They crossed the desert in ten days, travelling at night to avoid the dual menace of British reconnaissance sorties and the searing heat of the day. The advance of the smaller groups covering the flanks to the north and south proceeded at a similar rate. By 26/27 January, they were in a position to mount attacks on the extremities of the British line, at Qantara in the north and at Kubri near Suez on the Red Sea.

These actions, which were intended to deceive the British about the Turkish army's real plan of attack, made little impression either on their immediate targets or on the thinking of headquarters staff about where the main Turkish attack would fall. Unlike their opponents, the British had access to daily aerial reconnaissance intelligence which gave them regular insights into the progress of the Turkish army as it struggled across the Sinai desert. On 28 January, British aircraft located a Turkish force of up to 4,000 men some eight miles east of Deversoir (in the central sector), which confirmed the British view that the main Turkish attack would fall in the centre, probably in the area between Serapeum (four miles south of Lake Timsah) and El Ferdan (seven miles north of Ismailia). This warning gave the British time to reinforce the trenches on the key sections of the west bank, drawing on reserves which had been assembled close to the canal. British and French warships entered the canal and took up their stations. On 1 February, HMS *Clio* opened fire on enemy units in the desert east of El Ferdan.

By the beginning of February, some 15,000 Turkish troops had passed along the central Sinai route and arrived in the Ismailia area. They had been served well by their Bedouin guides and not a single Turkish soldier (or animal) lost his life. As elsewhere on the canal, the great majority of the British defending force was entrenched on the west bank, but defensive positions had also been built on the east side. In the central sector, there were five such posts, each manned by two companies of Indian infantry. On the west bank, between Lake Timsah and the Great Bitter Lake, there were twelve posts, each manned by two platoons. Each platoon was responsible for the defence of about 600 yards of canal frontage. These defensive arrangements were supported by a reserve of three companies, based at Serapeum, and two gun batteries.

The first contacts with the Turkish army in this area were made on 2 February when small Allied detachments were sent out from Ismailia ferry post – and at other points along the whole 20-mile front from Deversoir to El Ferdan. Small arms fire was soon exchanged, but a sandstorm brought these engagements to a premature end and delayed the impending Turkish attack on the canal. A French naval officer based at Ismailia, who had been involved in this attack, described the deteriorating conditions: 'there had sprung up a sandstorm which hid everything from view. I went on to a dune with the English colonel. But there it was even worse. Even to keep one's eyes open was horrible torture . . .'[6]

The sandstorm continued into the night and only in the early hours of 3 February could the Turkish assault on the canal begin. British troops at an observation post at Tussum provided the first evidence of the final preparations for an enemy attack. At 3.25 a.m., members of the Turkish 25th Division, an Arab unit, passed southeast of the post in the direction of the canal, apparently in relatively good order at this point. Not long after Turkish troops had been observed at Tussum, the British saw the enemy making its first attempt to cross the canal. In the words of the official historian, 'dark masses were discerned moving slowly down the gullies on the east bank towards the water. Presently these masses were discovered to be pontoons and rafts carried by squads of men.'[7] The pontoons, which were of the German service pattern, were made of galvanized iron and could hold up to twenty men. Some vessels were successfully launched and were moving across the canal before the British realized that they were about to be attacked. The alarm was raised and the canal was soon raked by heavy machine-gun fire from Indian defensive positions on the high west bank.

The Turks' progress across the canal was quickly brought to a halt, with the pontoons being rapidly holed and sunk. Most of the pontoons did not even reach the water as the troops carrying them were cut down by British rifle and machine-gun fire from the opposite bank. Slightly later, another attempt was made to launch further pontoons but this effort had no more success than the first. Only three pontoons managed to cross the canal, supported by heavy Turkish fire, but their occupants were killed or captured by the defending Indian troops on the west bank. By morning, it was clear that the attack had been a complete failure. Even if the sandstorm had not delayed the attempted passage of the canal, thus costing the Turks much of the advantage of darkness, the crossing of a waterway 100 yards wide at night under the full weight of enemy fire would have challenged the most experienced and fully trained troops. The Arab division deployed for this manoeuvre lacked the discipline of Turkish regulars and, unsurprisingly, the intense British fire across the canal had caused a panic among the leading units. These Arab troops went over to the British in large numbers.

More from desperation than any real prospect of success, the Turkish attack was renewed at dawn the same morning (3 February), between Tussum and Serapeum. This time the targets were the British trenches and observation posts on the eastern bank as well as warships in the canal. The Ismailia ferry post on the eastern side of Lake Timsah came under attack. During this assault, Turkish artillery fire hit the British warship HMS *Hardinge*, which was forced to withdraw to Lake Timsah, beyond the range of enemy fire. Diversionary attacks were launched at El Ferdan, north of Ismailia, and at Qantara. By daylight, fighting had spread across the whole front. Despite this, the Turks made little more progress than at their first attempt. Heavy artillery fire from two French warships (French involvement at this period was still confined to a naval role) was concentrated in the area between Tussum and Serapeum and the enemy was forced to call off the action at about 2 p.m. Further French artillery fire during the afternoon encouraged the Turks to begin their withdrawal eastwards.

By the following morning (4 February), the British discovered, much to their surprise, that the Turkish presence in the central sector had already been reduced to a token force. The great bulk of the invading army had simply disappeared from the immediate area as quickly and as quietly as it had come. A similar pattern was evident elsewhere along the canal, with the enemy's trenches at Ismailia and Qantara being found empty. Over the next few days, the results of aerial reconnaissance confirmed that most of the invasion force had left the canal area. However, there was to be no precipitate retreat across the desert as the Turkish forces retired steadily in the direction of their base at Beersheba. By 10 February, only 400 Turkish troops remained in close proximity to the canal.

Despite their unhurried withdrawal, there was no immediate British attempt to launch a counter-attack, except for the minor action of two Gurkha companies garrisoning Deversoir post just north of the Great Bitter Lake, which hit back at the Turkish left as it retreated from the canal zone. Elsewhere along the line, the defending Allied troops remained at their stations until the next day, when the Imperial Service Brigade was sent across the canal near Ismailia to undertake a limited reconnaissance mission into the desert. No general pursuit, however, was authorized. The waterway was soon reopened to merchant shipping and a sense of normality returned.

★

British inaction gave the Turks time to consider their next move. Although they had suffered the loss of some 1,500 men, including 716 taken prisoner, their 10th Division remained unscathed. However, morale had undoubtedly been damaged by the failure of their first operation to make any impact either on the canal or its defences. Nor was there any sign of a popular response to the invasion within Egypt itself, and it was evident that no assistance from that direction could be expected in the future. Without such popular support, the wider objectives of the invasion could not be achieved, given the marked imbalance in strength of the opposing forces. In his account of the Sinai campaign, Kress claimed that

Djemal Pasha had expected that his appearance on the canal would be followed by a rising of the Egyptian nationalists. In this hope he was deceived. There remained, however, an attainable goal, to force his

way suddenly astride the canal, hold the crossing for a few days, and in
that time close the canal permanently.[8]

However, without the element of surprise, even this more limited
objective remained beyond the Turkish army's grasp.

Djemal Pasha, commander-in-chief in Syria and Palestine, had
accompanied the invasion force to the canal and it was he who, on 3
February, decided that an orderly withdrawal was all that could now
be achieved. Although he had little talent as a soldier, he was realistic
enough to recognize that renewing the attack could result in the
complete destruction of the Turkish force and a further heavy blow
to Turkish prestige. The only consolation for the Turks was the fact
that the invasion force had been able to disengage without difficulty
and return to its forward base without any interference by the British.
As far as the British were concerned, although they had been able to
repel the attack with relative ease and with only minor casualties, the
uncomfortable fact remained that the Turkish army had crossed a
substantial area of desert with a large armed force equipped with
heavy artillery. This considerable achievement served as a timely
reminder that Britain needed to take the defence of Egypt seriously
and to maintain sufficient force levels in the canal area to ensure that
it was reasonably secure.

The abortive invasion revealed serious shortcomings in the military leadership of both sides. The Turks had launched an invasion
which involved a 100-mile trek across a desert before hostilities
could begin. It was only by chance that more men had not been
lost. More importantly, it was clear that the objective of capturing
Egypt required far more troops than the Turks had at their disposal
(or were ever likely to have). The hope that weaknesses in Turkish
military strength could be addressed by support from a successful
popular uprising in Egypt had also been exposed as a serious miscal-
culation. The appearance of Turkish troops near the canal had done
nothing to trigger a revolt. The Turkish army had paid a high price
for a lack of accurate information about public opinion, and the
failure of its information sources was compounded by its own
failure to stimulate a revolt by covert action in Cairo and other
urban centres. Without this support, the Turks' grand design had
little prospect of success.

Later the Turks and their German allies would try to minimize the
stated purpose of the expedition, claiming that it was no more than a

reconnaissance or an attempt to destroy part of the fabric of the canal. Even if such rationalizations are accepted, the methods employed were hardly equal to the task. For reasons that are not clear they used their weaker division in the attack and kept the stronger 10th Division in reserve. (This latter division was used at no time during the invasion.) Moreover their diversionary actions to the north and south were weak and unconvincing, and failed to draw British troops away from the main expected area of attack. The Turks were thus obliged to face the full strength of the defending forces when they attacked the British centre. The results, according to Yigal Sheffy, a specialist in the history of military intelligence, were fatal to the Turkish cause:

> Had Cemal [Djemal Pasha] implemented the principle of force optimization by bringing in the sizeable force available in the rear, invested his better trained troops in the first wave, and pressed the defenders on the flanks, he would have had a much better prospect for securing the east bank opposite Serapeum and establishing a beach-head on the west bank.[9]

Given that the capture of the canal was possibly the most valuable contribution it could have made to the cause of its allies, it seems likely that the Turkish army's half-hearted attack with insignificant numbers had a wider political explanation. With pan-Turkism the dominant element in the political priorities of the ruling Young Turks, the outbreak of war provided an opportunity for the government to try to reinforce Ottoman Turkish links with other Turkish races; its military objectives (and resources) were thus directed more towards the Caucasus than Egypt. Nevertheless, almost as soon as his forces had returned to Beersheba, Djemal started making plans for a second attack. He reorganized his forces, built new roads, extended the railway to Beersheba and drilled new water wells.[10]

The British also had their share of weaknesses exposed. The failure to use mobile forces on the eastern bank rendered the canal vulnerable to enemy attack. The fact that the structure of the canal did not sustain any serious damage during the Turkish assault reflected the enemy's failures rather than the effectiveness of British preparations. The location of the British line of defence on the west bank of the canal, moreover, may explain the passive stance taken by the British when the chance arose to pursue the Turks during their retreat. In effect the canal formed part of the Allied defences; at that time there were insufficient trained troops to construct and man defences to the east of the canal, although these were later built when Sir Archibald Murray succeeded Maxwell as commander-in-chief in 1916. If the British had adopted a more active form of defence, the Turkish retreat across Sinai could have been disrupted relatively easily.

Another explanation for the British failure to pursue the enemy was the lack of available transport, although this hardly seems credible in view of the ready supply of camels to be found locally. A more likely constraint was the difficulty Allied forces would have had in using such resources. Although there were 70,000 defending troops in Egypt, only some of the Indian brigades were highly trained and prepared for a pursuit of this kind. Also, moving large numbers of troops across the canal quickly was difficult because there was only one bridge – at Ismailia – and troops were dispersed along the length of the canal; slow ferries provided the only alternative crossing.

There was also a wider political constraint applied from London. Kitchener had ordered Maxwell not to risk a reverse in the desert that could have wide-ranging political and military effects on the course of the war. Continuing uncertainty about the size and strength of the enemy's forces in Sinai also affected calculations. At a time when the enemy was withdrawing steadily eastwards, an intelligence report of 6 February suggested (incorrectly) that substantial reinforcements had been requested and would soon be arriving in the canal zone. It was not until mid-February that Maxwell received confirmation that the Turkish reserve forces had remained in Beersheba and that there were no signs of any preparations for them to move. Whatever the reason, the failure to pursue the enemy across the desert represented a lost opportunity; large numbers of enemy troops could otherwise have been captured and the whole Sinai campaign brought to a much earlier conclusion.

Following the withdrawal of the invasion force, another large-scale Turkish attack was ruled out for the time being. The only Turkish troops remaining on Egyptian territory were members of the Desert Force, Djemal's operational army in the Sinai desert, which was commanded by Kress von Kressenstein. Consisting of no more than three battalions, a squadron of camelry and two mountain batteries, it was ordered 'to take consistent steps aimed at the canal to bring about its permanent or temporary closure'.[11] Over the next few months it carried out several minor raids and tried to disrupt traffic along the waterway by sowing mines in the water; it also attacked the railway that ran alongside the canal. On 22 March 1915, for example, a Turkish force attacked the Shallufa post on the canal and had to be repelled by members of the garrison and guns of the Royal Indian Marine ship *Dufferin*. One of the final acts – and a rare success – occurred on 30 June when a passenger liner was struck by a Turkish mine in the Little Bitter Lake. The liner turned and blocked the channel but within a few hours the waterway had been reopened. T.E. Lawrence, who was then based in Cairo, captured the anxieties of the period in a letter of 29 June 1915:

> The canal holds out nervously. It expects an attack every full moon, & when it is dark also: & continually pretends to us that the Turks are coming on. It is divided by us. Fact is 3000 men at Arish, 1000 at Nekhl, 1000 at Beersheba, & the rest are behind Jaffa, Haifa & Beyrout . . .[12]

By the summer pressing needs on other fronts – the Dardanelles, Mesopotamia and the Caucasus – meant that Kress's force had to be withdrawn from Sinai and most of the regular officers and men were transferred to Gallipoli.

The continuing presence of this small enemy group on Egyptian territory had helped to keep British fears of a second invasion alive and, as a result, there was pressure to retain larger numbers of Allied troops in Egypt than would otherwise have been required. These concerns were increased by reports brought back by French reconnaissance aircraft that some 30,000 Turkish troops remained in the Beersheba area. Maxwell reported to Kitchener in late February that 'it would appear from [these reports] that we may look for another attack later on'.[13] These frequent if minor assaults concentrated the minds of the defending army, but did not prevent the British military authorities from later reducing the overall numbers involved in defending the canal. The pressure of events in other theatres affected the British as much as the Turks and units involved in the defence of Egypt had to be dispatched to Gallipoli, Aden and elsewhere. They were also called away to meet another danger to Egypt's security posed by the Senussi – a threat which had been growing during the autumn and, in November 1915, came to a head on the western frontier. The willingness of the War Office to reduce numbers on the canal may also have reflected their initial assessment of the quality of the Turkish army based on its performance in invading Sinai. There is no doubt that, as Sheffy puts it, they

> considered the failure as reflecting the overall military incompetence of Istanbul. This inaccurate British image of the Ottoman army as an ineffective fighting machine had serious consequences later on: British misfortune in Mesopotamia and in Gallipoli in 1915–16 soon taught them the hard way that their adversary was an enemy not to be dismissed lightly.[14]

The operations in Gallipoli were to make Egypt the largest British base outside the United Kingdom. Following an appeal by the Russians early in 1915 for a British diversionary attack, the Royal Navy had mounted a naval bombardment of the Dardanelles in March 1915. Once it was clear that the naval attack had failed, the British landed troops on Gallipoli in April and a full-scale struggle for the peninsula ensued. Instructed to prepare 30,000 ANZACS (commanded by Major-General W.R. Birdwood) for action at Gallipoli, General Maxwell and his staff found themselves increasingly preoccupied with supporting this expedition as well as reviewing the implications it had for local defence arrangements in Egypt. With the launching of this new campaign, the Suez Canal lost its protecting naval forces and the seaplanes that kept the Sinai desert under observation.

The Turks were also under increased pressure as a result of the British naval action in the Dardanelles and the subsequent Gallipoli landings. With the Palestine commitment scaled down to the bare minimum, there was no prospect of securing the troops needed for a renewed Turkish offensive against Egypt. In August 1915, Enver formally confirmed the postponement of a second offensive against the canal until 1916. It was to be a year before the Turks were able to launch another attack on the canal. In the meantime small-scale raids on the canal and logistic preparations for the next offensive were to continue.

★

By the end of 1915 it had become clear that the Turks were likely to make a second attempt on the canal. A series of Turkish victories in Mesopotamia and in Gallipoli late that year seemed to signal a change, if only temporary, in the balance of power in the Middle East. Discussions about a British withdrawal from Gallipoli began in

October and by the end of 1915 the British had abandoned their attempt to force the Dardanelles. The final departure of the Allied army from Gallipoli opened the way to preparations for another Turkish assault on the canal.

Turkey had never abandoned the idea of a second attack: in parliament Enver Pasha represented the first invasion as no more than a highly successful reconnaissance in strength in preparation for a much larger offensive to be undertaken at a later date. The key to a successful second invasion was to be an improved transport system. In the autumn of 1914, the Turkish railhead in Palestine had reached as far as Sileh, some 275 miles from the canal. Under the supervision of Meissner Pasha, by November 1915 the railway had been extended from Sileh to Beersheba (and by May 1916 was to reach to El Auja and beyond). This greatly improved network suffered from one major flaw: the need to transfer supplies from standard gauge to narrow gauge at Rayak en route from Constantinople. The alternative supply route from the imperial capital was a road that crossed the Taurus and Amanus mountains. In the first part of the war this major route was upgraded so that by 1916 it could take motor transport. Kress's view was that 'from the first day of the war to the last, the lines of communication worked badly, and to this must be largely attributed the series of disasters which befell the Turks in Mesopotamia, Palestine and the Hedjaz'.[15]

Other military developments were also encouraging the Turks in their preparations for a second invasion. The British campaign in Mesopotamia had run into difficulties and had suffered a serious defeat at Ctesiphon in November 1915. The British were soon to be faced also with the possibility that another theatre of war – Salonika – could open up in the east as Bulgaria made clear its support for the Turks. The Turks were now in a position to release troops from these fronts to help create a new expeditionary force for a renewed attack on Egypt. The defeat of Serbia by the Central Powers in the autumn of 1915 also enabled the Germans to open a supply line running directly from Germany to the Middle East. However, the tide was not turning entirely in Turkey's favour. A new Russian offensive in the Caucasus early in 1916 caused reserves to be diverted to this front, so reducing the number of troops that could be spared for operations against Egypt.

The British were fully aware of the potential threat represented by an increased Turkish military presence in Palestine and Syria, which was reinforced by improvements in communications in Asia Minor and Syria and within Palestine itself. The extension of the Palestine railway to Beersheba and the construction of a metalled road from Beersheba to El Auja on the Egyptian frontier meant that larger numbers of troops could be moved more quickly and resupplied more effectively. In the words of the official British history, it 'vastly increased the importance of Beersheba as a base for operations against Egypt'.[16]

British policy in regard to a possible second attack evolved slowly. In the event of another invasion, Maxwell informed Kitchener in October, his response would be similar 'to that of February [1915], save that he would arrange for a counter-offensive, which lack of water and the tenor of his instructions had on that occasion prevented'.[17] Towards the end of 1915 the War Office also decided to reinforce the troops guarding the canal by sending additional divisions from the United Kingdom. Numbers were swelled by the force evacuated from Gallipoli, which was sent to Egypt for a period of rest and recuperation. Though useful in the event of a Turkish invasion, these units were under strength, and in the short term it was clearly unwise to place undue reliance on troops that had suffered so badly at the hands of a determined Turkish force. The scale of the task of restoring the Gallipoli veterans to full effectiveness was described by Sergeant Harold Clark of the Middlesex Regiment, who arrived in Egypt from Gallipoli in December 1915. He was transferred from Alexandria to a location north of Cairo which was the site of a

> staging camp for two divisions with ample space for training and recreation . . . Troops poured in daily and after Christmas another division arrived . . . This was one exercise by the commander-in-chief and his staff and the supply services which entitled them to claim great credit. To move, to provide and then re-equip nearly 100,000 men was a colossal task, and to do it with the minimum discomfort, as they did, deserved high praise.[18]

By the New Year, 1916, 14 infantry divisions, several mounted brigades and dismounted yeomanry brigades had arrived in Egypt. Once their period of rest and recovery was complete, Egypt would have more forces than it was ever likely to need. The War Office did not regard Egypt as their permanent station; they were a strategic reserve ready to be dispersed to any other front that needed reinforcement.

Their availability during their temporary winter sojourn in Egypt did, however, enable the military authorities to reconsider the idea of an Allied landing at Ayas on the western side of the Bay of Alexandretta. One of the reasons for its revival was Maxwell's belief that the evacuation of Gallipoli would have 'disastrous effects, morally as well as materially, unless Britain struck hard at Turkey elsewhere'.[19] While there were clear advantages in severing Turkish communications with Mesopotamia and Syria, the scale of the naval and military resources required and the risk of failure were equally great. Kitchener was unenthusiastic, and French arguments against the idea, which proved to be decisive, reflected concern at the presence of British soldiers in an area which the French regarded as being within their post-war sphere of influence. The British fight with Turkey would have to continue to be based on the defence of the Suez Canal.

With the Alexandretta project shelved, surplus troops were soon dispatched from Egypt. The 13th Division had already been sent to Mesopotamia, to reinforce the troops attempting to secure the relief of Kut. The remainder – the majority – were sent to France in support of a new offensive planned for the summer of 1916. Before long Egypt was once again in the position it faced before the influx of troops over the winter, the numbers available being barely sufficient to defend the canal. According to the official account, there was a real danger of 'the force in Egypt [being] almost reduced to the functions of a training and reinforcement camp'.[20]

But British ideas regarding effective defence of the canal were changing. A scheme based on the canal's western bank left it vulnerable to attack and to disruption of its commercial traffic in the event of a Turkish advance from the east, especially since a second Turkish assault was likely to be very much larger than the first. Such fears had been officially voiced when Kitchener visited Egypt in November 1915. Now, as Britain abandoned the policy of defending the Suez Canal on its banks, General Henry Horne, a distinguished artillery officer, was sent from London to advise on new defensive arrangements intended to put the canal out of reach of the enemy's long-range guns and to enable a system of active defence to be adopted. He was also instructed to consider how many troops would be needed to support these new arrangements.

Moving the protective line to the east of the canal, Horne prepared a plan which was based on three lines of defence: the first – the front

line – was some 11,000 yards to the east of the canal; the second
about halfway between the first line and the canal; and the third – a
series of fortified bridgeheads – was based on the eastern bank of the
canal itself. The second and third lines of defence would be covered
by the fire of warships stationed in the canal or lakes.

The question of whether Qatiya (an oasis 25 miles east of the
canal) should be occupied in order to deny it to an enemy invading
force was also considered as part of these proposals. There was intelligence that the Turks were planning to take over the Qatiya region as
a base for future operations. However, in the end a decision was postponed until the construction of the new canal defences had been
completed. This new defensive system, which included the construction of trenches extending over great distances, would need to be
supported by new desert roads, light railways and pipelines.

In a few weeks, over 100 miles of track were laid, and the main
railway line between Cairo and the canal was increased to double
track between Zagazig and Ismailia. Fresh water supplies to the new
front line were also organized. Water from the Sweet Water Canal
was processed in plants on the west bank of the Suez Canal and then
pumped to reservoirs on the east bank supplying tanks for use by
front-line troops. In the construction of the new defences and the
supporting communications local manpower, organized as the
Egyptian Labour Corps, played a substantial role. Since the adoption
of a system of active defence called for desert reconnaissance, often
involving light horse patrols, recourse was had to an Australian inven-
tion, the spearpoint pump, which could give troops on the move
immediate access to water supplies. Consisting of a 2.5-inch (6.35
cm) steel tube with a solid point at one end and a section with holes
covered by wire gauze to keep out the sand, the spearpoint pump
could be driven into the ground to a depth, if extension tubes were
used, of up to 6 metres. Water could normally be produced in
minutes.

Ideally, these new arrangements required additional troops to
support them. In November 1915, the War Office had estimated the
force needed to defend the canal at eight infantry divisions, five
mounted brigades and supporting artillery. Elsewhere in Egypt, two
infantry brigades and two mounted brigades were needed for the
defence of the Western Desert, while a mounted brigade and fifteen
garrison battalions would be needed for the delta. Estimates available
to Maxwell in December 1915, however, suggested that there were

some 250,000 Turkish troops in Palestine and Syria (a figure that proved to be a gross exaggeration). Expecting the next assault on the canal to be much larger than the last, Maxwell believed that twelve British infantry divisions were needed to defend the country from attack. However, when Russian military successes in the Caucasus led to the diversion of Turkish reinforcements earmarked for Palestine early in 1916, the immediate threat to the canal was reduced.

A third factor bearing on Egypt's security apart from the canal defences and the size of the defending forces was the nature of the local British command structure. With the arrival of the Mediterranean Expeditionary Force from Gallipoli there were three independent military commands coexisting within Egypt. The expeditionary force, which quickly assumed responsibility for the canal zone, was put under the command of Lieutenant-General Sir Archibald Murray, who arrived early in January 1916. An experienced professional soldier whose reputation was established during the South African war, Murray went to France in 1914 as chief of staff to the British Expeditionary Force under Sir John French. The traumatic early days of the war took their toll on him, and he returned home in poor health early in 1915. A period as Chief of the Imperial General Staff preceded his posting to Egypt, when he was succeeded as CIGS by Sir William Robertson.

With the introduction of this new command, Sir John Maxwell's role as commander of the force in Egypt was correspondingly reduced, reflecting a War Office view that his responsibilities for the defence of Egypt's western frontier and other internal military matters would not allow him time to manage the organization of the new canal defences or to rehabilitate the troops arriving from Gallipoli. He also retained an Egypt-wide function for the administration of martial law. To add to the complexity of these arrangements, there was a separate Levant Base, located at Alexandria, which was under the command of Major-General Edward Altham. This base held the military stores for British forces operating in Egypt, Gallipoli and Salonika.

The existence of three separate commands was clearly incompatible with sound administration and good military practice. The War Office experienced difficulties in dealing with the different commands and came to the conclusion – shared with the official record of the campaign – that it was clearly 'anomalous that the headquarters of a major force should have no voice in Egypt's affairs, which were interwoven with the administration of the Mediterranean Expeditionary Force'.[21] Murray himself quickly realized that there was no room for two independent commanders in Egypt and he offered to step down. Maxwell shared these concerns and pointed out that the base of the Mediterranean Expeditionary Force was located in a part of Egypt that was actually under his control. Sir William Robertson, Chief of the Imperial General Staff, also took this view and was not prepared to accept the muddled command and administration of the expanding forces in Egypt. Although Kitchener favoured the retention of the dual command structure, he was over-ruled by the Prime Minister and early in 1916 the War Office was instructed to create a unified command headed by a single senior officer.[22] Under this reorganization, announced in March 1916, the Mediterranean Expeditionary Force was merged with the Force in Egypt and renamed the Egyptian Expeditionary Force (EEF). Apart from meeting the security needs of Egypt and in particular the defence of the canal, the EEF was to provide a source of additional troops for the Western Front.

Sir Archibald Murray, commander of the Mediterranean Expeditionary Force, was appointed to the new post, and Maxwell was ordered to return home to England. Murray had obtained his original posting to Egypt because he wished to end his career in an independent field command rather than in the War Office. Although he had a solid record of wartime service, his real strengths were in administration and organization and he lacked the drive and deter-mination that were to underpin the achievements of his successor, General Allenby, in expelling the Turkish army from Palestine. However, for the immediate tasks envisaged at the time of his appointment – particularly the reorganization of the 'tired and depleted divisions' of the EEF, the development of a training pro-gramme and the restructuring of the canal defences – Murray was a strong candidate. It was only when offensive operations in Palestine began that his limitations as a military leader were to become fully apparent.

Murray had been working on new plans for the defence of Egypt before his formal appointment as commander-in-chief and, in mid-February, he presented his conclusions to Sir William Robertson. He did not believe that Egypt's system of defences, even in their new form, was entirely satisfactory: static defences tied up too many human resources and might not be effective against a determined enemy. He pointed to the advantage of creating a large mobile column in each sector of the canal zone. Beyond this, a more cost-effective form of defence could be achieved if British forces were to advance further into Sinai, well beyond the limits of the canal zone.

He had originally envisaged doing no more than constructing a railway line to Qatiya, which would permit its long-term occupation, but his plans soon became more ambitious. In a letter to Robertson of 15 February 1916, he made the case for a much more extended advance across the desert towards the border with Palestine. This would involve occupying the area between El Arish and Kossaima, thus blocking the northern coastal route from Gaza to the canal to a Turkish invasion force. British forces based in this area would also be able to operate against Turkish forces advancing across Sinai by the central and southern routes, or even to mount offensive operations against Turkish troops in Palestine before an invasion had started. The advance into Sinai would have to be carried out in stages as it would need to be accompanied by the construction of a water pipeline and a railway link from Qantara. Since the most powerful pumps then available could push about 100 tons of water an hour a distance of up to about 30 miles, reservoirs and pumping stations would have to be constructed at regular intervals across the desert. Murray believed that these objectives could be achieved with fewer troops than would be needed to maintain the passive defence of the canal.

The War Office replied cautiously to Murray's proposals, which marked a radical change in the direction of policy. Robertson agreed that Qatiya should be occupied as soon as possible if that were feasible, but he was not yet willing to make a decision about an advance to El Arish, which raised much wider policy issues. He was not convinced that the Turks could send more than 100,000 troops against Egypt; Murray's estimate of 250,000 men strained credulity in Whitehall and seems to have been well beyond the scale of Turkish plans. The War Office ignored Murray's figure and increased the rate at which British divisions were dispatched from Egypt to the Western Front. Robertson was also under pressure from the French to extend the British commitment to the Salonika front. Commenting on this in a letter of 15 March 1916 to General Murray, Robertson summarized his position:

Briefly my policy is to get as many troops away from the Salonika front as possible and as soon as I can. Refuse to take offensive action in the Balkans unless the situation changes very much. To keep Egypt reasonably secure. To keep a reserve in Egypt for India as long as it seems likely to be required. To get everyone else to France . . .[23]

Until March 1916, British troops were fully occupied in working on the canal defences and in the training and organization of the defence forces. For those involved in maintaining the new defences the work was hard and monotonous. According to Sergeant William Barron of the Northamptonshire Regiment, a typical camp

consisted of about a dozen tents in the middle of a network of trenches, and surrounded by a good strong barrier of barbed wire, with two entrances . . . this was the place we were meant to hold, if the Turks made an attack and tried to take the canal . . . there were about a hundred of us to hold this fort, but the Turks never came . . .[24]

The occupants of the fort were required to improve the camp and its defences, and a demanding daily timetable was imposed which reflected the extreme conditions under which they were expected to work. Sergeant Barron recorded the sequence of events in his diary:

The camp was roused at 3.45 a.m. . . . and started work at 4 a.m., [we] carry on until half past five then we used to knock off for tea and some bully beef stew, and in that half an hour we had to clean our tents, and lay our blankets out in the sun to air. At six o'clock we started work again, and carried on until eight o'clock, when it was too hot to be outside one's tent let alone working . . . [we] finished until 4 o'clock in the afternoon when we went and [did] another hour's work . . . in between nine o'clock in the morning and four in the afternoon it was almost too hot to breathe and we used to . . . lay in the tent, trying to keep cool . . .[25]

Once the new canal defences were in place, it was possible to move towards Qatiya, Murray's first objective in Sinai. Positioned at the western end of a series of oases that extended for some 15 miles to Bir el Abd, Qatiya was an obvious first target in the British advance eastwards. Drinking water was available in large quantities and since it was the nearest point to the canal that could sustain a large force, it was an attractive goal for a Turkish invasion force. Before Murray left the canal zone, British reconnaissance aircraft established that there were no substantial Turkish forces in Sinai or troop concentrations in southern Palestine. The operation effectively began in February 1916, when construction was started on the standard-gauge Sinai railway link between Qantara and Qatiya. As the terminus of the Sinai railway, Qantara was to develop as a major base and the future location of EEF headquarters. Its appearance was transformed, and as one officer, Lieutenant J.W. McPherson of the Camel Transport Corps, commented: 'the once picturesque village of Kantara, with its mosque frequented by pilgrims on the route to Mecca, no longer exists, but an enormous camp stretches for miles on both sides of the canal.'[26]

As the railway extended beyond the advanced line of the canal defences it was necessary to build permanent posts ahead of it in the direction of the Qatiya oasis in order to protect it from attack. By early April 1916, the railway had reached Oghratina oasis, within five miles of Qatiya. Shortly afterwards the Qatiya area was occupied by an infantry division and a mounted brigade and these troops soon began regular reconnaissance patrols, extending the writ of the British army further to the east through the series of oases towards Bir el Abd, 15 miles away. Here, on 9 April, the Worcestershire Yeomanry found the Turkish army present in some strength. Allied activity in Sinai was not confined to blocking the northern route; using mounted troops and aircraft they destroyed many of the water storage tanks on which the viability of the central route depended.

★

Increased British activity in the Sinai desert after almost eighteen months' absence did little to deter the Turkish army, which continued to develop plans for a second invasion in the spring of 1916. The idea was not to cross the canal but to take up positions east of it near to Qantara, thus giving the Turks the opportunity to block all traffic passing through it. The planned attack, however, was subsequently postponed and substantially scaled down because of demands on the Turkish army elsewhere. The attack was rescheduled for July and in revised form envisaged the involvement of no more than a single division. The reasons for the delay may relate to the loss of Erzerum in February and Trebizond in April 1916, in battles against the Russians. Although the Turkish campaign in the Caucasus did not result in the removal of troops from Syria, it may have delayed the dispatch of reinforcements there. As a result of these operations the Baghdad railway was working to capacity and it was not until the summer that German and Austrian reinforcements could be delivered to Palestine in significant numbers.

In addition, during this period Turkish forces were concentrated in northern Syria rather than in Palestine because of concerns about the security of its railway communications in the Alexandretta area. There were probably no more than 60,000 Turkish troops in the Ottoman territories south of Aleppo. It was certainly well beyond the capacity of the railway network in Palestine to maintain supplies for 250,000 men at Beersheba – which was the estimate General Murray had once subscribed to.

Although forced to delay plans because of their inability to bring their forces up to strength, the Turks soon found that inactivity was not an option either. Concerned at news of the regular departure of British troops to the Western Front, the Germans were applying pressure on their ally to make a limited advance towards the canal, in the hope that such a move would divert the Allies' attention. Having learned in March of British plans to build a railway from Qantara to Qatiya, the Turks decided to launch a fighting reconnaissance on Qatiya and Dueidar, 13 miles south-west of Qatiya.

In mid-April 1916, therefore, Kress von Kressenstein was dispatched into the desert once more, with a force consisting of about 3,500 men (together with six guns and four machine guns) organized in two battalions, together with a company of the 32nd Regiment, a mounted Arab regiment and a battery and a half of mountain artillery. Advancing westwards from Bir el Abd, Kress's main force proceeded quickly along the northern coastal route towards Oghratina and Qatiya, while a second Turkish column advanced to Bir el Mageibra, some 10 miles south-east of Qatiya, where on 19 April it attacked a British outpost. This was the first belated warning to the British of a Turkish advance, since their intelligence services had uncovered none of the enemy's plans nor any earlier sign of movement. In the words of the British official historian, they could have had little idea that the enemy was about to strike a blow which for 'combined speed, skill, daring, and success is hardly to be matched in the records of the campaign'.[27]

By this time the British Fifth Mounted Brigade (which consisted of the Warwickshire Yeomanry, Gloucestershire Hussars and

Worcestershire Yeomanry) had established its presence in the Qatiya area, where construction of the railway was well under way: the line by now had reached El Arais, some four miles to the west, and was within sight of Romani. Tasked not only with reconnaissance but with developing additional water supplies and protecting the new railway, the Fifth Mounted Brigade was dispersed over the area when the Turks approached. Based at Qatiya was a single squadron of the Gloucesters, while the remaining two squadrons were located at Romani. At Oghratina, five miles east of Qatiya, where the Royal Engineers were working on the water wells, were two squadrons of the Worcesters. At the same time two squadrons of the Warwickshire Yeomanry and a squadron of the Worcesters had been ordered to assemble at Bir el Hamisah, where they were to attack the enemy force advancing from Bir el Mageibra, eight miles to the north-east. This Allied force was led in person by Brigadier-General E.A. Wiggin, commander of the Fifth Mounted Brigade.

Wiggin arrived at Mageibra at dawn on 23 April, only to find a large and almost deserted camp. He quickly rounded up a small number of Turkish soldiers before returning to Hamisah. While the British had been pursuing this false trail, Kress had pressed on west-wards, during a hard night march, towards Oghratina, arriving there at 4.30 a.m. on 23 April, his presence concealed by darkness and an early morning fog. Attacked from the north, east and south-east, the single squadron of Worcestershire Yeomanry defending the position was taken completely by surprise. Heavily outnumbered, they fought for three hours but the Turks eventually overwhelmed them. Kress then advanced a further four miles to Qatiya, arriving there at 8 a.m. The defending troops at Qatiya were the Gloucestershire Hussars, reinforced by the squadron of Worcestershire Yeomanry which had returned from Hamisah at 10.30 a.m. Wiggin, who had arrived back at Hamisah at about 9 a.m., learnt that Oghratina had been surrounded and that the enemy was advancing on Qatiya. He left for the Qatiya area at 10.45 a.m. with a squadron of Warwickshire Yeomanry, but seeing Qatiya burning in the distance he decided to withdraw. Against superior Turkish forces the defending British troops had had a difficult task but they held out in the hope of further reinforcements until 3 p.m., when they surrendered after a bayonet charge. The forces has-tening there from Bir el Mageibra and Romani arrived too late: by the time they had reached the Qatiya area the fighting was over and the British had surrendered. The reinforcements fell back on Hamisah.

In a separate operation, a second column of Turkish troops attacked a British infantry post at Dueidar, west of Qatiya and some 12 miles from Qantara. A raid rather than an attempt to occupy the area, the enemy had already withdrawn when the Second Australian Light Horse Brigade arrived to eject them. On 25 April Qatiya and Romani were reoccupied by the British when the Turks withdrew to Bir el Abd.

The Turkish raid as a whole had been a tactical success and exposed weaknesses in British organization and intelligence. The Battle of Qatiya resulted in the loss of three and a half squadrons of British yeomanry. On the other hand, the Turks had failed in their main strategic objective: the action had no effect on the continued withdrawal of British troops from the canal zone to France. There had been twelve infantry divisions in Egypt in January 1916; by the beginning of June this number had been reduced to seven. A month later a further three divisions were sent to France.

★

After this operation, Kress suspended action for an expected three months (during the hot season from May to July when the hot southerly wind – the *khamsin* – blew) as he waited for Turkish and German reinforcements. The long interlude gave the British army the opportunity to consolidate its hold on the area immediately to the east of the Suez Canal, including Qatiya. The troops who were defeated by the Turks in April were replaced by more effective opponents, drawn from the newly formed Anzac Mounted Division. Created in March 1916 under the command of Major-General H.G. Chauvel, the division was to establish a formidable reputation by the end of the war. This division now reoccupied Romani on 24 April and held the key positions on the front line.

The lull in the fighting also meant that the construction of the Sinai railway could proceed without interruption and by mid-May it had reached Romani, although work on the water pipeline proceeded less quickly. Before the railway was pushed on towards Qatiya the 52nd Lowland Division was brought forward with the aim of establishing a strong defensive position, taking advantage of several natural features in the Romani area. The new British front line ran southwards from Mahamdiyah, a small settlement on the Mediterranean, for some six miles where it was protected by a line of sandhills. The northern end of the position, near the coast, touched the western edge of the extensive Bardawil lagoon; the southern flank was protected by a large dune named Katib Gannit.

A series of eighteen infantry redoubts was now constructed along this front, with each redoubt able to accommodate 100 rifles and two machine guns. Running westwards from Katib Gannit was Wellington ridge which marked the southern edge of a sand-covered plateau. The new Sinai railway ran through this area. To the south of Katib Gannit were several large individual sand dunes, including Mount Meredith, four miles south of Romani, and Mount Royston, four miles to the south-west. To the south of Katib Gannit was a concealed defensive position some four miles long. The troops based here were charged with delaying the enemy so that other mounted troops had the opportunity to launch a flank attack. The entire British position was supported by a branch of the new mainline railway which ran from a junction at Romani to Mahamdiyah; this port was also supplied direct from Port Said by means of a narrow-gauge railway link. As soon as the new British position at Romani was secure, the construction of the Sinai railway restarted. Qatiya was the next stop on the route to the Palestine border.

During this period, the outbreak in the Hejaz of the Arab revolt against Ottoman rule, in June 1916, marked a significant extension of the war against the Turks in the Middle East. Following British assurances about the future of the territory of Syria and Arabia, the Arabs under Sherif Hussein launched an uprising in Medina which soon spread to other parts of the Hejaz. With large numbers of Turkish troops tied down in the region, the revolt triggered a War Office review of British policy on the question of a further advance towards the Palestine border. Though previously dismissed in London as no more than a remote possibility, Robertson, following an appraisal of the situation by Murray, no longer ruled out the idea, but believed that such an advance would not be possible before October 1916. In a letter of 10 July 1916 he reinforced the message that little additional help would be available in the immediate future:

> we ought not to regard the dispositions as between different theatres in too rigid a manner, but be ready and willing to transfer from one theatre to another according as the situation and the season requires. Next winter you may require a good deal of help. On the other hand you may not. We shall see later on . . .[28]

In the meantime, Robertson believed that the 'great thing is to push on the El Arish railway as quickly as you can'.[29]

Meanwhile the British could do little to unsettle the Turks whose presence on the ground was limited to a few isolated garrisons out of range of their opponents. The Turks did, however, maintain a strong aerial reconnaissance capability and their aircraft 'hopelessly out-classed' those of the British. Lieutenant McPherson of the Camel Transport Corps described an incident in which 'fifty rounds of shrapnel have been lost on [the Taube], and an enormous number of machine gun bullets. One of our battle planes has engaged him and, I regret to say, has come down with a run, and he is still making circles round us and dropping bombs when he thinks fit.'[30] The Turkish camp nearest to the canal was at Bir el Mazar, some 42 miles east of Romani, where 2,000 troops were based. However, there were no apparent efforts to mobilize these troops and with 'the season being so far gone, [it was generally believed that] the long anticipated Turkish offensive would now be postponed until the winter [of 1916/17]'.[31] However, the situation quickly changed when increased numbers of enemy aircraft – faster and more effective than their British equivalents – suddenly appeared over Romani on 17 July. It was the first sign that the Turkish army might be starting its long-planned second attempt to invade Egypt.

This new Turkish force was better trained and equipped than that deployed in the first attempt of February 1915. Organized by the Germans, its objectives were more limited. It was ordered to capture the Romani position and then establish strong entrenchments oppo-site Qantara. Here its heavy artillery would be within gun range of the Suez Canal and would be able to use its firepower to ensure that normal traffic was disrupted. It had no remit to cross the canal. Liman von Sanders described the Turkish aim as 'not whole and not half'; it made 'one think of a man trying to wash his hands without wetting his fingers'.[32] However, the possibility of extending these modest objectives remained. If the Turkish army could defeat the British at Romani and break through to the canal zone, more troops could be moved across the desert and the option of trying to cross the water-way could be adopted once more.

Under the leadership of Kress von Kressenstein, the force consisted of 16,000 men (11,000 combatants) including the Third Division (from Anatolia), a Camel regiment and the German Pasha I forma-tion. The latter contingent, drawn up in Germany and dispatched to

the front via Constantinople, included eight machine-gun companies, five anti-aircraft groups and four heavy artillery and mountain
batteries. With a total of 12,000 rifles, 30 guns and 38 machine guns
this force now assembled at Shellal, north-west of Beersheba, and
departed for Sinai on 9 July 1916. This time it followed the northern
coastal route and after ten days of night marches it had reached Bir el
Abd and Oghratina.

Despite its attempts at concealment, the Turkish presence in Egypt
was soon discovered by British reconnaissance aircraft. On 19 July,
some 15 miles from British forward posts, the RFC found a Turkish
force of about 2,500 men occupying Bir el Bayud, with a smaller
force to the west at Gameil. In addition there was another force on
the northern coastal route at Bir el Abd. By 21 July, the Turkish army
had reached as far west as Oghratina, in sight of the British lines. The
British took immediate action to strengthen their defences in the
sector that separated the enemy from the canal. The 42nd Division
was allocated to No. 3 Section of the canal defences, which covered
the forward position at Romani. This represented a considerable
enhancement of the forces already deployed in the area under the
overall command of Lieutenant-General H.A. Lawrence, which
included the 52nd Division and a brigade of the 53rd Division, with
36 guns at their disposal. In addition, there were the several mounted
brigades in the section: the First and Second Australian Light Horse
Brigades were based at Romani, while the New Zealand Mounted
Brigade and the Fifth Mounted Brigade (Yeomanry) were positioned
at Hill 70 to the east of Qantara. Additional mounted troops, based in
No. 2 Section of the canal, could be sent northwards in the event of a
Turkish attack.

Kress's options as he advanced westwards towards the British line
near Romani were limited. An attack on the British left flank, which
rested on the Mediterranean shore, was clearly not practicable. The
envelopment of their right followed by an advance on the railway at
Romani was the Turkish army's only way forward. But it would be
far from easy to achieve success. The area beyond the British right
contained no water and was dominated by large dunes whose soft
sand made them difficult to negotiate. General Lawrence had also
come to the conclusion that this was the Turks' only possible route
and he made plans accordingly. Once the Turks had advanced into
the area, a British counter-attack would be launched. The infantry
would attack the Turkish centre, while the cavalry would envelop

their left. The aim would be to complete the destruction of the entire invasion force in a single action.

It soon became clear that events might not unfold in the way that General Lawrence had expected. On 24 July, the invasion force's westward march was brought to a halt a few miles east of Romani and remained in that position for ten days. The delay was caused by water shortages and the difficulty of moving heavy guns over the sand dunes near El Arish and up to the front line. There is no doubt that this operation was, in the words of the official British historians, an 'extraordinary feat', achieved only by the laborious process of laying down boards 'over the smaller islands of soft sand' and picking them up again 'when the wheels had passed over them'.[33] Elsewhere in the desert tracks for the wheels of gun carriages had to be dug and packed tightly with brushwood. Even normal movement in this part of the desert, where there was 'very, very heavy sand', was difficult. Guy Dawnay, a senior British staff officer, drawing on personal experience, calculated that 'ten miles over Sinai sand is equal to 25 miles anywhere else, from the point of sheer physical effort alone – to say nothing of the lack of water, fuel and shade, and the heat.'[34] Typically, horses could travel no faster than four kilometres an hour in such terrain.

However, the extended delay gave the British ample opportunity to plan their response. Their defensive preparations completed, General Murray's thoughts turned to the idea of offensive action. If Kress's force had not moved forward by 13 August, Murray was determined to launch a direct attack. British preparations were rapidly made and by the beginning of August over 10,000 camels had been brought to the front line to provide transport for the new offensive; British monitors anchored off Mahamdiyah shelled the Turkish invasion force as it assembled east of Romani; and an armoured train waited in a siding at Qantara ready to be brought up to help to defend the British right flank if necessary. The British also had the advantage of having uncovered the enemy's plans, which recorded on a map taken from a captured German officer.

During this period of uncertainty the Turkish forces were kept under close observation by the First and Second Australian Light Horse Brigades. A regular routine was soon established. One of the brigades spent the day before Qatiya observing the enemy position, while the other rested, returning to Romani when darkness fell. Kress seized the opportunity offered by the regular appearance and withdrawal of these mounted brigades. As soon as he was ready to attack, on the evening of 3 August, when it was mild and still, he followed the Second Australian Light Horse Brigade as it returned to camp after a day on reconnaissance duties. Intending to launch a surprise night attack he hoped to pass round the flank of the Allied position on the heels of the Australians with the aim of taking Wellington ridge before daylight.

The British were not, however, caught completely unawares by the Turkish action. An attack had been expected at any moment and the First Australian Light Horse Brigade had been deployed between the Turks and the flank of the British position. This outpost line, which extended southwards for four miles from Katib Gannit to Hod el Enna, brought the Turks to a temporary halt at 1 a.m., and when the Turkish attack was launched an hour later it provided heavy opposition along the whole front. In the end, however, the weight of Turkish numbers had its effect and the Australians were forced back. Fierce fighting developed and by 3 a.m. the Turks had captured Mount Meredith, a substantial dune in the centre of the front line. It had taken two attempts to capture it, the first having failed, according to the official British history, because the Turks could be easily seen by the Australian defenders: 'Their masses, visible against the silver sheen of the sand, offered excellent targets to magazine fire and their first assault was beaten back with heavy loss.'[35]

Australian troops of the two light horse brigades south of Mount Meredith were forced to fall back to their second line of defence but by daybreak they realized that their right was being outflanked by a strong Turkish force. They abandoned their position and fell back slowly to Wellington ridge, putting up strong resistance throughout. The Turks advanced up the valley between Wellington ridge and Mount Royston, another substantial dune two and a quarter miles to the west. Despite the arrival of two additional Australian regiments to reinforce the Allied right, the Turks maintained the momentum of their advance. At 5 a.m. an Australian withdrawal from Wellington ridge began and within three hours the Turks appeared on the crest. The enemy's outflanking movement continued as it skirted the slopes of Mount Royston, turning the right of the Second Australian Light Horse Brigade. At this point the commander of a squadron of Gloucestershire Hussars, based at Pelusium station, had seen at a distance the Turkish soldiers advancing in the Mount Royston area. He ordered his squadron into action and checked the Turkish outflanking movement. The Turkish assault in any case was beginning to fail: the troops were tired; they had run out of water; and Allied resistance had been stronger than expected. Attacks continued along the whole front but the Allied defences held.

At this point British headquarters, based at Qantara, put in train concerted action against the Turkish left. By 2 p.m. units of the New Zealand Mounted Regiment began an advance on Mount Royston, which by now had been captured by the Turks. The mount was retaken after a protracted four-hour struggle in which 500 Turkish prisoners were seized and 'the outer flank of the enemy's force was completely routed'.[36] During this period the Turkish inner flank made a final attempt to advance across Wellington ridge but they were thrown back by heavy artillery fire. The British then moved to recapture the ridge and had advanced to within 100 yards of the crest by the time darkness fell; it was recaptured on the following morning (5 August) and 1,500 prisoners were rounded up. It soon became clear that Kress would have to try to withdraw his force before he was encircled by the British. Although the Turkish force had exhausted itself, the Allies had new units at their disposal. On the enemy's left, the Third Australian Light Horse Brigade and a small mobile column, commanded by Lieutenant-Colonel C.L. Smith, were beginning to close in. On the Turkish right, the 52nd Division was well placed to launch an attack, while the 42nd Division was brought forward from reserves.

The forward movement of the British infantry, however, was slowed by heavy sand and summer heat, and Kress managed with great skill to extricate most of his troops (and heavy guns) from the immediate battle area before his opponents were in a position to launch a full-scale counter-attack. On 6 August, as British mounted troops pressed down on him, he fought an intense rearguard action. On the 7th he fought a similar action at Oghratina before evacuating the position, the Allied infantry having failed to make sufficient progress to support the cavalry in its assault on the Turkish positions. According to the official history, as they advanced the 'heat was terrific and the heavily burdened infantry suffered tortures on its march'.[37] The next day, the Bikanir Camel Corps, together with a squadron of aircraft, was sent out 'to search the desert for the unfortunates who had fallen out on the march and now lay upon the sand, often in a state of delirium'.[38] A day later Kress successfully resisted an attack by the Anzac Mounted Division on his positions at Bir el Abd, where he had first appeared three weeks earlier, before withdrawing further east to El Arish. He left an outpost at Bir el Mazar.

This marked the end of the Battle of Romani, which represented a costly failure for the Turkish army. About half of Kress's force of 16,000 men had been killed, wounded or taken prisoner. He also lost four heavy guns and several machine guns. British losses, at just over 1,100 in total, were relatively light. It is clear that Turkish losses would have been much higher had the British succeeded in preventing their escape from the battlefield. As it was, Kress kept his force in being and his artillery largely intact. Despite the intensity of the fighting, the British formed a favourable view of their opponents. Robert Wilson, a volunteer in the Royal Berkshire Yeomanry, who served in Sinai and Palestine from 1916, reported:

> The Turks are good sports, one day a Taube flew over and dropped a message saying 'Please mark your hospitals more distinctly', three days afterwards they came and dropped about 25 bombs – at one place we found a message 'Good fight, don't drive us too hard, your cavalry has beaten us' and, 'Don't stop here long it is infected with cholera', so we cleared out.[39]

Various factors had worked against a properly coordinated British counter-attack. Their headquarters – located at Qantara – were too far away from the battlefield for the high command to control the course of events with any degree of precision. Its work was complicated by the fact that the infantry at Romani was not under a single commander, while the mounted troops brought in from the adjoining area of the canal defences – No. 2 Section – were under yet another command. The difficulties inherent in the British command arrangements were compounded by the limited intelligence available to them during the battle as a result of the shortage of reconnaissance aircraft.

The combined effect of these constraints was to reduce British responsiveness and to delay the pursuit of the enemy. This was unfortunate because the British infantry needed a time advantage over their opponents: neither the 42nd nor the 52nd Division was trained in desert warfare and they were unable to maintain the same pace as the Turks, whose powers of endurance were remarkable. They were also slowed by water supply problems. British mounted troops were unable to compensate for these shortcomings. Indeed, it has been argued that their own tactics were flawed and, in concentrating on direct assaults rather than flank attacks, they helped to facilitate the Turkish withdrawal. Even though a more determined pursuit might have secured the destruction of Kress's force, the Battle of Romani remained a considerable British achievement and was a turning point in the campaign to restore Egypt's territorial integrity and security. There is little doubt that the battle marked the end of the Turkish campaign against the canal. It was clearly no longer an attainable goal. According to the official historians, 'further attacks might be projected in Constantinople, but they were always found to be impracticable.'[40]

The military initiative now passed to the British who were poised to continue their stage by stage advance across the Sinai desert, forcing the Turkish army back across the frontier into Palestine. In Robertson's view, expressed in a letter of 1 August to General Murray, there was no advantage in another delay: 'the longer he [the Turk] stays where he is the stronger he will become, and therefore the sooner he is dealt with the better.'[41] Another reason for maintaining the momentum of this protracted campaign during the summer of 1916 related to the changing fortunes of the Arabs of the Hejaz, far to the south of Romani. Their revolt against the Turkish army of occupation was soon to run into serious difficulties.

# 3

# *The Arab Revolt*

THE ARAB UPRISING against the Ottoman empire began near Medina in the Hejaz province of Arabia on 5 June 1916.[1] The Hejaz was part of the Arabian peninsula and the largest of the three provinces under Turkish control that faced the Red Sea. To the north it extended almost as far as the Gulf of Aqaba; to the south the province encompassed Jeddah, the port of Mecca. Built by German engineers, the Hejaz railway provided a direct link between the province and the rest of the Ottoman empire. This metre-gauge line ran from Damascus via Amman to the southern terminus at Medina, some 250 miles north of Mecca. The construction of the railway, which reached Medina in 1908, was a useful mechanism to strengthen Turkish control and increase German influence in the area.

Beyond Jeddah were the provinces of Asir and Yemen, which were isolated from the outside world by the Royal Navy's blockade of the Red Sea. Asir was an inhospitable place where there was strong local opposition to the Turks; it played no active part in the war. A single Turkish division, the 21st, was maintained there. Further south, the ruler of the Yemen, the Imam Yahia of Sanaa, had offered active opposition to the Turks in the pre-war period and had fought several campaigns against them. Just before the outbreak of the First World War, the Turks concluded a treaty with the imam, which ensured that the two sides coexisted peacefully until 1918. Under the terms of this agreement the imam supplied the two Turkish divisions – the 39th and 40th – that were based in the Yemen, but did nothing actively to support them. The only interruption to the peace of this isolated province was an invasion of the British protectorate of Aden in July

1915 by the Turkish forces based in the Yemen. When the invasion force threatened the fortress of Aden, Britain responded by sending a brigade from Egypt, which was able to ensure the security of the fortress itself. No effort, however, was made to expel the Turks from the large area of the Aden protectorate, which they occupied until their collapse at the end of the war.

The Arab decision to raise the standard of revolt was the result of extended and complex negotiations with the British dating back to the early days of the war. The British had viewed the Hejaz Arabs as a potential ally since 1914 and had sought an alliance with them as much for political as military reasons. The Turks had used religion as a weapon to increase anti-British feeling throughout the Muslim world, including Persia, Afghanistan and India. An alliance with the ruler of the Hejaz, Sherif Hussein, Amir of Mecca, would help to undermine the impact of the declaration of a *jihad* and counteract German propaganda, as well as opening a second front against the Turks in the region.

Kitchener had been briefed on Arab national aspirations as early as February 1914 when Abdullah, the Sherif's second son, had visited Cairo. Abdullah made it known that it was the Sherif's ambition to secure greater autonomy for the province. The Sherif himself informed Kitchener in September that he would not support Turkey by choice in the event of war being declared, and from that point the Hejaz Arabs were viewed as potential allies. Following the outbreak of war with Turkey Sir John Maxwell urged that these earlier contacts should be pursued. Sherif Hussein was given an assurance that if he actively supported the Allies, then Britain would endorse Arab aspirations for independence. In his reply, in December 1914, the Sherif said that he would do nothing that was hostile to British interests but that he was not yet ready to make a final break with Turkey because of his position within Islam. Despite his caution, the Sherif had declined a request from Constantinople to proclaim a *jihad* from the Hejaz and the declaration – issued in Constantinople on 14 November 1914 – was seen as a purely Turkish action without Arab endorsement.

Serious negotiations with Hussein reopened in mid-1915 when the Sherif wrote to Sir Henry McMahon, who in January 1915 had been appointed to the new post of High Commissioner in Egypt.[2] As the price for Arab cooperation Hussein made wide-ranging demands, seeking British recognition of Syria, Palestine and Arabia as an independent Arab-governed area in the event of a Turkish defeat. Subsequent correspondence between Cairo and Mecca focused on British attempts to limit the nature of the post-war gains that the Arabs could expect to secure in return for their military support. The British end of these discussions was assisted by the creation early in 1916 of the Arab Bureau, a Cairo-based unit that was responsible for the collection of information and the development of policy on Arab issues.

Britain was always careful not to constrain itself by giving away too much and there was often a degree of ambiguity in the correspondence between McMahon and Hussein. On the other hand, it was soon evident that Britain would need to make real concessions if it wished to secure the Arabs' military support. There was also a danger that a breakdown in the discussions would drive the Arabs into the hands of the Turks or Germans: the Turks were showing signs of having recognized the ambivalence of the Arab position and were being untypically flexible in their approach to the emergence of a secret society of Arab officers within the Turkish army. In October 1915, McMahon finally sent a positive response to Hussein's demands, indicating a British willingness to recognize and support the independence of the Arabs in some of the areas that Hussein had identified. British agreement was subject to a number of qualifications, including the exclusion of the area that now comprises Lebanon. The assurance was also limited 'to those parts of the Arab territories in which Great Britain was free to act without detriment to the interests of France'.[3]

The Hejaz Arabs read the agreement as signifying that in return for their help in defeating the Turks independent Arab governments would be established in Ottoman Palestine and Syria; the British, on the other hand, intended to concede to the Arabs no more than parts of Syria and Arabia. Sir Henry McMahon's ambiguous prose, however, was notable for the confusion it caused.

Britain needed room for manoeuvre because of the separate negotiations it was simultaneously conducting with the French about the shape of the post-war Middle East – negotiations that led to the signing of a secret Anglo-French agreement (known as the Sykes–Picot agreement) in April 1916 which allocated well-defined spheres of influence to Britain, France and Russia. This agreement aimed to divide the area on a different basis from that proposed by McMahon, and in particular identified two areas, one allocated to France, the other to Britain, in which they were each to oversee a self-governing

Arab state. The western boundary of the British area extended from a point south of Lake Tiberias and followed the Jordan to the Dead Sea. Here it turned west to the coast at Gaza and ran along the Sinai frontier to Aqaba. Beyond this, the British area extended eastwards as far as the Mesopotamian border. The French area formed a triangle running from Aleppo to Lake Tiberias to Rowanduz near the Persian border. It included the cities of Homs, Aleppo and Damascus in Syria. To ensure recognition of their claims, the French decided that they could not rely indefinitely on diplomatic means and agreed to maintain a military force in the area. Supplementing a few technical units already present in the Hejaz, French aircraft and artillery units were duly dispatched to serve with the Egyptian Expeditionary Force on the Palestine front, but did not arrive until May 1917.

Hussein was unaware of the existence of this agreement at the time the Arab revolt began. It was evident that it ran counter to the understanding he had reached with McMahon, particularly as it affected the territory that was to fall within the French sphere of influence. It quickly became clear to those who had access to the agreement that Sherif Hussein would have to occupy Damascus, Hama, Homs and Aleppo before the end of the war. Without this physical presence, he would be unable to secure the conditional control of Syria and Mesopotamia that was provided for in the Sykes–Picot agreement. A daunting task – the capture of Syria – therefore faced the Arabs before their revolt could be brought to a successful conclusion, and it was essential that their strategy fully reflected these hidden political imperatives. In an article on *Seven Pillars of Wisdom*, his celebrated account of the Arab revolt, T.E. Lawrence expressed the Arabs' wartime objectives in the following terms:

> I thought of the Arab aim, and saw that it was geographical, to occupy all Arabic-speaking lands in Asia. In the doing of it we might kill Turks: we disliked them very much. Yet 'killing Turks' would never be an excuse or aim. If they would go quietly, our war would end. If not, we would try to drive them out: in the last resort we would be compelled to the desperate course of blood . . . but as cheaply as possible for ourselves, since the Arabs were fighting for freedom, a pleasure only to be tasted by a man alive.[4]

Although the architect of the agreement with Sherif Hussein, Sir Henry McMahon, was General Allenby's oldest friend, most of the military establishment in Cairo were at first opposed to the deal. Prior to Allenby's arrival on 27 June 1917 there was little enthusiasm for the Arab revolt among the high command of the British army. General Murray, the commander-in-chief, saw the Allied war against the Turks in conventional terms as a war of movement between two modern armies (he later moderated his views). The Arabs were disorganized and ill-equipped and their impact would be limited. Vast sums would be needed to bring them up to date, with uncertain results. These funds would be better spent on the Allied forces moving across the Sinai desert. Other British military officers in Cairo, however, had a wider political vision and saw the potential benefits of collaborating with the Arabs. Some of these more enlightened officers were members of the Arab Bureau, whose bulletins helped to change the climate of opinion within the British army in Egypt.

An essential member of the Arab Bureau was T.E. Lawrence, 'Lawrence of Arabia', British scholar and archaeologist, who became one of the most prominent and controversial figures to emerge during the war.[5] Despite his relative youth – he was twenty-six at the outbreak of war – he was highly knowledgeable about the Middle East as a result of his pre-war archaeological expeditions and his involvement in a military survey of the Sinai desert. He was particularly well informed about Syria and had a rare understanding (for an Englishman) of the Arab psyche. His military mapping experience led directly to an appointment to a newly created intelligence department of the general staff in wartime Cairo where he was one of a number of able young men – including archaeologists Stewart Newcombe and Leonard Woolley as well as Members of Parliament Aubrey Herbert and George Lloyd and *The Times* journalist Philip Graves – who formed the nucleus of the new department. Both Newcombe and Woolley were former colleagues of Lawrence: Woolley and Lawrence had worked together in Syria, while all three men had contributed to the 1914 survey of Sinai. At first, Lawrence was largely desk-based and his responsibilities included that of map officer, monitoring the strength and disposition of Turkish forces. His remit was gradually extended and, in March 1916, he was sent to Mesopotamia as part of the delegation negotiating with the Turks to secure the lifting of their siege of the British force trapped at Kut el Amara.

During this period Lawrence became deeply involved in developments in the Hejaz and was appointed the first editor of the *Arab*

*Bulletin*, which published intelligence summaries of developments in the Arab world. The *Bulletin* included reports produced by members of the Arab Bureau, to which Lawrence had transferred as a founding member early in 1916. On the staff of the bureau he worked actively in support of the Arab cause and the launch of the revolt. In a letter to his mother of 1 July 1916, Lawrence referred to its long period of gestation, while being fully alive to its wider significance:

> It has taken a year and a half to do, but now is going very well. It is so good to have helped a bit in making a new nation – and I hate the Turks so much that to see their own people turning on them is very grateful . . . This revolt, if it succeeds will be the biggest thing in the Near East since 1550.[6]

★

Once agreement had been reached with the British towards the end of October 1915 and Sherif Hussein had decided, in the spring of 1916, to initiate military action, all that was awaited was a suitable occasion for the Arab uprising. The timing of the revolt was triggered partly by the repressive action being taken by Djemal Pasha, Turkish governor of Syria, against leading Arab nationalists in Damascus. Another consideration was the arrival at Medina in late May 1916 of 3,000 Turkish troops on their way south through Asir province to the Yemen, where they were to reinforce the 39th and 40th Divisions.

The revolt, which broke out at Medina on 5 June 1916, was led by Sherif Hussein and his four sons – Ali, Abdullah, Feisal and Zeid. Supported at first by some 50,000 tribesmen, they launched attacks on the principal concentrations of Turkish troops in the main towns of the Hejaz. These formed the foundation of Ottoman rule in the province and without them imperial authority would cease to exist. Only a small proportion of the Sherif's forces had modern rifles and initially they had no machine guns or artillery. The reliability of the rank and file could not be taken for granted as individual contingents made their own decisions about when to arrive or return home. The occupying forces could muster a single division – the 22nd – in the Hejaz, although they were supported by battalions from another division (the 21st) based in Asir. In total, the Turks had about 15,000 men available.

The uprising in Medina was initiated by Feisal, who led an assault on the town's defences the following day (6 June). Some 30,000 men were involved in the action, although only 6,000 of them were armed. The action was unsuccessful and after a few days they withdrew from the immediate area, out of range of the fort artillery, and there initiated a blockade. Meanwhile, Ali advanced northwards with the intention of cutting the Hejaz railway at a point some 180 miles away, while Sherif Hussein himself commanded a force dispatched to attack the holy city of Mecca, some 250 miles south of Medina.

Mecca proved to be a relatively easy target since most of the Turkish garrison had relocated to its summer quarters at Taif, a town in the hills some 70 miles to the south-east. The remaining Turkish troops – some 1,000 elite troops – though enjoying the protection of their forts, were isolated from the outside world and heavily outnumbered by Arab tribesmen. Three days of street fighting followed the initial attack on Mecca, but the Arabs gradually captured the essential points – the mosque of the Holy Kaaba, the administrative quarter and the main bazaar. The principal barracks were destroyed by fire and, on 12 June, the majority of the surviving Turks, overcome by smoke, were forced to surrender. A few survivors held out in two small forts until mid-July, when they finally surrendered after the arrival of several artillery pieces from Egypt.

The Turkish garrison at the nearby Red Sea port of Jeddah was in an even less secure position than the troops at Mecca. On 9 June, the sheikh of the Harb tribe organized and led an attack by 4,000 tribesmen which was repelled by the Turks with no real difficulty; the Arabs were unable to make much impact against a garrison armed with machine guns and artillery. Soon, however, the Royal Navy came to their rescue. On 11 June, two warships bombarded the port, while seaplanes from the carrier *Ben-my-Chree* dropped several bombs. The continuing impact of the naval assault – combined with a severe shortage of water – forced the Jeddah garrison to surrender on 16 June, with some 1,500 prisoners and 16 guns and machine guns being captured. Rabegh, another Red Sea port 100 miles to the north of Jeddah, fell some time afterwards. Within days of its fall, on 27 July, a third Red Sea port, Yenbo, 100 miles beyond Rabegh, was captured by Sherifian forces.

Elsewhere in the southern Hejaz, the Arabs made less rapid progress. The Turkish troops based at Taif, the summer station of the Mecca garrison, maintained their strongly fortified positions until the latter part of September. Some 3,000 Turkish troops, protected by

German artillery, faced 5,000 Arabs led by Abdullah. The deadlock was broken following the arrival of an Egyptian artillery battery, together with a battery of captured Turkish howitzers from Egypt, which substantially altered the balance of forces. The bombardment began on 16 July and lasted for over ten days, causing serious damage. Abdullah decided to maintain the siege rather than launch a final assault, which could have caused him heavy losses and undermined Arab morale. With no prospect of external assistance, the beleaguered Turks decided that they had no choice but to abandon the fight and on 22 September they surrendered unconditionally.

Further to the north, at Medina, the other principal Arab target, the prospect of an even longer siege had become a reality, even though the Arabs were no match for their opponents in terms of military experience or access to modern equipment. Under the command of an old-fashioned and determined military leader, Fakhri en din Pasha, 'the Tiger of Medina', the Turkish troops fought effectively from well-entrenched positions. Their constant machine-gun fire meant that the Bedouin could make little impact on this essential centre of Turkish power and the intensity of their attacks soon died down. Even a few recently acquired artillery pieces were no match for Medina's ancient city walls. On 3 July, Fakhri Pasha underlined his local strength by making a sortie from the centre of the town, during which he engaged and defeated Feisal's forces, compelling them to withdraw. Soon afterwards, he launched a brutal attack on the residents of Awali, an undefended suburb that he had occupied. Innocent men, women and children were murdered and their homes destroyed. It was the first indication that women and children – hitherto inviolate – were to be considered legitimate targets in the struggle between Arab and Turk. An Arab counter-attack once more failed against the walls of Medina.

On 3 August, the Turkish forces based at Medina launched a second attack on Feisal's forces which surrounded the city. In the running battle that ensued, Feisal was pushed back some 20 miles along the road running west from Medina in the direction of Rabegh. The Arab levies were subsequently withdrawn 50 miles to the south, where they were instructed to block the road to Rabegh and Mecca. At this point there was a barrier of hills some 20 miles wide which helped the defensive efforts of Feisal's tribesmen. In the meantime, Fakhri Pasha reinforced his position by extending his lines in the Medina area. The railway to the north was repaired and reinforcements were soon being sent down the link from Maan and beyond. Before long a permanent garrison of 2,000 troops was in place which would enable Fakhri Pasha to maintain control of Medina for another two and a half years. The siege was only finally brought to an end when his officers staged a mutiny in January 1919, more than two months after Britain and Turkey had signed an armistice.

★

In the lull in the fighting which now occurred, while the Turks made preparations for a new offensive to recapture Mecca, the British were able to evaluate how best to support the initial Arab successes. While it was clear that their victory was far from complete, news that the Turks were waiting for reinforcements to arrive at Medina encouraged General Murray in his belief that the Hejaz revolt was likely to draw off a sizeable number of Turkish troops who would otherwise be deployed in Sinai against a British advance towards the Palestine border. He also supported War Office plans, approved on 6 July 1916, for the British occupation of Aqaba simultaneously with the British advance on El Arish. The action would remove a potential threat to the Allied right flank as it advanced across the northern Sinai desert, while a British presence in Aqaba, within striking distance of the Hejaz railway, would threaten Turkish communications between Medina and Syria and give moral and material support to the Arab revolt. The project was rejected by the military authorities in Egypt on practical grounds. Although a landing from the sea presented no great difficulties, the landing force would be vulnerable to continuous flank attack from the hills beyond Aqaba, where the Turks had a series of strong defensive positions. Murray's staff calculated that it would take three divisions – almost equal to the strength of the Egyptian Expeditionary Force – to dislodge the Turks from their positions north of Aqaba.

At the practical level, there had been a rapid build-up in the logistical support offered by the British from the moment the revolt had begun. General Sir Reginald Wingate, Governor of the Sudan and commander-in-chief of the Egyptian army, was given overall responsibility for British operations in the Hejaz. One of Wingate's first actions was to appoint Colonel E.C. Wilson, governor of the Sudan's Red Sea province, as his personal representative in the Hejaz and to charge him with advising Sherif Hussein on strategy. In August, Feisal made contact with Colonel Wilson for the first time. Wilson reported to Wingate that 'Feisal spoke bitterly about the lack of supplies from Britain and of ammunition shortages during a month's continuous fighting. As a result his forces had been obliged to retire gradually towards the coast at Rabegh.'[7] However, Wilson was able to point to an inconsistency in approach between Feisal and his father. While Feisal was complaining about the lack of British support, Sherif Hussein was stopping men and supplies from Egypt entering the country, in an attempt to minimize British influence on the course of operations.

The relatively static military situation continued during the summer while the Medina garrison waited for sufficient reinforcements to arrive from the north. The build-up was slow and it was not until late September that the Turks were ready to advance from Medina. Their forces were to be dispatched southwards into the province with the aim of recapturing the main towns lost to the Arabs. The plan was to deploy a mobile column to advance on the port of Rabegh and then aim for Mecca. In preparation for the offensive, in August 1916 the Turks also stripped Hussein of his title as Amir of Mecca; his replacement, Ali Haidar, was being dispatched from Constantinople and would accompany the Turkish army as it made its way from Medina to Mecca. When the holy city had been captured, Ali Haidar would 'be ready to make a triumphal entry into Mecca, with the Turkish holy carpet'.[8]

Reinforcements continued to arrive at Medina, eight additional battalions in total being added to the surviving Turkish garrisons. These new troops strengthened the Turkish Hejaz Expeditionary Force which consisted of some 15,600 men, six batteries of field guns, three mountain batteries and four Maxim batteries. Most of the Hejaz force was concentrated in the Medina area: 2,000 troops formed the garrison of the town itself, while 6,500 were deployed up to 40 miles to the south and 1,500 on the railway to the north. In advancing from Medina to Mecca, it was likely that the Turks would use the route through the port of Rabegh, 150 miles to the southwest, as this provided access to reliable water supplies. The defence of Rabegh was the key to the security of Mecca and therefore the essential issue of concern to the Arabs and their British advisers.

At this point in the revolt, the Arabs were braced to respond to a strong Turkish thrust from Medina. Their failure to capture the town meant that the Turks had a relatively secure base from which to continue operations against them. The three Arab field armies, led by

Hussein's three eldest sons, had difficulty matching the strength of their regular opponents, particularly when the Bedouin tribesmen were so unreliable and could leave the field at a moment's notice.

Based south-west of Medina was Ali with eleven guns and an army of 8,600 men, the majority of whom consisted of Arab tribesmen, although included in their number were some 1,800 Arab regular troops with a degree of military training. Positioned to the south-east of Medina, and now moving in a north-easterly direction, was Abdullah's army with up to 10,000 men and ten guns at his disposal. Based at the port of Yenbo, but in practice normally operating from positions several miles inland, was Feisal, supported by a force that was divided by tribal allegiances – his men came from the Ageyi, Billi, Juheina and Ateiba tribes – as much as it was united against a common enemy. Feisal's force fluctuated considerably in size from 2,000 to 8,000 men depending on whether family and tribal ties called on them to leave the front line. Feisal was supported by Zeid, his younger brother, and by Abdul Aziz al Masri, a Turkish exile in Egypt who had served as a cavalry officer in the Ottoman army. A smaller force, consisting of 900 Egyptian volunteers and 700 irregulars, was based at Rabegh.

The long expected Turkish expedition to recapture Mecca finally left Medina in late September 1916 and marched down the Sultani road towards Rabegh. At first it made less progress than the Arabs had expected. The mountainous section of the route proved to be difficult to negotiate and Feisal's army helped to slow its progress even further. The will to resist the enemy was greatly strengthened by the arrival of news that the Turkish fort at Taif had finally fallen to Abdullah's forces on 22 September. To help stabilize the position Ali sought Sherif Hussein's agreement to move his forces from the Medina area to Rabegh, where they could be used in support of Feisal and would significantly increase the prospects of defeating a Turkish force advancing on Rabegh. On arrival there, accompanied by 1,000 men, he was ordered to secure a strong defensive position and given the task of building a force of 5,000 Arab regulars under the command of Abdul Aziz al Masri, with Nuri es-Said as his deputy. These troops would help to provide a more reliable core to the forces fighting in support of the Arab revolt and would encourage the tribesmen to maintain their positions during an engagement.

Advancing from Medina down the Sultani road, the Turks fought a number of engagements with Feisal's army in the area around Bir

Abbas, beginning on 6 October, during which the Arabs gained a temporary advantage. Within a day, however, the Turks had recovered from their setback and the advance towards Rabegh continued. By 23 October, the Arabs had been forced to retreat some 30 miles to Hamra. Fears that the port of Rabegh could finally fall to the Turks had already triggered the dispatch of a high-level British mission to the Hejaz. Ronald Storrs, a diplomat on the staff of the British residency, was sent to Jeddah to discuss the situation with Sherif Hussein's son Abdullah. Lawrence asked to be allowed to go with him and 'no one at G.H.Q. was anxious to detain him'.[9] During the course of his visit, Lawrence hoped to identify an Arab military leader whom Britain would be able to support in the confidence that he would make effective use of the arms and money supplied. Lawrence also expected to improve his knowledge of the organization of the Arab armies.

By this time extensive military aid was being given to the new Arab state through the Sudan, where Wingate continued to offer active support to the Arab cause. Specialist advice was also available, although the key individuals were not active on the ground until early in 1917. Commanded by Colonel Wilson, the team included Colonel Newcombe; Hubert Young, transport and supplies chief; and P.C. Joyce, who secured Arab cooperation in the northern desert of the Hejaz. Joyce's chief of staff was W.F. Stirling, who was to found the Special Air Service during the Second World War. Feisal, who had already been forced back to Kheif, warned Wilson that the Turks would try to break through to Mecca in time for the annual Muslim pilgrimage. He reiterated the need for a landing of British forces at Rabegh and requested more aeroplanes, arms and equipment. He also urged a British military intervention to the north with the aim of severing the railway link to Medina. Wilson himself supported the idea of a landing at Aqaba as a way of extending the scope of the revolt.

Feisal's complaints about gaps in the delivery of military supplies were not entirely the fault of the British. Entering the country through the port of Rabegh, these supplies were intended to be distributed by the Sheikh of Rabegh, Hussein ibn Mubeirik, who was suspected of diverting some of them to the enemy. Whatever the truth of the matter, Feisal's forces were not in good enough shape to oppose a Turkish force intent on recapturing Mecca via Rabegh and the coastal road to the south. In the short term both Feisal and

Wilson believed that the dispatch to the Hejaz of a British force was the only way to save the revolt. For this purpose Feisal requested a force of 200 regulars and two aircraft. General Murray, however, when discussing this request with the EEF, believed that a much larger force – a brigade of infantry, plus supporting troops – would be needed if it were to be capable of defending itself when deserted by Arab troops. This was too large a commitment, though, to be contemplated at a time when the British were planning to advance across northern Sinai to El Arish and considering a landing in Aqaba. The issue was referred to London, where any further extension of British involvement in the Middle East would need to be approved. This did not prevent Wilson and others continuing to campaign for British intervention in the Hejaz as Arab difficulties began to mount.

Feisal remained unhappy about the course of events and attributed much of his ill fortune to logistical problems. Despite his despondent mood, it was clear to Lawrence from his first meeting with Feisal at his camp, on 23 October, that he was the only one of Hussein's sons who had the necessary qualities to lead the Arab revolt and bring it to a successful conclusion. Aged thirty-one, Feisal was

> tall, graceful and vigorous, with the most beautiful gait, and a royal dignity of head and shoulders . . . He showed himself hot-tempered and sensitive, even unreasonable . . . His personal charm, his imprudence, the pathetic hint of frailty as the sole reserve of this proud character made him the idol of his followers.[10]

When asked by Feisal how he liked his camp in Wadi Safra, Lawrence replied, 'Well; but it is far from Damascus.' Feisal could appreciate more readily than most of his colleagues the importance of Lawrence's message that the capture of the Hejaz was no more than the beginning of the Arab revolt; their real target should be Syria and the northern towns mentioned in the Sykes–Picot agreement. Unless these towns were under Arab control by the end of the war, the danger that the nationalist cause would be marginalized would become a reality.

On his return journey to Cairo, Lawrence went first to Khartoum and at a meeting with Wingate he endorsed further Arab requests for additional support in the form of advisers, equipment and supplies. Wingate took a different view, seeing the need for the landing of British troops in the Hejaz as a necessity if the current military deadlock were to be broken. Such an intervention, Lawrence realized, would be unacceptable to the Arabs themselves as well as leading to the involvement of French ground troops. On his return to Cairo in mid-November, Lawrence summarized the situation in the Hejaz for his political and military superiors in Cairo:

> All the forces fighting for the Sherif are made up of tribesmen, and it is the tribal army 3,000 to 4,000 strong under Sidi Feisal . . . that has held up the advance on Mecca or Rabegh of Fakhri Pasha's army for five months. Rabegh is not, and never has been, defensible with Arab forces, and the Turks have not got there because these hill tribes under Feisal bar the way. If the hill tribes yield the Turks need not look to any further opposition to their advance until near Mecca itself.[11]

In Cairo Lawrence continued to argue for the provision of more British support for the Arabs. He complained that the three batteries of mountain guns which Feisal had asked for almost four months ago had still not arrived. If they

> were given these guns . . . they will . . . be able to hold up the present Turkish force as long as they require. Their morale is excellent, their tactics and manner of fighting admirably adapted to the very difficult country they are defending, and their leaders understand that to provoke a definitive issue now is to lose the war. To continue the present *guerre de course* is sooner or later to wear out the Turks completely, and force them back on a passive defence of Medina and its railway communications.[12]

Lawrence's views on sending British ground forces to the Hejaz, though based chiefly on concern at local reactions to the intervention of a white, non-Muslim force in the area, coincided with those of General Murray, the commander-in-chief, and his staff, who were anxious not to lose a single soldier as they advanced across the Sinai desert. The issue was finally settled when Hussein declined to accept British aid in this form. British military headquarters in Cairo had, however, begun to recognize the potential importance of the Hejaz revolt and supported it with more instructors and supplies.

Beyond improving the supply of equipment to the Hejaz, there was a need to increase the size of the Arab forces and improve the quality of its leadership. Desertions from the Turkish army proved a fruitful source of trained Arab soldiers and officers. In addition, an

Arab Legion was formed from Arab volunteers held with other members of the Turkish army as prisoners of war in Egypt and India. Arabs in Turkish service held prisoner at Rabegh were another source.

As long as there were insufficient professional trained officers in the Arab forces, the role of British military advisers was of great importance in ensuring that the Arabs responded effectively to the situation on the ground. While it would take months to identify and send sufficient advisers to the Hejaz, Lawrence had already shown himself virtually indispensable in this capacity. No sooner had he arrived back in Cairo, in mid-November 1916, than he was planning to return to the Hejaz. Reappearing in Yenbo at the beginning of December, Lawrence was to serve with the Sherifian forces for the rest of the war. His appointment as a liaison officer and adviser to Feisal, which took effect shortly after his arrival, was originally intended to be temporary but the arrangement worked so well that it became permanent. Brigadier-General Gilbert Clayton, the senior British staff officer involved in the Hejaz operations, commented in March 1917: 'the value of Lawrence in the position which he has made for himself with Feisal is enormous.'[13]

Lawrence's return coincided with important military developments. With the Turks unable to break through the Arab barrier south-west of Medina, the risk to Rabegh and Medina was receding and Sherif Hussein turned his thoughts to breaking the stalemate. A proposal to extend the campaign northwards to Wejh, a small Turkish-occupied port some 200 miles north of Yenbo, soon emerged. This extension of the front would have the benefit of easing the pressure on Rabegh by reducing the number of Turkish troops potentially available for service there as they were redeployed further north. More important, Wejh was in striking distance of the Hejaz railway at a point where it could not be easily defended. If the Arabs could sever the link with Syria, the Medina garrison would eventually be forced to surrender.

The first stage in implementing this plan was to redeploy Arab forces so that the Turks would be unable to advance from Medina to Rabegh, Yenbo or Wejh. As a first step, Arab forces were to be concentrated in the hills west of Medina, Ali advancing from Rabegh to Bir ibn Hassani on Wadi Safra. Feisal would move northwards with most of his forces from Wadi Safra to Kheif on Wadi Yenbo. Once the position south-west of Medina had been secured, it was intended that Feisal should move his base from Yenbo to Wejh. The remainder of Feisal's army would be placed under the command of Emir Zeid who was to hold Bir Said and prevent the Turks advancing towards Yenbo. Abdullah's army was also instructed to move northwards from his base at Mecca. He was to operate from a position east of Medina, attacking the railway and helping to isolate the garrison. When these moves had been completed a force of 2,000 tribesmen, raised in the Yenbo area, would advance on Wejh under the leadership of Sherif Nasir.

Implementation of the plan began at the end of November when Feisal proceeded to move northwards to Wadi Yenbo, secure in the knowledge that Zeid's army was apparently holding the Turks in check at Bir Said. However, early in December, he received news that Turkish forces had outflanked the Arabs near Khalis and advanced into Wadi Safra. The effect of this development was described in a report by Lawrence:

> the front line of Arabs, hearing news of this enemy six miles in their rear, broke with a rush to rescue their families and property in the threatened villages. Zeid's main body followed suit. Zeid himself fled at top pace to Yenbo; and the astonished Turks occupied Hamra and Bir Said unopposed.[14]

The way was now open to the Turks to attack the port of Yenbo, once they had cut the route between Yenbo and Rabegh. Feisal moved to block their advance while relocating his encampment, which was in a vulnerable position on the Wadi Yenbo.

Lawrence curtailed his discussions with Feisal at Nakhl Mubarak – a position difficult to defend – in order to help organize the defence of the Arab base at Yenbo for which he enlisted the assistance of the Royal Navy. Fortunately Captain Boyle, commander of the Red Sea patrol, was on board HMS *Suva* which had recently arrived at Yenbo with new supplies, and as a result of his intervention five warships converged on the port. Shortly afterwards Feisal came under attack and during the engagement the Juheina tribesmen who constituted his left wing suddenly abandoned the field. Feisal had no choice but to give up the fight and retreat rapidly in the direction of Yenbo. His force of 1,500 men arrived there on the morning of 9 December. The human barrier preventing the Turks advancing on Rabegh (and then on to Mecca) had now gone. At this moment of crisis the issue of sending a British brigade in support of Rabegh was reopened, with both Feisal and Lawrence, who had previously opposed such intervention, supporting the plan. Hussein remained opposed to the idea and would only countenance the use of Muslim troops.

As these inconclusive engagements were being fought, time was gained to organize the defences of Yenbo. Ancient town walls were repaired and reinforced with barbed wire. Machine-gun emplacements were installed and communications established with the five British warships anchored offshore. In the event of an enemy attack, the ships' searchlights and guns were expected to play an important role in the town's defence. The action was sufficient to deter the Turks, who were planning to launch an attack on 11 December, and at the gates to the port they turned back. They had intended, so Lawrence recalled,

> to rush Yenbo in the dark [so] that they might stamp out Feisal's army once for all; but their hearts had failed them at the silence and the blaze of lighted ships from end to end of the harbour, with the eerie beams of the searchlights revealing the bleakness of the glacis they would have to cross. So they turned back: and that night, I believe, the Turks lost their war.[15]

★

Against this uncertain military background, discussions with Arab leaders about British armed intervention continued. It was finally decided, in mid-December, that Wingate should send Hussein an ultimatum asking him to decide within two weeks whether he was prepared to accept assistance from a European force to be landed at Rabegh. The Foreign Office took the view that if he failed to respond the 'responsibility for the collapse of the Sherif's movement . . . will rest with him, owing to his final refusal of British military assistance for which he had asked and which we were prepared to send'.[16]

Meanwhile, on 16 December, the first evidence of a general Turkish withdrawal from the Yenbo area became apparent. On 18 December, Nakhl Mubarak was evacuated and rapidly reoccupied by Feisal's forces. It was not clear what the Turkish objectives were, but fearing an attack on Ali's force, which had left Rabegh in support of the Arab forces at Yenbo, Feisal almost at once was on the move again, advancing inland with the hope of trapping the Turks between his own force and that of his brother. This plan soon fell apart when

Ali decided to abandon his advance and return to Rabegh. Feisal could no longer hope to surround the Turks in the hills and he was forced to return to Nakhl Mubarak, where he arrived on 22 December. At the same time, Fakhri's army was regrouping and although its next move was not clear, there was a strong possibility that it would advance on Rabegh. The Arabs would need to apply heavy military pressure on the Turks if they were to divert their attention from Rabegh and other objectives further south.

Towards the end of December, the proposal to extend the Arab revolt to the northern Hejaz, which had first been raised in mid-November, was revived as a way of breaking the current deadlock. As before, it involved the capture of the Red Sea port of Wejh, some 200 miles north of Yenbo, which was held by a small Turkish garrison. This would provide the base for a continuous campaign against the Hejaz railway, which ran some 100 miles to the east of Wejh, and was bound to draw Turkish attention – and troops – away from Rabegh and force them to abandon plans to advance on Mecca. Under the previous plan, Feisal had not intended to move to Wejh until the position of the Arabs had been secured in the hills south-west of Medina. This time it would not be possible to achieve this level of security and the risks associated with the new scheme were correspondingly greater. Lawrence summarized the position as follows:

> Our fear was not what lay before us, but what lay behind. We were proposing the evacuation of Wadi Yenbo, our only defensive line against the Turkish division in Wadi Safra, only fifteen miles away . . . We were going to march nearly two hundred miles up the coast, with no base behind and only hostile territory in front . . . If the Turks cut in behind us we would be neatly in the void.[17]

As part of the new plan, Lawrence also found a way to disrupt the Hejaz railway nearer to Medina as well as in the north. Abdullah's army, which had been positioned north-east of Medina, had made no impact on the operation of the railway. It was at too great a distance from the line and badly located. Lawrence suggested that they be moved to the Wadi Ais, which had easier access to the Medina line. The wadi ran from the coast near Yenbo towards the railway and would provide a base from which Abdullah could attack the line or prevent a further Turkish advance on Yenbo or Mecca. As a result of these moves 'the two Arab armies would dominate a two-hundred mile stretch of the railway and the Medina garrison would be at their mercy'.[18]

Feisal's flank march northwards finally began on 4 January 1917 when he left Nakhl Mubarak with 10,000 tribesmen (together with four Krupp guns and ten machine guns) on the first stage to Owais, a group of wells 15 miles inland from Yenbo. A flotilla of five British naval ships, which carried fifty guns and several hundred Harb and Juheina tribesmen, left for Wejh at the same time. The departure was almost ceremonial in style and matched the importance of the event. Lawrence himself took part in it:

> The march became rather splendid and barbaric. First rode Feisal in white, then Sharraf at his right, in red head-cloth and henna-dyed tunic and cloak, myself on his left in white and scarlet; behind us three banners of faded crimson silk with gilt spikes; behind them the drummers playing a march, and behind them again the wild mass of 1,200 bouncing camels of the bodyguard . . . the men in every variety of coloured clothes . . . Everyone burst out singing a full-throated song in honour of Emir Feisal and his family.[19]

Feisal's concern for the security of Yenbo had been eased by news of the expected withdrawal of Turkish troops from Wadi Safra. During a reconnaissance on 3 January, which sought to establish whether the Turks were in fact moving, Lawrence as a member of a small Arab raiding party became personally involved in the fighting for the first time. Feisal was further reassured when he received, on 9 January, confirmation that Abdullah was moving to Wadi Ais. On the same day, Feisal left Owais and, having made steady progress northwards, set up camp at Um Lejj, a Red Sea port halfway between Yenbo and Wejh, choosing a location a few miles inland where water could be found. As described by Captain Boyle, commander of the Red Sea patrol which brought Lawrence to Um Lejj by sea, it was 'a great encampment of camel-skin tents in the centre of which stood Feisal's. It was a striking scene, but the absence of any sanitary precautions made it an unpleasant place on a hot day.'[20]

On 16 January, Feisal, Lawrence and British military and naval representatives met to finalize arrangements for the attack on Wejh, which was still a week's march away. It was agreed that Feisal would attack the town from the south, while a smaller group of 550 Arabs would be taken by the Royal Navy and landed to the north of the town to prevent the Turkish garrison's escape. It was also agreed that there would be a final meeting between Feisal and the navy before the attack took place.

Feisal had planned to resume his advance northwards on 18 January but news that Abdullah's force had captured a prominent enemy figure caused a delay while celebrations were held. As a result, the planned meeting with the Royal Navy did not take place and Admiral Wemyss was forced to decide whether to wait for Feisal or attack without him. Boyle was concerned at the possibility that the garrison of 1,200 men might escape before the main attack began. The fact that he had more than 500 Arab troops on board one of his ships was the deciding factor. Unable to feed them for much longer, Wemyss decided to go ahead with the attack without Feisal's support.

On 23 January, therefore, this small force, accompanied by two British officers, was landed north of Wejh, where the Turkish defences were at their weakest. Supported by heavy naval gunfire, the Arabs advanced into the town and rapidly defeated the Turkish garrison. A British naval landing party reinforced the Arabs who were in full control of the town well before Feisal arrived. Some twenty Arabs were killed in the fighting. There was little evidence of discipline among the Arab forces during the attack or after the surrender of the Turkish garrison when the town was systematically looted. Lawrence was concerned by the course of events: 'We wanted Wejh as a base against the railway and to extend our front; the smashing and killing in it had been wanton.'[21]

The relocation of the Arab army to Wejh, which served as Feisal's headquarters from January to August 1917, marked a turning point in the Hejaz revolt, with the Arabs in the ascendancy for the first time. As their fortunes changed, so the revolt gathered momentum, with the tribes that had formerly stood to one side now actively encouraged to participate. In Lawrence's words:

> We wanted this march, which would be in its way a closing act of the war in northern Hejaz, to send a rumour through the length and breadth of western Arabia. It was to be the biggest action of the Arabs in their memory; dismissing those who saw it to their homes, with a sense that their world had changed indeed; so that there would be no more silly defections and jealousies of clans behind us in future, to cripple us with family politics in the middle of our fighting.[22]

Following this victory, the Turks were forced on to the defensive for the rest of the war. They were obliged to redistribute half of their available manpower to protect the length of the Hejaz railway: this reduced the size of the Medina garrison and effectively prevented Fakhri from launching a further offensive unless large-scale external support was provided. More and more Turkish troops were drawn into the area. Reinforcements from the Seventh Division were among the first to arrive; a new Turkish force was established at Maan, while other units were positioned at Tebuk, some 300 miles to the north of Medina. The potential threat to Rabegh and Mecca soon disappeared. Indeed, Fakhri would find it increasingly difficult to maintain a presence in the hills south-west of Medina as he had done for some months. His abandonment of a number of advanced posts in the direction of Yenbo and Rabegh marked the start of a general withdrawal to Medina.

In planning the next military actions beyond the capture of Wejh, Feisal looked increasingly to Lawrence's advice and in January 1917 personally requested that Lawrence should remain with him indefinitely as his liaison officer. Distinguished by his commitment to the Arab cause and his exceptional political and military knowledge of the region, Lawrence found his relationship with Feisal strengthened by two further developments. First, early in February, on his arrival at Wejh, Lawrence exposed the real motives behind a French plan to land an Allied force at Aqaba, which Feisal had been pressed to accept. With Aqaba taken, the Allied force was to advance against the Hejaz railway, cutting the line permanently and forcing the Turkish garrison at Medina to surrender. Having faced months of friction with the French over various issues, Lawrence revealed that they planned to use the capture of Aqaba as a means of containing the Arab revolt within the Hejaz. The advance of an Anglo-French force inland from Aqaba could be presented as an exercise in imperial conquest. The reputation of the leaders of the Arab revolt would be damaged by their association with Britain and France and this would make it difficult for them to mobilize the popular support needed to extend the revolt northwards into Syria.

At the same time Lawrence also decided to reveal the full significance of the French attempt to contain the revolt. At an interview with Feisal, Lawrence informed him of the existence of the Sykes–Picot agreement between France and Britain, with its secret plans for the division of the Middle East after the war. Feisal was to place no reliance on the McMahon–Hussein understanding. Under the terms of the later agreement, the French had been allocated the Lebanon and Syria unless by the end of the war the Arabs had captured the towns of Aleppo, Damascus, Hama and Homs. If the Arabs failed to extend the revolt to the north, the post-war settlement was bound to be determined solely by the imperial powers. Given success, there was the prize of Arab self-government of a large area east of the Jordan for the proposed new state of Syria. They might also be in a position to secure improvements in the terms of the Sykes–Picot agreement by obtaining, for example, a strip of land north of Lebanon to secure access to the sea for this otherwise land-locked state. Lawrence's briefing proved to have a lasting influence on Feisal and helped to determine his strategy and objectives for the rest of the war. It also helped to set the limits for an Arab campaign in the north. Palestine was clearly the preserve of the British and the Lebanon was earmarked for the French; any Arab military incursion in either area was likely to be counter-productive. Although Lawrence's briefing was a serious breach of official confidence, and later proved flawed, it demonstrated his commitment to the Arab cause and his wish to build a relationship with Feisal that was based on mutual trust.

Under these circumstances, it was not surprising that the Arabs soon began to look northwards from their new base at Wejh. Aqaba was identified as their next main goal and plans were laid, in conjunction with the Royal Navy, to capture the intervening coastal villages of Dhaba and Muweilah. The latter, which was 120 miles north of Wejh and halfway to Aqaba, would serve as a base for the landing. Lawrence had the same concerns about this scheme as he had about the French plan. A landing by sea would almost certainly succeed in capturing Aqaba, but it would be virtually impossible to take the track that led from the town through the Wadi Itm – where the Turks had strong defensive positions – and on to the Maan plateau. Unless the Allies could capture this vital route, the future success of the entire northern campaign would be jeopardized.

To avert this, Lawrence produced an alternative and highly original plan – based on a surprise inland attack – which he persuaded Feisal to accept. The success of the scheme depended on cutting the Aqaba road to the north so that the Turks would be unable to send reinforcements from Maan to support the Wadi Itm defences. With the road blocked, the Arabs could deal with the lightly defended Turkish positions of the Wadi Itm with relative ease. This advantage depended on the Turkish garrison at Maan being unaware of what was planned. Once aware of the operation the Turks would launch a counter-offensive from Maan and a large Arab force would need to be landed at Aqaba to deal with the threat.

Before ordering a general advance northwards, however, Feisal wanted to consolidate his position. Of immediate concern was the unfinished task of capturing Medina, which was encircled by the forces of Ali and Abdullah. As a preliminary to another attempt to take the city, Feisal was charged with cutting the Hejaz line permanently at El Ula, some 100 miles east of Wejh. Once Medina was captured, the Hejaz would be entirely under Arab control and Feisal would be sufficiently confident to proceed northwards. He planned to advance along the route of the railway, taking Maan, Damascus and, eventually, Aleppo. These plans reinforced the need for a credible plan to take Aqaba. Unless it could be used as a base, it would be impossible to resupply the advancing Arab forces.

Feisal also needed to broaden the basis of his support among local chiefs. Most had been quick to declare their support, although some remained reluctant. Support was also received from more distant tribes to the north and east of Wejh, including the eastern Howeitat,

> those famous abu Tayi, of whom Auda, the greatest fighting man in northern Arabia, was chief. Only by means of Auda abu Tayi could we swing the tribes from Maan to Akaba so violently in our favour that they would help us take Akaba and its hills from their Turkish garrisons: only with his active support could we venture to thrust out from Wejh on the long trek to Maan.[23]

The progress of the Arab revolt also depended on the success of the British forces which had advanced across Sinai and were preparing, early in 1917, to launch an attack on Gaza, the gateway to Palestine. If it succeeded the British would soon make direct contact with Arab forces in Syria, and the War Office agreed that General Murray should control their future operations north of the Hejaz. Operations within the Hejaz – south of a line running from Aqaba to Maan – would continue to be overseen by Sir Reginald Wingate.

★

By February 1917, the need to make progress towards the ultimate targets of the Arab revolt – the cities of northern Syria – was uppermost in Lawrence's mind. He was concerned at the lack of action in the Medina area, reflecting the fact that neither Ali nor Zeid was apparently prepared to take any undue risks in launching offensive attacks against the enemy. Operations initiated from Wejh against the railway were also slow to start partly because the Billi, the local tribe, were less than enthusiastic supporters of the Arab revolt.

It did not, however, take long before a night raid led by British officers succeeded in derailing a train. This was followed, early in March 1917, by an attack by Abdullah's forces on the line to the north of Medina, which resulted in the destruction of several sections of track and a bridge. Attacks on the line subsequently increased in frequency and, on 17 March, the Turkish high command, concerned that their forces would be unable to defend the Hejaz railway as it came under concerted attack at several different points, ordered the evacuation of the entire Medina garrison, instructing it to withdraw to a new defensive position south of Maan, some 500 miles north of Medina.

These orders were issued just as General Murray was about to launch his first attack on Gaza, where his forces outnumbered those of the enemy. Murray was concerned that his apparent advantage could be lost if the whole Medina garrison were transferred to the Palestine front. The Arab forces at Wejh were urged to do everything possible to prevent the Medina garrison moving northwards. Although the Arabs had been seeking to bring the Hejaz campaign to an early conclusion, Feisal was persuaded to agree to the British request, even though the continued Turkish occupation of Medina underlined the fact that the liberation of the Hejaz had still not been completed. Convinced by Lawrence's argument that it was in their longer term interests to cooperate with Murray whose support would be essential to the furtherance of Arab aims in Syria, Feisal asked his brothers to begin by attacking the railway to the north of Medina and launching a full-scale attack on any Turkish forces attempting to leave the city. Other Arab forces were encouraged to attack the line at various points so that it was beyond the Turks' capacity to repair. Lawrence suggested that the 'weak point of the Turk plans lies in the trains of water and food. If we can cut the line on such a scale that they cannot repair it, or smash their locomotives, the force will come to a standstill.'[24]

Lawrence decided to deliver Feisal's message to Abdullah in person and travelled south to Wadi Ais early in March. Delayed there during a bout of illness, Lawrence reviewed the strategy of the Arab revolt. Although he accepted Murray's view that nothing should be done that would tend to increase the number of Turkish soldiers on the Palestine front, he was not now convinced that the Arabs should capture Medina and imprison its garrison; it was preferable, he believed, for the garrison to be maintained where it was. Larger numbers of Turkish troops would be needed to keep the Hejaz line open as the Arab attacks increased. Lawrence concluded that

> We must not take Medina. The Turk was harmless there. In prison in Egypt he would cost us food and guards. We wanted him to stay at Medina, and every other distant place, in the largest numbers. Our idea was to keep his railway just working, but only just, with the maximum of loss and discomfort.[25]

Arab guerrilla action rather than conventional attacks would force the Turks to deploy ever increasing resources in order to maintain their vital lines of communication. In the long run, this war of attrition could exhaust the Turkish army and lead to their surrender. Lawrence summarized the character of the new warfare as follows:

> Most wars were wars of contact, both forces striving into touch to avoid tactical surprise. Ours should be a war of detachment. We were to contain the enemy by the silent threat of a vast unknown desert, not disclosing ourselves till we attacked. The attack might be nominal, directed not against him, but against his stuff; so it would not seek either his strength or his weakness, but his most accessible material.[26]

Lawrence's experiences in Abdullah's camp tended to confirm his conclusions. In his view, Abdullah was more of a politician than a general: 'he is incapable as a military commander and unfit to be trusted alone with important commissions of an active sort.'[27] He was equally deficient in small arms and spares; for example, only two of his five machine guns were in working order. If the Turks were to be left in Medina, Lawrence could see no reason not to extend the Arab revolt northwards into Syria.

Before he returned to Wejh, Lawrence led two expeditions against the railway with the aim of showing the Arabs how to conduct such operations and to demonstrate how land mines should be used to cause maximum damage. For various reasons, the laying of an explosive charge was by no means a simple operation:

> The Turks search the line very carefully by daylight before a locomotive passes. A trolley came first, and then an infantry patrol of 11 men, of whom three were each side of the way, looking for tracks and fire on the way itself, walking bent double, scanning the line for signs of disturbance. For this reason tracks should be made through (i.e. both E and W of the line as though by a party crossing over) and the burying of the charges and fuse should be done most carefully. The railway is well laid, ballasting ample, and earth work and bridging solid. The rails are very light, and badly worn, and the sleepers (all steel) light in section and shallow. The heads of many bolts have been buried to prevent loosening of the nuts, which makes it impossible to undo them with any ordinary short wrench.[28]

Lawrence feared that Abdullah was 'too lazy and luxurious' to keep the momentum of the attacks going. Inaction was also a problem at Wejh because Feisal was more concerned about building support for operations further north than he was about raiding the railway. Feisal's intention of pushing northwards was given added impetus by rumours that the French were planning an invasion of Syria with a force of 60,000 men. Lawrence's ideas and those of Feisal now coincided. The Arab forces would need to move soon if they were to have any chance of capturing the northern cities of Syria. Discussions in Feisal's camp focused on how this objective might be achieved and, according to Colonel Newcombe, two alternatives were proposed.

The first option, favoured by Feisal's advisers (except Lawrence), involved proceeding 'direct with a small force to the Druse mountains [east of Deraa] and from there to descend on the railway between Damascus and Maan and from Deraa to Afuleh, using the Druse, Beni Sakhr, Huitat, and Anazeh'.[29] One advantage of this scheme from the British perspective was that it avoided the need to take Aqaba; there was a great reluctance in Egypt to see Aqaba in Arab hands. The result might be, as Clayton expressed it, 'the Arabs claiming that place hereafter, and it is by no means improbable that after the war Aqaba may be of considerable importance to the future defence scheme of Egypt. It is thus essential that Akaba should remain in British hands after the war.'[30]

The second option, favoured by Lawrence, was far less risky. The

Arabs would advance progressively northwards along the route of the railway with the aim ultimately of capturing Maan. Operations would then continue further north using Aqaba as a base. Lawrence's commitment to this option deepened after his discussions with Auda abu Tayi, the Howeitat leader, in Wejh in April, following his return from Abdullah's camp. Auda, who agreed that Lawrence's plan could work, would himself be an essential ingredient in its success. Indeed, without him the plan for a landward attack on Aqaba would have come to nothing. As described by Lawrence,

> Auda was their [the Abu Tayi's] master type. His hospitality was sweeping . . . He had married twenty-eight times, had been wounded thirteen times; whilst the battles he provoked had seen all his tribesmen hurt and most of his relations killed. He himself had slain seventy-five men, Arabs, with his own hand in battle. Of the number of dead Turks he could give no account: they did not enter the register. His Toweiha under him had become the first fighters of the desert, with a tradition of desperate courage, a sense of superiority which never left them.[31]

Lawrence pressed ahead with the Aqaba plan without the knowledge of his superiors in Cairo, who would almost certainly have instructed him not to pursue it. In contrast, Lawrence believed that both British and Arab interests would benefit from the capture of Aqaba. As well as opening up a supply route for the Arabs once the advance northwards into Syria began, it would provide a direct link between British forces and the Arabs through which supplies from Egypt could be routed. The occupation of Aqaba would also deprive the Turks of a base from which to threaten the right flank of the EEF as it advanced into Palestine. With the Arabs in possession of Aqaba and advancing northwards, it would be Turkish lines of communication into Palestine that would be potentially vulnerable to attack.

The expedition to Aqaba left Wejh on 9 May 1917. Consisting of Lawrence, Sherif Nasir, Auda abu Tayi and some forty-five Arabs, it prepared the way for a later Arab advance northwards which Feisal was to lead. The plan, which Lawrence and Auda developed, involved travelling in a north-easterly direction to the Maan area. Here they would recruit from the Howeitat and other tribes, using the reserve of £20,000 they were carrying as an inducement.

Following diversionary attacks in the Maan area they would advance towards Aqaba, capturing Turkish posts on the way. Lawrence described it as an 'extreme example of a turning movement, since it involved a desert journey of six hundred miles to capture a trench within gunfire of our ships . . .'.[32] Among the highlights were the demolition of a section of the railway, which they reached after ten days, and crossing the vast desert beyond it. Lawrence commented on the scale of the landscape through which they passed: 'We, ourselves, felt tiny in it, and our urgent progress across its immensity was a stillness or immobility of futile effort.'[33] It was also a hostile environment, as Lawrence recorded in his notebook: 'Sun reflects from [the mud flats] like a mirror – flame-yellow, cutting into our eyes, like glare burning glass on closed lids. Heat in waves and eyes often going black . . . Camels exhausted and foot-burnt.'[34]

The expedition established its first camp in the Wadi Sirhan and most of the group dispersed to recruit more men to the cause. It was during this period of waiting, on 5 June, that Lawrence left Nebk on a secret northern journey deep into enemy territory, triggered by a crisis of conscience brought about by the need constantly to reassure the Arabs that victory would bring them independence, when it was evident that if Britain 'won the war these promises would be dead paper'.[35] Although the reasons for undertaking this dangerous adventure were mainly personal, relating to his concern at the deception being practised on the Arabs by the British and the French, it also had a wider purpose. He wanted to renew his knowledge of Syria and assess the commitment of local tribal leaders to the revolt. A journey of 300 miles, which extended to the north of Damascus, enabled him to achieve these objectives. He returned to Nebk on 18 June, by which time recruitment to the expeditionary force had been completed. The force, which now consisted of more than 500 men, moved to Bair, where it was to join with tribesmen from the west of Maan, who would help in seizing control of the vital road to Aqaba. By this time, the Maan garrison had become aware of these movements and Lawrence was asked to lead a diversionary raid on the Hejaz railway far to the north intended to convince the Turks that the main force would move in a different direction from the one it had planned.

Lawrence set out from Bair once more on 20 June with the aim of destroying a bridge that carried the railway from Deraa into Palestine. The operation failed and he rejoined the main force on the 28th. It soon moved to Jefer, about 30 miles east of Maan, in preparation for the final advance on Aqaba. While the main force waited, local tribesmen captured the key Turkish post at Fuweila, which guarded access to the Maan–Aqaba road. The Maan garrison, which did not permit itself to be distracted by a series of local raids on the railway, soon learned of the events at Fuweila, but was still not aware that Aqaba was the real goal of the expedition.

A Turkish battalion was dispatched from Maan and soon recaptured the Fuweila post before occupying the Abu el Lissan springs in the vicinity. The expeditionary force could not make further progress until the enemy had been contained or defeated. Before daylight on 2 July, the Turks were surrounded and gunfire was exchanged for most of the day. In the evening the Arabs charged the Turkish positions and overwhelmed them. While Auda led fifty men in an attack on the Turkish rear, Lawrence and Sherif Nasir led a charge against the Turkish infantry in which Lawrence accidentally shot his own camel. Arab losses amounted to only two men, while the Turkish battalion was destroyed: 160 were taken prisoner and 300 were killed during the action and in the massacre that followed, carried out in revenge for recent Turkish raids on Arab villages.

The way was now open to capture Aqaba. The Arabs advanced across the Guweira plain and passed through a narrow defile at Wadi Itm. Having taken the Turkish post at Khadra, at the mouth of the wadi, they soon confronted the final obstacle – the 300 troops that garrisoned Aqaba itself. The morale and condition of these troops were poor and they were in no position to fight an Arab force that had grown to some 2,000 men. Faced with the choice of surrendering or being massacred, they raised a white flag, and at dawn on 6 July the Arab force galloped into Aqaba through a sandstorm to take possession of this valuable strategic asset.

There were insufficient supplies at Aqaba to sustain the large Arab force or their 650 prisoners and almost immediately Lawrence left for Suez, 160 miles away across the Sinai desert. News of the achievement – which, according to Newcombe, was 'entirely conceived by Lawrence, who was its real leader and animating spirit'[36] – was welcomed by the military authorities in Cairo, who were still coming to terms with a second defeat at the hands of the Turks at Gaza. The next step was to establish whether the EEF would value the potential benefits of future cooperation with the Arabs and was willing to make available the necessary supplies.

# 4

# *Advance Through Sinai*

T HE GRADUAL EROSION of Turkish power in the Hejaz in the
months after the Arab uprising at Medina in June 1916 was
matched by regular setbacks in the Sinai campaign as the British
advanced across the desert. There was, however, a much more clearly
defined turning point in the course of the war in the Sinai than there
was in the Hejaz. The Turkish defeat at the Battle of Romani, August
1916, ended for good their offensive operations against the British in
Egypt. All hope of capturing the vital strategic prize of the Suez
Canal and inspiring a pro-Turkish nationalist revolt in Cairo had
gone for ever. Turkish military planners in Constantinople may have
continued to develop new schemes for disabling the canal, but there
was virtually no hope now of successfully executing them. In reality
the strategic initiative had passed decisively to General Murray and
his forces and remained with them until the end of the war, just over
two years later.

Over the next few months Murray's forces would advance steadily
eastwards until, early in 1917, they reached the Egyptian frontier with
Ottoman Palestine. Egypt was secure against further occupation and
attack, while the British now had the opportunity to advance into
Palestine. But, in August 1916, following the Romani victory, the
British government in London did no more than agree to the east-
ward advance of General Murray's forces to El Arish, which was not
expected to be reached before the winter. Work on the railway and
the accompanying pipeline resumed as soon as the enemy invasion
force had withdrawn east of El Arish in August 1916. At this time
British military objectives continued to be restricted to improving

the security of Egypt by increasing the distance between the Turkish army and the canal. There were no plans at this stage for a general push eastwards; the British stance in Sinai remained defensive.

Murray shared the government's view that the active defence of Egypt should be based on his occupation of El Arish even though, according to his own assessment, his force was under strength by at least a division. But he believed that he could go one step further without jeopardizing his position. In a letter of 21 October 1916 to the Chief of the Imperial General Staff, he expressed the view that there was scope for using his troops more aggressively in a thrust towards the border, with the aim of preventing the redeployment of Turkish troops from Palestine and Syria to other theatres. However, the requisite political approval from London for such action was not yet forthcoming. Nor was the War Office likely to view such a proposal favourably. In a letter to Murray of 16 October 1916, Robertson had already explained his views:

> I am not intent on winning in any particular quarter of the globe. My sole object is to win the war and we shall not do that in the Hedjaz nor in the Sudan. Our military policy is perfectly clear and simple . . . [It] is offensive on the Western Front and therefore defensive everywhere else.[1]

With the British now within 40 miles of the enemy and with the net rapidly closing round them, the Turks were faced with a number of difficult choices. These included strengthening their defences at El Arish; launching a further offensive from the Turkish railhead at Kossaima along the central Sinai route; or abandoning the Sinai peninsula for good. Murray found it difficult to predict which direction Turkish policy would take, but he felt confident that he could capture the important staging post of El Arish without much difficulty.

Discussions between London and Egypt continued on the wisdom of taking the fight into Palestine and Syria and the number of British troops needed to sustain it, but the issue was not to be resolved for some time. General Robertson acknowledged the benefits a wider Palestine campaign might have in drawing away Turkish soldiers from other fronts, a view held yet more enthusiastically by the Prime Minister, Lloyd George. However, Robertson's belief in the central role of the Western Front in determining the outcome of the war was unshakeable. It is perhaps not surprising, therefore, that the idea of

extending the campaign found little favour among War Office officials. In December 1916, after months of debate, the message from
London remained the same: the primary role of the Egyptian
Expeditionary Force was the defence of Egypt; the likelihood of any
reinforcements arriving in support of a strategy with wider objectives
was reduced accordingly.

There was no early resumption of hostilities in Sinai after the
British victory at Romani. It was a hard-fought battle and Allied
forces needed a period of rest and recuperation before they could
move forward again. That autumn, General Murray gave priority to
air and land reconnaissance operations, with the aim of keeping large
areas of the desert under regular observation and trying to maintain
control of the Bedouin, whose loyalties were always suspect. While
ground operations were suspended, Murray moved his headquarters
from Ismailia, his base since the beginning of the year, back to Cairo,
their traditional location. There were several pressing problems –
including the continuing threat from the Senussi and the faltering
Hejaz revolt – which Murray believed could be more effectively
handled from the Egyptian capital. He appointed Major-General Sir
Charles Dobell to command the troops on the canal and in the
desert, now known as Eastern Force; Dobell was promoted to the
rank of lieutenant-general and given the title of GOC Eastern
Frontier Force. But the change came at a price. Murray lost direct
contact with the officers of his expeditionary force and his lines of
communication were seriously weakened. It was one of the factors
that led to the decision to replace him by General Allenby after the
British defeat at the second Battle of Gaza in April 1917.

The timing of the renewal of Allied military operations was also
affected by progress in installing communications across the desert.
The pace of the advance from the canal to Romani had been dictated
by progress in laying the standard-gauge, single-track railway and
water pipeline and this was to remain the case. Following the Battle
of Romani railway construction was restarted and progressed eastwards across Sinai at the rate of about 15 miles a month. When completed, it ran for about 140 miles from Qantara on the Suez Canal to
the Wadi Ghazze, the river opposite the town of Gaza, and had the
capacity to run thirteen trains a day.

Continuous supplies of good quality water were essential both for
advancing troops and railway engines. British army engineers had
sunk wells between Qantara and El Arish but the water they yielded

was not suitable for human consumption or even for use by the trains. There was no alternative but to use water from the Sweet Water Canal which was brought to the front line by means of a pipeline that followed the railway across the desert. Pipeline construction eventually caught up with the railway at El Arish in February 1917. Although the quality of local water supplies improved significantly east of El Arish, the pipeline was extended almost to Gaza, where it was to become an indispensable source of supply for the troops who were to invade Palestine.

Further Allied progress across the Sinai peninsula also depended on improvements in the deployment of troops by road. Soft desert sand was a serious barrier to rapid troop movement except when camels were used. The construction of 'wire roads', using rabbit-netting laid across the sand, helped to ease the passage of light vehicles and infantry. The process was described by Noel Drury, a lieutenant in the 6th Royal Dublin Fusiliers:

> A track ten feet wide is roughly levelled in the sand and two rolls of one-inch rabbit meshing are laid down side by side and then just rolled along the ground, and then two more joined to the ends, and so on. At intervals, of about a yard or so, wooden spikes are driven in at the edges to keep the netting in place. One would imagine the wire would sink into the sand, but it does not do so to any appreciable extent, and it makes an almost perfect road for cars and ambulances.[7]

By the beginning of December 1916, the railway had reached El Mazar, which was about halfway between Qantara and the Palestine frontier. The new line was virtually within sight of El Arish, which had been occupied by the Turks for much of the war. Some 1,600 well-entrenched enemy infantry held the town, supported by other Turkish forces based 25 miles south-east of El Arish on the banks of the Wadi el Arish – known as the 'River of Egypt' – at Magdhaba and Abu Aweigila. The primary function of these troops was to maintain a Turkish presence on Egyptian territory, even though the foothold served little real military purpose. A more specific objective was to protect the Turkish railhead at El Kossaima, some 75 miles away.

It was not until 20 December that the British finally renewed their offensive, having been delayed by the need to accumulate substantial water stocks at the railhead since the Turkish army controlled all the local supplies. The British movement was led by a new force, the Desert Column – the advanced guard of Eastern Force – commanded by Lieutenant-General Sir Philip Chetwode, a distinguished cavalryman who as commander of XX Corps was to play a leading role in the capture of Jerusalem. The Australian and New Zealand Mounted Division, commanded by General Sir Harry Chauvel, was a major component of the new column. A veteran Australian cavalry officer, Chauvel too was to make a major contribution to Allenby's Palestine victories.

Leading units of the Anzac Mounted Division and the Imperial Camel Brigade surrounded El Arish unopposed on the morning of 21 December, after a 20-mile march. The town was found to be completely unoccupied, confirming earlier RFC reconnaissance reports that the Turks, believing they could not defend it, had deserted the area on the very day that the British had renewed their eastwards advance. Although described as a 'disappointing place' with 'only one stone building besides the mosque', El Arish marked the end of the Sinai desert and offered British forces direct access to the Mediterranean.[3] No time was wasted in making use of this facility: the first supplies were landed there two days later.

General Chetwode had arrived by boat a day earlier. He gave immediate orders to pursue and surround the retreating Turkish forces, which had withdrawn in two different directions. Although there was uncertainty at the time about the direction taken by the bulk of the retreating forces – had they followed the direct route to Palestine eastwards along the Mediterranean coast via Rafa or had they turned inland along the Wadi el Arish in the direction of Kossaima? – it later became clear that most of these forces had departed to the south-east along the wadi en route for the railhead at Kossaima. This was the nearest point of the Turkish railway, which met the Egyptian frontier well away from the coast. Kress summed up the position confronting the Turks at the turn of the year:

> In face of the steady hostile advance along the coast . . . the Turkish army could not hope to remain there for long, and early in January 1917, it fell back into Palestine, leaving posts at Magdebbe and Rafa. Colonel Kress would have preferred to evacuate the desert zone altogether, but Djemal, on political grounds, decided to keep these two garrisons there, and both shortly after were surrounded and captured by hostile mounted troops.[4]

General Chauvel was instructed to pursue the enemy with the Anzac Mounted Division and the Imperial Camel Corps Brigade, whilst a detachment of the Camel Corps was to be sent along the coast towards Rafa to capture the remainder of the Turkish forces that had fled from El Arish. This latter operation was subsequently cancelled when British air reconnaissance revealed a considerable concentration of Turkish forces inland at Magdhaba, on the main line of retreat from El Arish. General Chauvel's departure was delayed until fresh water supplies had arrived at El Arish and it was not until midnight on 22/23 December that he finally left the town.

After a 25-mile night march along the banks of the Wadi el Arish, Chauvel was within sight of the new Turkish position before dawn on 23 December. The enemy had occupied a circle of about six redoubts, linked by a series of entrenchments, on both sides of the wadi and extending for about two miles from east to west. Magdhaba was some 40 miles from the then British railhead and 25 miles from El Arish and at these distances the Turks must have believed that they were out of immediate danger of a British attack. However, the Turks underestimated Chauvel's determination and the 'prodigious effort' he made to bring the pursuit to a successful conclusion.[5]

Chauvel quickly initiated a strong enveloping action with the aim of capturing the Turkish positions before they were abandoned. The Third Australian Light Horse and New Zealand Mounted Brigade (under Brigadier-General E.W.C. Chaytor) were sent to the north of Magdhaba with the aim of attacking from the north-east. The Camel Brigade was to advance directly on Magdhaba from a position north of the road to El Arish. Units of the Third Australian Light Horse Brigade were subsequently sent round the enemy position with the aim of cutting off its lines of retreat to the south and south-east.

However, headquarters soon received a report – which later turned out to be false – that the enemy might escape this offensive movement. This produced an immediate response from Chauvel who ordered a direct attack on Magdhaba by units of the First Australian Light Horse Brigade. A cavalry charge on Turkish positions was cut short by heavy machine-gun and rifle fire, indicating that there had been no general Turkish withdrawal from their fortified positions. Continuing heavy fire from the redoubts – and the prospect of rapidly mounting casualties – checked further British progress, even though by noon almost the entire Turkish position had been surrounded. The attack was renewed by the Third Australian

Light Horse Regiment, which advanced slowly up the wadi. It was in touch with the Camel Brigade and, by late morning, was within 100 yards of Redoubt No. 1, one of the Turks' principal positions and a major barrier to further progress.

Chauvel had no fear of an early attack from Turkish reinforcements, but his ability to remain at Magdhaba for any length of time was severely constrained by lack of water for his men and their horses. The nearest water supply was back at El Arish and at 2 p.m., with no apparent prospect of an early breakthrough, he decided to call off the action. But as he was in the process of issuing orders for withdrawal, the Third Australian Light Horse Regiment and the Camel Brigade carried out a 'spirited charge' against Redoubt No. 1. The Camel Brigade on the plain above the wadi and the light horsemen in the wadi 'dashed at the redoubt'. Despite heavy opposing fire the cavalry was able to maintain the momentum of the advance and the Turks surrendered before they were forced to engage in hand to hand fighting. This short action was 'the climax of the whole fight' and a high proportion of the losses suffered at Magdhaba were incurred in the course of it. Other Turkish positions then progressively fell under the weight of the British onslaught, including a successful encircling movement by the 10th Australian Light Horse Regiment. By 4.30 p.m. the entire enemy force had surrendered.

Turkish losses, which amounted to 1,242 men and four mountain guns, were heavy in comparison with those of the British, who had only suffered 146 casualties (22 dead). No more than 200 Turks escaped before they were surrounded. This imbalance was explained in part by poor Turkish marksmanship and also by the dominance of British artillery. The action had also demonstrated the effectiveness of mounted troops against heavily defended fortified positions. The new Camel Brigade likewise played a valuable role and when it went into action dismounted, so the British official historians claimed, 'the strength of its three battalions almost equalled that of two light horse brigades'.[6]

★

The collapse of the Turkish defences at Magdhaba marked, with one or two minor exceptions, the effective end of the Ottoman occupation of Egypt. The destruction of their rearguard was a major setback which left them with little choice but to abandon virtually all their remaining posts in a retreat across the border to Palestine. This process was completed by New Year's Day, 1917, and meant that for the first time since the outbreak of war the Sinai peninsula was virtually clear of the Turks. There were wider implications also to the British victory. As Guy Dawnay suggested at the time, it

> will likely make them nervous about the safety of their forces further south in Arabia; and I hope it will create difficulties for them in southern Syria, where they are very unpopular and may have a bad time if the native population is imbued with the idea that they are the beaten side.[7]

The only exception to the general Turkish withdrawal from Sinai was their continuing occupation of the border town of Rafa, some 25 miles further east, where they continued to maintain a strong presence. RFC reconnaissance flights discovered that some 2,000 enemy troops of the 31st Regiment – together with field artillery and a battery of mountain guns – held the commanding location of El Magruntein, south-west of Rafa. (The next Turkish encampment was further east on the left bank of the Wadi Ghazze in Palestine.) However, despite the heavy blow dealt by the British at Magdhaba, no immediate offensive action could be taken to dislodge the Turks, as the occupation of El Arish had first to be properly secured. Railway and waterpipe construction had also to be given a chance to catch up.

The first train reached El Arish on 4 January 1917 and four days later Chetwode continued his advance eastwards along the northern coastal route, commanding the raid on Rafa in person. With forces which included the Anzac Mounted Division, the Fifth Mounted Brigade (Yeomanry) and the Imperial Camel Corps Brigade – accompanied by six Ford cars, each equipped with a machine gun, of No. 7 Light Car Patrol – he covered the ground without delay during a brisk night march at a time of the year when cold rather than excessive heat was the main problem for the rank and file. Harry Hopwood, a non-commissioned officer in the 6th Battalion, Manchester Regiment, had direct experience of the difficult conditions in the final stages of the march across Sinai:

> It has been very wet and very cold in fact quite winterly and it was hard work to keep warm especially at night. The old song about 'when the sands of the desert grow cold' is a misnomer. You have only got to lie on them just now to find whether they grow cold or not.

We have not seen a tent since Romani which is about ten weeks back
now. Our bivouacs are made out of blanket, mackintosh sheets, old
sacks etc and remind you of the gypsies encampments at Blackpool.[8]

Arriving at El Magruntein, the site of the Turkish defences near
Rafa, on 9 January as darkness was lifting, Chetwode's forces found
the enemy well entrenched and difficult to dislodge. The Turkish
forces were concentrated in four positions – a series of three systems
of defensive works on higher ground, known as A, B and C, supported by a formidable central keep on a hill above them. The
ground between the opposing forces offered the British no cover of
any kind. The 'works were well dug and excellently sited, with a
perfect field of fire of up to 2,000 yards in almost every direction'.[9]

Chauvel divided his forces so that he was in a position to launch an
attack on each of the defensive works. At an early point in the fighting, a detachment of New Zealanders captured the village of Rafa
itself, but elsewhere the advance was slow. In the face of constant fire
from heavy machine guns and the occasional shrapnel gun, the
cavalry was forced to dismount. By noon, the New Zealand
Mounted Brigade, which had been allocated C works, had made the
most progress and was within 600 yards of the enemy's position. As
the advancing forces converged on their target, individual Allied
formations made direct contact with one another. It was not long, in
the words of the British official history, before 'the cordon of troops
round the enemy's fortifications [was] complete'.[10] Progress was
maintained at the same gradual pace for the next couple of hours as
the Allied noose was tightened by the cavalry advance. But it was
hard going as 'the very slight undulations of the ground gave hardly
any cover, and every yard seemed to be beaten by machine-gun
fire'.[11]

Though Chauvel called on his men to renew the effort, by mid-
afternoon the British attack appeared to falter as supplies of
ammunition began to run low. Reports that Turkish reinforcements were on their way also alarmed Chauvel and, at 4.30 p.m.,
following discussions by telephone with General Chetwode,
orders were prepared on the latter's instructions for the immediate
withdrawal of all Allied forces from El Magruntein. However,
before these orders could be conveyed to the whole force, the
New Zealand Mounted Brigade, seizing their opportunity, charged
the central keep and overwhelmed its occupants. Chaytor, com-

manding the New Zealand Mounted Rifles Brigade, described this decisive action:

> This attack was carried out in a perfect manner. The brigade had to advance over a mile across an open, grassy slope, devoid of any cover. The covering fire from machine guns and rifles was excellent, made the redoubt appear a smoking furnace, and kept the Turkish fire down. The men covered the last 600 to 800 yards in two grand rushes, everyone having made up his mind to get home, and the result was that the position was taken with very little loss to ourselves.[12]

Hereafter the determined and brave resistance of the Turks, which had characterized the whole battle so far, began to fall apart. This first Allied success, which was attributable to the exceptional performance of the New Zealanders, was quickly followed by the fall of the C group of defensive works and then of the B group as a result of action by the Camel Corps. The remaining defensive system – A group – was evacuated by the Turks themselves and by dusk El Magruntein was in British hands. Without this first dramatic breakthrough, however, the further stages of the battle would have been finely balanced and the outcome almost impossible to predict. The Turks had lost 200 killed and 1,635 taken prisoner; the British suffered 71 fatalities and 415 wounded. Once the action had been concluded, the British were obliged to withdraw as quickly as possible. A detachment of the Wellington regiment was already engaged at long distance with enemy troops advancing westwards from Shellal and Khan Yunis. The victors of El Magruntein fell back to Sheikh Zowaiid.

The British victory at El Magruntein marked the final expulsion of Ottoman troops from Egyptian territory, apart from a few isolated units in southern Sinai that were mopped up in February. It also marked the end of the desert campaign. The area across the border, which was soon to be discovered by British reconnaissance patrols, was a revelation to many who passed through it. Lieutenant Robert Wilson thought it was

> delightful country, cultivated to perfection and the crops look quite good if not better than most English farms, chiefly barley and wheat. The villages were very pretty – a mass of orange, fig and other fruit trees . . . The relief of seeing such country after the miles and miles of bare sand was worth five years of a life.[13]

Following their defeat at Rafa, Kress von Kressenstein now concentrated his remaining forces on the Wadi Ghazze at Wali Sheikh, to
the west of Shellal. Although managing to delay the British advance
into Palestine, the Turks never managed to recover the Egyptian
ground that had been lost. Indeed, Kress would shortly be forced to
withdraw further into Palestine. The main British objective of the
Sinai campaign – securing the defence of Egypt and the canal by
pushing back the Turks – had been achieved.

★

Within two days of this victory, on 11 January 1917, General Murray
received further guidance from London on government policy for
the direction of future operations in Palestine. A War Office telegram
reiterated the fact that early in 1917 strategic priority was to be given
to the Western Front in the preparation for a spring offensive. For the
foreseeable future no reinforcements were likely to be available for
Egypt; indeed, the new offensive would require the transfer to France
of one or two divisions – and soon after, on 17 January, the War
Office ordered the dispatch of an infantry division (the 42nd) from
Egypt. Meanwhile, plans for a large-scale offensive in Palestine would
need to be developed although they could not be implemented until
the autumn. Provided they could be managed from existing
resources, the War Office made it clear that it had no intention of
curtailing Murray's activities. Indeed, in a letter to General Murray of
10 January, Robertson seemed to urge a more active approach:

> I hope you will do all you can to upset the Hedjaz railway communi-
> cation. Even if it is only an occasional bombing it will be better than
> nothing. Personally I have never been worried about the Hedjaz.
> There has been trouble in the Hedjaz for the last 20 years to my per-
> sonal knowledge and I am quite sure that there will be trouble there
> for the next 20 years.[14]

Lloyd George continued to be much more flexible in his strategic
approach than some of his political and military colleagues and did
not believe in concentrating all his resources on the Western Front.
Successful campaigns elsewhere could, in his view, help to undermine
the effectiveness of the enemy's war effort in Europe. Lloyd George
had already authorized the renewal of offensive operations in
Mesopotamia as General Maude sought to avenge Britain's humiliat-

ing defeat at Kut on 29 April 1916. There was every reason to believe that the invasion of Palestine would be sanctioned later in the year. Sir William Robertson said as much in a letter of 31 January 1917 to Sir Charles Monro, then commander-in-chief in India:

> If we do not get a big success in the west this year we shall have diffi-culty in retaining popular support of the war. Not so much in this country as among some of our allies, and therefore it is very necessary that we should have a second string to our bow and be able to show that we have a good kick left in us . . . The Turks in general are fed up. If therefore we are still fighting next winter and could have a good thing based on Egypt we ought to get good value out of it, and more-over it is the only theatre where we can operate in wintertime and so keep up public interest.[15]

Within these constraints, General Murray had to ensure that his forces were prepared for future action and that they were correctly positioned to move rapidly through southern Palestine. Neither El Arish (where Eastern Force's headquarters were now located) nor Rafa was a suitable base from which to launch operations. Although the desert did not extend as far as Rafa, the area had no roads and it was separated from Gaza and Beersheba – Palestine's gateway towns – by the vast Wadi Ghazze. This river, dry during the summer when the springs in the river bed form a valuable source of water, is during the winter 100 yards wide at some points and up to 40 feet deep, and runs from the Judean hills to the Mediterranean coast some five miles south of Gaza. There is a second natural barrier – a series of hills – to the east of the wadi which runs from Gaza in a south-easterly direc-tion to Beersheba and beyond. Gaza and Beersheba, which are about 25 miles apart, provided another defensive opportunity for the Turks. In particular, Gaza, which is located on a low hill some two miles from the coast, is on the direct invasion route from Egypt to Palestine and control of the fortress had been regularly disputed over the cen-turies. To occupy Gaza would give the British direct access to the main roads in southern Palestine, including routes to Jaffa, Jerusalem and Hebron.

Between January and March 1917 there was a further lull in the fighting as General Murray's forces prepared to take action to over-come these barriers to a successful invasion of Palestine. The depar-ture of the 42nd Division from Egypt early in February triggered a reorganization of Eastern Force, which remained under the command of Sir Charles Dobell. As a result of the changes, the infantry component now consisted of three divisions – the 52nd, 53rd and 74th. The cavalry element was also reorganized and two divisions – the Anzac Mounted Division and the Imperial Mounted Division – each consisting of four brigades, were created. The Imperial Camel Corps Brigade, as before, was the final component of Eastern Force. The Desert Column, which consisted of the two mounted divisions (less one of its four brigades in each case), the 53rd Division and two light car patrols, was retained.

Now that its supply arrangements were in place – the water pipeline had reached El Arish early in February, not far behind the railway – the British coastal advance was able to resume. On 22 February the Anzacs moved forward with the aim of occupying Khan Yunis, a position some five miles east of Rafa, which was thought to be free of Turkish troops. The report proved to be false, although the Turks soon vacated their defences which were subsequently occupied by the Desert Column on 28 February. Kress was greatly assisted in his tactical decisions by the fact that the Turks continued to enjoy air superiority during this difficult period. On 20 March, Murray notified the War Office of his concern at the arrival over the Sinai theatre of new German Halberstadt aircraft which outclassed existing Allied types. Kress reported:

> The standard of efficiency of the 300th Flight Detachment was wonderful. Though the [British] had superiority both in numbers and quality of machines, the detachment won and kept an undoubted mastery of the air from its arrival in the desert in the spring of 1916 until the autumn of 1917.[16]

Meanwhile, Eastern Force commanders continued to be preoccupied with securing supplies. The advancing British force would soon be at the Gaza line, over 200 miles from Cairo. By the beginning of March the railway had almost reached Rafa. This was still some way from the front line but General Dobell did not believe that an attack on Gaza could be delayed until the gap had been closed. Alternative methods of transport had to be employed. An early surprise attack was essential if the Turks were to be brought to battle, otherwise it was widely believed that the enemy would withdraw without a fight. Despite some additions to his forces, Kress had, on 5 March, been forced to abandon his strong position at Shellal on the Wadi Ghazze while awaiting a British attack. With a 'heavy heart', Kress had with-drawn 14 miles north to the Gaza–Beersheba line, but it was feared that he would retire again rather than face a major British attack unless he felt confident about the strength of his new position. Kress also recorded that his 'army was much weakened by sickness and desertion, and its mobility hampered by loss and sickness among the transport animals'.[17]

As he withdrew Kress allocated some troops to both Gaza and Beersheba, but held the majority of his forces in reserve at Tell esh Sheria and Jemmameh until the direction of the expected British advance became clear. In mid-March, the Turkish detachment defend-ing Gaza was strengthened and the 53rd Division was called down from Jaffa, where it had been held en route from Constantinople to the front line to deal with an expected British landing there. A decision to concentrate forces on Gaza was made following the arrival of reports that an attack was imminent (although the 53rd Division had still not arrived by the time the battle started on 26 March). At this point the garrison could muster 3,500 rifles and 20 guns; it was organ-ized in seven battalions and five batteries, together with several machine companies. They were supported by a squadron of German fighter aircraft, which gave the Turks local air mastery.

Turkish expectations of an early British assault on Gaza were not based on firm intelligence but accurately reflected General Dobell's plans. He secured approval from General Murray for an attack at the end of March, which would involve the crossing of the Wadi Ghazze before making a direct assault on the garrison at Gaza. However, the official line in London had remained unchanged since the War Office telegram to Murray of 11 January 1917 which made it clear that an advance into Palestine – together with a planned attack on Jerusalem – was to be postponed until the autumn. But a general change in Allied strategy, agreed less than two months later, was to have an impact on the course of events in Palestine. An Anglo-French Congress held in Calais on 26 February agreed on the need to launch new offensive action in the spring in several theatres, including the Western Front, Macedonia and Baghdad. The outbreak of the Russian Revolution in March 1917 reinforced the need for urgent Allied action. The British War Cabinet, aware of Murray's plan to attack Gaza, wanted the Allied force on the Palestine border to play a part in the general spring offensive.

Surprisingly, despite Turkish expectation of an early enemy attack the Allied forces had been assembled south of Gaza without attracting their adversary's attention. Virtually every available fighting unit was brought to the front line, with the Desert Column being positioned at Deir el Belah, the 54th Division at In Seirat, the 52nd Division at Khan Yunis and the Camel Corps Brigade at Abasan el Kebir. This heavy concentration of Allied firepower so close to the Turkish front line was made possible by steady progress in constructing the Sinai railway. On 1 March, the railway had reached Sheikh Zowaiid, 30 miles from Gaza, and three weeks later it had been extended to Khan Yunis and Rafa station had been opened. The water pipeline followed close behind and was supplemented by a good local source at Khan Yunis. Despite this progress, supply arrangements were stretched to breaking point. There was insufficient transport to enable the British to conduct a campaign at any significant distance from the railhead at Khan Yunis. The force could only be maintained in the field for a maximum of twenty-four hours, and it would not take long for ammunition and water supplies to begin to run low.

The capture of Gaza would enable the British to renew their water supplies, but they had only limited time in which to achieve success: if they had not secured this prize by nightfall on the first day, it would almost certainly be necessary to abandon the action. The plan produced by General Dobell and his staff was a development of the approach used at Magdhaba and then at Rafa. Like Rafa, Gaza was protected by a small detached Turkish outpost, although stronger forces were based in the area – principally at Tell esh Sheria and Jemmameh – and could be called upon to support it. These forces amounted to two and a half under-strength divisions, consisting, according to Turkish sources, of about 16,000 rifles. The British could expect the same determined response from the Turks here as they had experienced at Rafa, particularly as Kress had ordered the commandant 'to hold Gaza, whatever might happen, to the last man'.[18]

The 53rd Division, commanded by Major-General A.G. Dallas, would lead the direct assault on Gaza while the cavalry (some 11,000 men) would encircle the town to the north, east and south-east. The aim of the cavalry screen, which would be some 15 miles long, was to prevent the arrival of Turkish reinforcements and to stop the withdrawal of the Gaza garrison. Philip Chetwode, GOC Desert Column, was placed in command of the task force. The other two infantry divisions (54th and 52nd) remained under the direct command of Sir Charles Dobell. The 54th Division was given the task of supporting the southern end of the extended cavalry screen, while the 52nd Division would serve as a general reserve (it played no role in the battle).

The plan was firmly based on the local superiority of British ground forces but in other respects suffered from a number of risks. There were some 15,000 Turkish front-line troops (and up to 50 guns) in the area, in addition to the garrison at Gaza which had been increased to some 4,000 rifles. On the British side, as well as the cavalry force of 11,000, some 12,000 infantrymen (together with 36 field guns) were to be involved in the assault. The 52nd Division provided a reserve of 8,000 men.

One of the reasons for the greater strength of British forces was the need to overcome the powerful natural defences that Gaza enjoyed. Located on a small hill, the town is separated from the Mediterranean coast some two miles away by a series of sand dunes. There was no harbour and ships had to anchor a mile out to sea, where they loaded and unloaded their cargoes using smaller ships. In 1914, Gaza had a population of 40,000 and an extensive export trade with Britain. The town itself was surrounded by fields that were divided by cactus hedges which, growing in some places to a height of 10 feet and a width of 15 feet, proved a formidable barrier to an advancing army. The main natural barrier to an invading force emerging from the Sinai desert was the narrow ridge that ran from a point two miles north-east of Gaza to the Wadi Ghazze, south-west of the town. The northern section of the ridge took its name – Ali Muntar – from a knoll east of the town; the southern section was known as the Es Sire ridge. There was a parallel formation to the east of Ali Muntar which, at its southern end, was known as Sheikh Abbas ridge. The Turkish garrison exploited these natural features by constructing trenches among the cactuses and strong defensive positions on the Ali Muntar ridge.

As well as the time limitations imposed by supply problems and the need for an extended cavalry line, the British position was further undermined by weaknesses in command and control. General Murray operated from a command post on his train, which had moved up to El Arish, but he was physically too remote from the battle to have any real influence on it. The 53rd Division was also inconveniently located at El Breij, west of the Wadi Ghazze, placed there apparently to ensure the most effective use of the limited number of available telephones. The joint headquarters of Eastern Force and the Desert Column were located at In Seirat, where the overlapping responsibilities of General Dobell and General Chetwode promised to cause difficulties: Chetwode, as the subordinate of the two commanders, felt 'himself cramped in his conduct of an action if his superior [was] "on top" of him'. These problems were compounded by a general feeling that the staffs of Eastern Force and the Desert Column were too small. The price paid in battle, so the official British history puts it, was 'excessive strain, lack of sleep, and consequent liability to error'.[19]

★

Two days before the operation was launched, on 24 March 1917, the orders of Eastern Force were issued. The GOC Desert Column was directed to 'dispose his mounted troops so as to block the enemy's lines of retreat from Gaza, and to watch for any movement of [the enemy's] main body from the neighbourhood of Huj or Tell esh Sheria'; and then to 'attack the enemy's force occupying Gaza'.[20]

The first stage of the British attack began at 2.30 a.m. on 26 March, when the mounted troops left their bivouacs west of the Wadi Ghazze. They reached the wadi as dawn was breaking but their passage across the dry river bed was concealed by dense fog. The weather did nothing to delay the cavalry and there was no immediate sign of the Turks. Progress was unexpectedly rapid and, despite one or two encounters with enemy patrols, Gaza was almost encircled by 10.30 a.m. By this time the leading squadrons of the Anzac Mounted Division had ridden round to the northern side of the town, occupying a hill – subsequently known as Australia Hill – overlooking Gaza from the north-east. Soon afterwards the Seventh Australian Light Horse Regiment had reached the Mediterranean shore and had thus effectively surrounded the town. The other mounted troops – the Imperial Mounted Division and the Camel Brigade – were also by this time in their allotted positions east of Gaza. The mounted troops had therefore succeeded, as their orders required, in 'interposing their main force between the town and the Turkish encampments to the east, thus making a corridor for the main attack'.[21]

The cavalry was closely followed across the wadi by the 54th Division which took up a position of observation on the Sheikh Abbas ridge. The passage of the 53rd Division across the wadi went less smoothly. Two valuable hours were lost as the division waited for the fog to clear. Even so the leading brigades of the division had reached their first staging post – some three miles or so from the Turkish positions on Ali Muntar knoll – by 8 a.m. With the difficult task of taking Ali Muntar, which dominated the whole area, and then occupying the town itself, it was nearly four hours before General Dallas, despite continuous pressure from Chetwode, finally gave the order to attack. Dallas blamed the delay on the late arrival of the artillery but the real reasons related to the effect of fog on the overall timetable and the need to brief subordinate commanders on the plan of attack.

The Turks became aware of the British action by about 9 a.m. when an aviator reported to army headquarters that the British were advancing with two infantry divisions, and three cavalry divisions, assisted by armoured cars, against a front which extended from Gaza to Tell esh Sheria. This was reinforced by a message from the commandant of Gaza that he was being attacked from three sides. Kress von Kressenstein immediately ordered all troops within reach to converge on Gaza as quickly as possible. Not only the Turkish 53rd Division, which was already on the move southwards from Jaffa, but also the Third Division at Huj and a group based at Beersheba were included in the orders. These forces were, however, slow to react and would still be a long way from Gaza when darkness fell.

Just before noon, the British infantry finally moved: accompanied by an artillery bombardment, the 158th Brigade advanced from Mansura towards Ali Muntar over an exposed open plain, while the 160th moved on Es Sire ridge. The 159th Brigade, which had not yet arrived at Mansura, had not been assigned a specific role in the attack but was now ordered to protect the right flank of the 158th Brigade. This brigade made determined progress under heavy Turkish machine-gun and artillery fire but their advance was slowed by the appearance of the first cactus hedges as they closed in on Ali Muntar knoll. Advancing uphill, they were highly vulnerable to concealed machine-gunners and snipers and exposed to an unremitting sun with no shade or water to protect them.

In order to increase pressure on the defending garrison, Chetwode issued orders at 1 p.m. for the Anzacs to attack Gaza from the east and west. The resulting gap in the northern section of the cavalry screen surrounding Gaza would be filled by extending the responsibilities of the Imperial Mounted Division and the Camel Brigade. There was a long delay before Chauvel received these orders and it was not until 4 p.m. that the Anzac attack began. It made good progress towards the northern outskirts of the town. The defending Turkish forces were primarily concerned with the main infantry attack to the south and, initially, few troops were redeployed to stem the cavalry advance. To the south, at about the same time, General Dallas ordered the 161st Brigade to advance between the 158th and 160th Brigades with instructions to take Green Hill, a knoll on the ridge which was the source of Turkish enfilade fire that had prevented the capture of Ali Muntar. The effort was successful and by about 6.30 p.m. the Turks had been ejected from the whole ridge.

At about the same time, the Anzacs had reached the northern and eastern outskirts of the town and victory seemed to be in sight. To the north the Second Light Horse Brigade had faced little real resistance until it reached the cactus hedges, where the Australians encountered fierce opposition. There was also evidence of stronger enemy action to the east of the town as the New Zealand Mounted Brigade advanced from the Jebaliye area. By the early evening Gaza had been almost completely surrounded (except for the south-west side) and the advancing troops expected the garrison to surrender before long despite the resistance it had offered.

The prospect of victory proved to be an illusion. General Dobell, in consultation with General Chetwode, had already decided – on the basis of incomplete and misleading information – to abandon the fight if Gaza had not been captured by nightfall. Although supply difficulties played a part in the decision, their main concern was the reports of the arrival of substantial Turkish reinforcements from Huj to the north-east, and from Beersheba to the east, at about 4 p.m. Dobell believed that the cavalry squadrons operating to the north of Gaza were in danger of being cut off unless urgent action was taken. As a result of British delays earlier in the day, it was unlikely that Gaza could be taken without engaging with these Turkish reinforcements – an engagement that Dobell was certain would not take place until the following day.

Soon after 6 p.m. therefore, as darkness fell, orders were issued for the withdrawal of all mounted troops to the relative safety of the far bank of the Wadi Ghazze. The absence of any clear information about the progress of the 53rd Division (although Ali Muntar was to be captured within half an hour) reinforced GHQ's determination to withdraw. It was not until some hours later that an intercepted Turkish radio message revealed that the Gaza garrison was on the point of collapse and would have rapidly surrendered under the pressure of further attack. It also became clear only later that the Turkish reinforcements in transit had been stopped for the night for the same reason – Kress believed that Gaza was already effectively in British hands. The delay would thus have provided the British with the opportunity of success, had they still been there to use it.

However, infantry units were already being redeployed with the aim of facilitating a general withdrawal. As a precautionary measure, the 54th Division had been ordered to move up from Sheikh Abbas to Mansura ridge so that it could work in support of 53rd Division. With the impending withdrawal of the mounted troops, the right flank of the 53rd Division would otherwise have been exposed. Unfortunately, owing to a communications blunder, General Dallas, as commander of the 53rd Division, was not informed of this movement, an omission that was to have disastrous consequences. In order to complete the manoeuvre, Chetwode ordered Dallas to withdraw his right so that it could make contact with the left of the 54th Division as it moved into its new position. Not surprisingly, Dallas, who still believed that the 54th Division was positioned at Sheikh Abbas, objected to the order. He was unhappy about abandoning the ground he had won and asked for more troops to close the gap between the two divisions. Dallas was overruled and in these circumstances he withdrew his entire division southwards from the town and during the night it returned to its original starting point for the attack. The withdrawal was already well under way when, at about midnight, Dallas discovered what was happening – the 54th Division was drawing into a new position north of Mansura. There is little doubt, in the judgement of the British official history, that 'had he known this movement was in progress, he would certainly not have abandoned all the captured position'.[22]

It was not until 5 a.m. on 27 March that Chetwode learned that the entire position had been abandoned. An urgent attempt was made to rescue the situation. Dallas was ordered to retake the Ali Muntar ridge and the 160th and 161st Brigades were instructed to advance once more. Such an action was evidently 'a severe test, moral and physical, for troops who had been without rest for over 36 hours, who had gallantly captured the position and then been withdrawn from it.'[23] But it proved to be too late. Although the leading troops briefly retook Ali Muntar and Green Hill, a large Turkish force, strengthened by the recently arrived reinforcements, recovered the positions.

The British themselves were now vulnerable to a counter-attack at the point at which the right flank of the 53rd Division joined with the left of the 54th Division, in open ground east of Ali Muntar. The 53rd Division, on the Es Sire ridge, came under attack from artillery positions on Sheikh Abbas, which the enemy had recently captured. There is no doubt that the 'holding of the advanced line on Ali Muntar, with the Turkish artillery on Sheikh Abbas, would have been an exceedingly difficult matter, unless Gaza could be taken immediately'.[24] With all chance of success now gone, the British were forced to withdraw and, by the evening of 27 March, they had retired to the west bank of the Wadi Ghazze. British losses were relatively heavy, with 400 killed, 2,000 injured and 200 missing. Turkish losses were about 2,400 in total – 300 killed, 1,085 wounded and 1,061 missing.

The British failure at the first Battle of Gaza underlined the importance of effective battlefield communications and the serious consequences that can arise when there is a lack of up-to-date information about progress. The decision to withdraw the cavalry from the Gaza area was taken by the high command in the absence of such information. In a large and dispersed battle it was difficult to form an accurate overview and Chetwode was clearly not aware that victory was almost within his grasp. He had no knowledge of the capture of Ali Muntar or of the Anzacs' occupation of parts of the northern and eastern outskirts of the town; he was unaware at the time of the despairing radio messages sent by the Turkish commander of the Gaza garrison. His principal concern was the vulnerable position of the cavalry – on the first or second day of the British attack – once Turkish reinforcements had arrived from the east, although he made exaggerated assumptions about how quickly they would get there.

In these circumstances the delay in the arrival of the infantry caused by fog on the Wadi Ghazze was a significant factor in the British withdrawal. It made it impossible for the operation to be completed and for news of the outcome to be passed to headquarters within the hours of daylight on the first day – the assumption on which the battle plan had been framed. However, if headquarters had possessed a full understanding of the course of the battle this delay would not have had the disproportionate impact it did. There is little doubt that the British failure at Gaza was one of command rather than intelligence and it became clear that adequate systems were not in place.

★

The conclusion of the first Battle of Gaza coincided with a Cabinet review of strategy triggered by the British capture of Baghdad on 11 March and the outbreak of the Russian Revolution two days earlier. There were unrealistic expectations in London that the change of government in Moscow would lead to a more vigorous military effort by the Russians which would force Turkey to the negotiating table. The British government was seeking coordinated action to eject the Turks from Mesopotamia: as General Maude continued his offensive north of Baghdad, the Russians, it was hoped, would advance on Mosul. The Turkish position would be further weakened if there were a British breakthrough in Palestine. In considering British military prospects in Palestine, the Cabinet was influenced by General Murray's positive – and inaccurate – account of the outcome of the fighting at Gaza, which he sent to London on 28 March. In a reply dated 30 March, Sir William Robertson, the Chief of the Imperial General Staff, referred to Murray's 'recent success' and to British progress in Mesopotamia. He said that the Cabinet was about to authorize an invasion of Ottoman Palestine, with the defeat of the Turks south of Jerusalem and the capture of the holy city being identified as Eastern Force's immediate objectives.[25]

In a response sent the following day General Murray, who had consistently argued that such an operation required more troops than he had been allocated, expressed his reservations about the plan. The Turks made very good defensive fighters and any British advance would depend on the availability of water and other supplies; he could proceed no faster than the pace of railway construction would allow. However, the government was determined to press on with its plans and questioned Murray's claim that he needed five infantry divisions under his command if he were to mount a successful invasion. British forces already enjoyed a sufficient numerical advantage over their opponents and Murray was well placed, in the Cabinet's view, to advance energetically and capture Jerusalem. In the meantime there was growing civil unrest in Turkey and 'she was undoubtedly more exhausted than any other of Great Britain's enemies'. There was no longer any question of a delay until the autumn.

Concern was growing at the strain of the war on the British home population and the government believed that 'the moral effect of success was extremely valuable'.[26]

This new optimism in London partly reflected recent progress in Mesopotamia, but the content of Murray's reports was also a strong influence: these 'created in their minds the impression that the result of the battle had been more favourable, and that the enemy had been harder hit, than was actually the case'.[27] However, the reality of the position was a major setback to British war aims. According to Chauvel's biographer, it also caused serious damage to the morale of those directly involved: 'if the Anzacs were angry and frustrated, they could not feel the bitterness of the infantry. They too had been withdrawn, but after suffering [heavy casualties].'[28]

Increasing political pressure gave the local military leadership little time to prepare for a renewal of offensive action and there was a gap of no more than three weeks between the first two Gaza battles. In a telegram of 4 April, Murray sought to reassure the War Office that not 'a single day in the last 15 months had been wasted. Preparations were in progress for a renewed attack on Gaza, but he was anxious not to hurry over this operation, as he felt that a methodically prepared attack had chances of winning a considerable success.'[29] These intensive preparations were frequently interrupted by air reconnaissance and bombing missions carried out by the air forces of both sides. Nothing, however, could be permitted to interfere with the start date of a fresh assault on Gaza as the first obstacle to an invading force advancing along the Palestine coast.

Following their victory at the end of March, the Turks had considered moving on to the offensive but Djemal Pasha decided against it. Instead, they threw their energies into preparations for a renewed attack by the British. Action concentrated in two areas – strengthening the defences of Gaza itself and securing the line between Gaza and Beersheba. Gaza was well protected by a series of trench systems to the south of Ali Muntar knoll, but strong defensive positions were extended westwards from the southern outskirts of the town to the Mediterranean. To the east, a series of redoubts was constructed on the ridges between Gaza and Sheria with the aim of preventing the encirclement of Gaza by British cavalry. As a result of these works, according to the official history of the campaign, Gaza was transformed from 'an outpost held by a strong detachment to the strongest point in an entrenched position running from the sea along the Beersheba road as far as Abu Hureira [a distance of 12 miles]'.[30]

The Gaza garrison was strengthened by the arrival of two more regiments of the Third Division and there is no doubt that the Turkish coastal flank was now very strong; elsewhere, more troops were poured in to defend the line extending eastwards towards Beersheba. There were few troops based at Beersheba itself. According to official estimates, Turkish forces consisted of 18,000 rifles, 86 machine guns and 101 guns, although Kress and others give lower figures. The defence also benefited from the fact that morale had been considerably raised by its victory in the first Battle of Gaza. In these improved circumstances, there was no question of a Turkish withdrawal at the first sign of trouble. The Turks were determined to hold on to Gaza and firmly believed that they could do so. At least in the short term, events were to prove them correct.

As preparations continued it was clear that the British now faced a firm defensive line. Murray recognized that the second Battle of Gaza would be very different from the first. Unlike the first attack, it would not be a *coup de main* but 'a deliberate attack upon a strongly defended position, an attack largely dependent on effective artillery support'.[31] General Dobell had no option but to plan for a heavy frontal assault much in the style of an attack on the Western Front. An attempt to turn the Turkish left at Beersheba was ruled out, given the perceived difficulties of supplying a large attacking force with water, even though the position was not heavily defended and appeared to offer better prospects.

In planning this direct attack, Dobell would need to deploy three weapons – heavy artillery, gas and tanks – strongly associated with the war in the trenches in northern France. The bombardment would play a leading role in such an offensive and Eastern Force's artillery resources were increased to 170 guns. However, this seemed barely enough to make an impact over such a widely dispersed battlefront. The fact that he could also call on the heavy guns of the French battleship *Requin* and two British monitors anchored offshore did not seem to compensate for this shortfall. Gas and tanks were to be used for the first time in this theatre, though not in large quantities: no more than eight tanks were delivered before fighting resumed, although as many as 4,000 4.5-inch gas shells had arrived on the Sinai railway. (Even though gas was never used again in the Palestine campaign, 700,000 gas shells – some 8 per cent of all chemical weapons produced during the First World War – were subsequently shipped to the area.) On the other hand, the British suffered from a severe shortage of operational aircraft: only 25 were available for the second Battle of Gaza.

Under the plans formulated by Dobell, the battle would take place in two stages. As in the first battle, the infantry would make a frontal attack but this time three divisions would be deployed rather than one. It would advance so as to be within easy firing range of the Turkish defences south of the town. This would mean taking a line from the Mediterranean eastwards to the Sheikh Abbas ridge. The main attack would then follow, with the 54th and 52nd Divisions attacking the ridges to the south and south-east of Gaza, Ali Muntar ridge being one of the principal objectives. The aim of the right of the attack was therefore, as before, 'to wheel up to envelop the ridges covering the town from the east, and by this enveloping attack it was hoped to destroy the Turkish right'.[32] The Desert Column would contain the Turkish forces entrenched on the right of the British infantry, while the 53rd Division was to advance up the coast. Part of the mounted formation would be deployed against these entrenchments and the remainder would be held in reserve. In the event of any gap opening up, these reserve forces would pursue retreating enemy troops or surround Gaza from the north.

The first moves began on 17 April as the 54th and 52nd Divisions crossed the Wadi Ghazze and moved with little difficulty to their allotted positions. The British land and sea bombardment of Gaza began at 5.30 a.m. on 19 April. This included the use of six British guns that fired 'special shells' at ten entrenched redoubts located mainly to the south and south-west of Gaza. The howitzers fired their entire supply of some 350 shells in half an hour. The attack was so weak that the gas evaporated before the Turks had noticed it. The artillery barrage was followed, at 7.15 a.m., by the advance of the 53rd Division up the coast. The 52nd and 54th Divisions launched their assaults shortly afterwards. On the right, the Imperial Mounted Division attacked the Atawineh redoubt, while the Anzacs protected the right flank of the British from a Turkish assault from the east.

The assault was determined and courageous but made little impact on the Turkish defences. The artillery bombardment silenced few enemy guns as the British batteries were too thinly spread along a front extended over several miles. Kress confirmed that the naval bombardment did little physical damage, although it had a certain moral effect. The tanks were a disappointment, proving to be mechanically unreliable and vulnerable to enemy shells. In fact, in Kress's view, they 'did little to justify their reputation'.[33] Despite these setbacks there was some limited progress on parts of the front. On the right, the Camel Brigade succeeded in protecting the right of the 54th Division and preventing the enemy from sending in reinforcements. Otherwise the Allied cavalry was condemned to playing a secondary role until the infantry could open up a gap for them.

The left of the 54th Division advanced as far as the Turkish front line but could advance no further because of enfilade fire from Ali Muntar. Further to the left, units of the 52nd Division briefly took Outpost Hill, halfway to Ali Muntar, but could make no further progress. Along the coast 53rd Division fought its way to Sampson ridge, within two miles of the town, before being turned back. The reason given was unchecked enemy fire from high ground to the east, but the real explanation, in the view of the British official history, was that the division still felt the 'effects of their losses, disappointments and fatigue in the battle fought three weeks earlier, for their advance, even up to Sampson Ridge, had been much slower than that of the other two divisions'.[34]

Negative reports on the course of the battle, which reflected this very patchy progress, soon arrived at headquarters, where there was growing concern as the day wore on about rapidly diminishing ammunition and water supplies. Although more infantry could have been called up, much needed artillery reinforcements were not available. The performance of the defence was another factor. The battle illustrated once more 'the high quality of Turkish troops in prepared positions'. The redoubts were 'well sited for mutual support' and since the Turkish infantry did not 'flinch from counter-attack, the result was never in doubt'.[35]

The British action was called off in the evening but for a while it was intended to renew the offensive early the following morning. Murray reported in his dispatches:

> I issued personally instructions to the General Officer Commanding Eastern Force that all ground gained must, without fail, be held during the night with a view to resuming the attack on the Ali Muntar position, under cover of a concentrated artillery bombardment at dawn on the 20th [April 1917].[36]

Murray's plan for a dawn artillery bombardment was soon called into question as further intelligence arrived during the night which convinced General Dobell that the battle had already been lost. Reports from divisional commanders referred to the weakened state of British troops and dwindling ammunition supplies. The only result of a renewed action would be to increase the heavy casualties already suffered by British units. The relative strength of the Turkish position was demonstrated by the fact that they were able to mount several limited counter-attacks on the first day; a general Turkish assault was planned for the following day but circumstances conspired against it. According to Kress, 'our weakness and exhaustion of the defending troops and the shortage of munitions and supplies made a counter-offensive on a large sector out of the question, and the enemy effected his withdrawal to his old positions unmolested.'[37]

Dobell postponed the renewal of the British operation for twenty-four hours and reported to Murray that in his view no further advance could be achieved. The commander-in-chief agreed that further offensive action had no prospect of success and should be abandoned. However, there was to be no withdrawal of British forces; they were to maintain the positions that they held when the battle ended.

★

The second Battle of Gaza was, in the assessment of the Marquess of Anglesey, author of the definitive history of the British cavalry, a 'costly total defeat' for the British army.[38] British losses, which amounted to 6,444 (of which 509 were killed, 4,359 wounded and 1,576 missing), were much heavier than those in the first attempt to take Gaza; Turkish losses amounted to about a third of the British total. It was to be the largest set-piece battle fought in this theatre throughout the course of the war. The second British failure to take Gaza 'cast a gloom on the whole army' in the view of Sergeant Harold Clark of the Middlesex Regiment and many of his contemporaries.[39] It also pointed to a serious failure of military command. Murray had initiated a frontal assault without the additional troops and heavy artillery that he believed necessary to ensure success.

On the other hand, as the second Turkish victory over British forces within a month, it provided a great boost to Turkish morale and spurred them on in their efforts to complete their defensive works. The railway was extended and the water supply improved. The Turkish defensive line ran eastwards from Gaza as far as Sheria, a distance of about 30 miles; further along the road Beersheba was fortified as a separate enemy position. General Allenby described Gaza as a 'strong modern fortress, heavily entrenched and wired, offering every facility for protracted defence'. The remainder of the enemy's line, Allenby continued, consisted of

> a series of strong localities, viz: the Sihan group of works, the Atawineh group, the Baha group, the Abu Hareira-Arab el Teeaha trench system, and, finally, the works covering Beersheba. These groups of works were generally from 1,500 to 2,000 yards apart, except that the distance from the Hareira group to Beersheba was about four and a half miles.[40]

Within a few weeks of the second Battle of Gaza there was a further increase in Kress's force as more Turkish (7th and 54th Divisions) and Austrian troops were sent to southern Palestine. It now amounted to some 33,000 infantry, 2,200 sabres, 120 guns and 130 machine guns. According to intelligence historian Yigal Sheffy, the arrival of these reinforcements underlined the fact that the Turks and the Germans 'were in a defensive position in Palestine, but if attacked would put up stubborn resistance. Should they be forced to withdraw northwards, they would do so gradually, blocking the British momentum and wearing down their attackers.'[41]

The British line, which was reasonably secure, was based on the positions established when the first battle ended. It varied in distance from 400 to 2,500 yards from the Turkish line as it ran from the Mediterranean through Sampson ridge, south of Outpost Hill and on to Sheikh Abbas. At this point the British line turned away and ran to the Wadi Ghazze at Tell el Jemmi. The second British failure in quick succession inevitably led to a reshuffle of some of the senior commanders. General Murray remained in overall command for the moment, but General Dobell left his post at Eastern Force headquarters and returned to England shortly after the second Battle of Gaza, to be replaced by General Chetwode. General Chauvel succeeded Chetwode as commander of the Desert Column and Chauvel was in turn succeeded by General Chaytor as head of the Anzac Mounted Division.

As the opposing troops dug in, the Gaza line took on something of the character of the Western Front trenches, although distinguished by the extreme weather conditions and the fact that each side had a flank open. For these reasons, the stalemate was to last months rather than years as British military planners quickly came under pressure to find a feasible route round the obstacle. In the meantime, neither side was capable of more than limited military activity, consisting of small-scale attacks on the ground and by air on the opposing trenches. Regular patrols were mounted on the open flank on the British right. A notable breach in the stalemate was the successful British assault on the Turkish railway branch line from Beersheba to Auja, towards the end of May, which resulted in extensive damage. The action was described by Robert Wilson of the Royal Berkshire Yeomanry:

> we have just returned from a very interesting two-day show. We rode out to a Turkish railway just beyond Beersheba, arrived there at dawn and blew about fourteen miles of it all to blazes besides three small bridges. Whether we took them by surprise or whether they were afraid of us I don't know but we met practically no opposition and got back safely the next night with hardly a casualty in the two divisions.[42]

Britain continued to improve its railway communications and work started in April on a branch line from Rafa to Shellal, in support of possible future operations against the Turkish left. To support increased troop movements once the invasion began, the possibility of doubling the single-track line from Qantara to Gaza was given serious consideration for the first time.

In London the second Gaza defeat led to a major review of military policy. The main issue was whether the further investment of the resources necessary to open the Turkish gateway to Palestine could be justified. Alternatively, should the British government seek to maintain the new status quo, secure in the knowledge that the military security of Egypt had been enhanced by the ejection of the Turks from Sinai? It was quite clear that an invasion of Palestine was going to require a more substantial British military presence than had so far been envisaged. General Murray lost no time after the second battle – he wrote on 22 April – in reminding the War Office of the minimum extra forces – two infantry divisions plus additional artillery – that would be needed to ensure success.

With no prospect of reinforcements being sent to Palestine at an early date, the postponement of the Russian offensive planned in the Caucasus, and the British defeat in the first Battle of Gaza itself, the War Office modified its recent instructions to Murray. A letter from Sir William Robertson, sent in late April, confirmed that he was no longer required, as his immediate task, to defeat the Turkish forces based at Jerusalem and occupy the city. Instead, he was instructed 'to take every favourable opportunity of defeating the Turkish forces opposed to him, and to follow up any success gained with all the means at his disposal, with the object of driving the Turks from Palestine, as and when this becomes practicable'.[43] Robertson subsequently confirmed that Murray's request for additional field artillery would be met in full, but for the present the two extra divisions could not be supplied.

Discussions in Whitehall on wartime strategy were conditioned by the existence of two groups. The 'Westerners', led by Sir William Robertson, believed that the outcome of the war could only be determined in a direct confrontation on the Western Front. Scarce resources should be allocated accordingly. The 'Easterners', led by Lloyd George, believed that the military deadlock could be broken if progress were made on other fronts against Germany's allies. The failure of the French offensive in Champagne in May 1917 and the continuing stalemate on the Western Front strengthened Lloyd George's hand. He remained firm in his view that successful action on other fronts would be needed if civilian morale was to be maintained and if a breach was to be made in the enemy coalition that might lead to the defeat of Germany. Other, longer term considerations for increasing British military activity in Palestine were also gaining ground. A post-war British presence would help to stabilize a region that was a vital staging post between Britain and her colonies in the east. Success in Palestine would ultimately help to underpin the stability of the whole empire.

The progressive collapse of Russia after March 1917 offered an additional reason for British offensive action in Palestine. As a result of Russia's impending withdrawal from the war, large numbers of Turkish troops would soon be available for use on other fronts. However, many of these troops were in poor shape after having spent a long, hard winter in the Caucasus. Moreover, many of their most seasoned fighters had been sent to support the Germans on the Eastern Front in the latter part of 1916. Turkey urgently needed a significant victory on her Near Eastern fronts. Apart from her defeat at Baghdad she had also effectively lost control of the Hejaz following Feisal's capture of Wejh early in 1917. Although she had checked the British invasion of Palestine at the second Battle of Gaza, the likelihood of attack remained. If British forces passed through this gateway, Jerusalem would come under early threat. The loss of Jerusalem, one of the principal religious centres of Islam, would be a massive blow to the spiritual authority of the Ottoman empire.

Growing German concern at the deteriorating fortunes of its ally led to the dispatch of General Erich von Falkenhayn to Turkey at the end of April. For the first two years of the war he had been Chief of the General Staff in succession to General Helmuth von Moltke and had been highly influential in the formation of German strategy on the Western Front. In 1916, his position was weakened by the German army's failure at Verdun and Romania's entry into the war and he was replaced by General Erich von Ludendorff. Falkenhayn went on to display great qualities as a field commander in the successful German invasion of Romania. Arriving in Constantinople on 7 May 1917, Falkenhayn was asked to investigate the feasibility of a proposal to recapture Baghdad. Following a tour of inspection of Turkish forces in Syria and Iraq, he reached the conclusion that the project was feasible in principle. It would mean assembling a force of sufficient strength at Aleppo and would depend on the present stand-off at Gaza being maintained.

Following discussions between the Turkish and German governments it was decided to proceed with the offensive against Baghdad, which was given the codename 'Yilderim' (or 'lightning'). The German contribution would include the dispatch to Aleppo of the Asia Corps, a specially assembled group of infantry, cavalry and artillery units together with supporting personnel. The corps would total some 6,500 men under the command of Colonel von Frankenburg und Proschlitz. The core of the Yilderim force would be Turkish Army Corps III and XV, which had been working with the Germans in operations against the Russians and Romanians. The direct reinforcement of General Maude's army in Mesopotamia in response to these developments was a difficulty for Falkenhayn, while a strengthened British force for the Palestine offensive would help to ensure that Turkish forces were drawn away from the Baghdad operation. The need for additional troops was accepted by the War Office and they were to be obtained in part from the Salonika front, where the British wished to scale down their commitments.

The need for a successful British attack on the Palestine gateway also raised the question of whether the leadership of the Egyptian Expeditionary Force needed to be changed. The matter of Murray's future had first been discussed by the War Cabinet early in April after the first Battle of Gaza, but a decision was deferred. However, two successive defeats had revealed Murray's weaknesses as a military leader and undermined the War Office's confidence in him. In particular he had been shown to be out of touch with his forces and had displayed on occasion a lack of judgement in his assessments of the real position on the front line. The verdict amongst the rank and file was to be even harsher. Arthur Fletcher, a private in the Lincolnshire Yeomanry, spoke for many when he attributed successive defeats in Egypt and Palestine entirely to Murray's 'bad generalship'.[44] On the other hand, Murray was never supplied with the number of troops he regarded as being essential to achieve the objectives set for him: 'Like the commanders of many other British "advanced guards" sent to open a campaign with insufficient resources, he was superseded because he had failed to achieve the success expected.'[45] He had also lost political support at the highest level. The Prime Minister was gravely disappointed at the British military record in the Middle East: 'In Palestine and Mesopotamia nothing and nobody could have saved the Turk from complete collapse in 1915 and 1916 except our General Staff.'[46] According to Wavell, Lloyd George's attitude was crucial. He 'was always seeking a strategical "soft spot" and a way of escape from the slaughter of the Western Front, [and] demanded that this campaign should be set going again with fresh troops and a new leader'.[47]

Lloyd George's first choice to succeed Murray was the South African general Jan Smuts, who had recently arrived in London from an East African campaign that had achieved only limited success against the Germans. Smuts declined the offer on the grounds that the War Office had little enthusiasm for the Palestine campaign and would not give him sufficient support. With Robertson continuing to make known his objections to enlarging the scope of operations in Palestine, there was to be no active support in London for requirements in this theatre until he was replaced early in 1918.

When Smuts refused, Lloyd George turned to General Sir Edmund Allenby, Third Army commander on the Western Front, who had been recommended by Robertson. Allenby's initial reaction was one of disappointment. He believed that he had been 'removed

from France and relegated to an unimportant command because of
the limited success of the Arras battles'.[48] It was not until he returned
to London for meetings with the Prime Minister and the Chief of the
Imperial General Staff that he began to take a more positive view of
the posting, which was confirmed by the Cabinet on 5 June 1917.
Lloyd George wrote of his meeting with Allenby:

> I told him in the presence of Sir William Robertson that he was to ask
> us for such reinforcements and supplies as he found necessary, and we
> would do our best to provide them. 'If you do not ask it will be your
> fault. If you do ask and do not get what you need it will be ours.' I said
> the Cabinet expected 'Jerusalem before Christmas'.[49]

Whatever his initial reaction had been to the move, it did not
prevent Allenby paying generous tribute to his predecessor after the
war; he was to refer to Murray's preparatory work as forming 'the
cornerstone' of his successes. Though clearly not seen as the general
to lead the army into Palestine, by expelling the Turks from Sinai
Murray had undoubtedly laid the foundation for future victories
there and beyond. It was through his efforts that the infrastructure to
support an invasion – particularly the railway and pipeline that
spanned 120 miles of desert – had been constructed, and a coherent
organization provided to support a multinational military force.
Murray, however, never received full public credit for what he had
done and on his return to England he was sidelined, being given the
Aldershot command, which he held until November 1919. In the
Palestine arena, Allenby was now in charge.

# 5

# *Victory at Gaza*

MURRAY'S SUCCESSOR ARRIVED in Egypt on 27 June 1917, taking over command of the Egyptian Expeditionary Force a day later. General Sir Edmund Allenby had been commissioned into the Inniskilling Dragoons in 1882 and spent his formative military years in colonial Africa, serving in the Bechuanaland (1884–5) and Zululand (1888) expeditions. He entered the South African war (1899–1902) as adjutant to the Third Cavalry Brigade, with the rank of major. He was a major-general by 1910 and served as inspector-general of cavalry, 1910–14. During the First World War, Allenby commanded the cavalry in the retreat from Mons and at the first Battle of Ypres. He headed the V Corps at the second Battle of Ypres, 1915, and the Third Army at the Battle of Arras, 1917.

Although success had eluded him on the Western Front, even there he had demonstrated those personal characteristics that were to be such an important influence on the successful outcome of British operations in Palestine. Noted for the confidence he inspired, Allenby was a strong character who had a violent temper. On arrival in Palestine, according to the British official history, he soon

> restored the old personal relationships between leader and troops which was one of the finest traditions of the British army in the past and one of the keys to its successes. He was constantly up and down his line, so that there can have been few commanders in modern warfare who were so well known to their troops.[1]

To the rank and file, 'never was a change [in the leadership] so popular . . . as each individual cried out aloud his pleasure when the announcement was made'.[2] The ordinary soldier saw Allenby as determined and dominant, though often slightly threatening, and he quickly earned the sobriquet 'Bull'. These formidable characteristics were matched by the demanding objectives that the new commander was ultimately expected to achieve. These included the capture of Jerusalem, the defeat of the Turkish army and its expulsion from Palestine. Field Marshal Lord Wavell was to assess him as the 'best British general of the Great War'.[3]

Allenby's approach was very different from that of his predecessor. He relocated his headquarters from the relative comfort of the Savoy Hotel in Cairo to a camp at Um el Kelab, near Rafa. It was a 'hot and unpleasant, fly-plagued camp of huts and tents a few miles behind the line'.[4] Here he was in constant touch with his combat troops at the front and his physical presence had a marked effect on morale. Action to restore morale was a major priority because, in Wavell's words, it was clear when Allenby arrived that the rank and file 'were discouraged and cynical: they had lost faith in the higher command and in themselves and [were] . . . weary of the hardships of the desert. The force was in the doldrums, becalmed and dispirited, held between failure and success.'[5] Although the first objective of British policy – maintaining the security of the Suez Canal – had been achieved the Turks seemed well positioned in their new entrenchments on the Palestine border and a protracted stand-off appeared to be in prospect. This discouraging outlook and its consequences – widespread desertion and unauthorized absence, together with petty crime and drunkenness – quickly faded as the new commander's personality made itself felt. According to an Australian view, he radiated an 'impression of tremendous resolution, quick decision and steely discipline'.[6] As a result, the effect of the previous defeats was soon shaken off.

Allenby reinforced the good impression he had created on his first arrival by making some long overdue personnel changes. Sir Arthur Lynden-Bell, chief of the general staff, was returned home on medical grounds after he expressed reservations about Allenby's more vigorous approach. He was replaced by Major-General Louis Bols, an able staff officer, who had worked closely with Allenby in France. Allenby also welcomed the arrival of Lieutenant-Colonel A.P. Wavell who had been sent to the front by Sir William Robertson to act as the CIGS's liaison officer or, more accurately, his eyes and ears. Wavell, who later wrote a standard history of the campaign, came to enjoy the confidence of both Allenby and Robertson and proved to be an effective channel of communication between Palestine and London. By this means more interest in the campaign was generated in England, where so far it had made little impact on the public mind. But the shakeout went beyond this and a 'number of staff officers who had been spending too much time propping up the bar at Shepheard's Hotel [in Cairo] soon found themselves on the boat home, as did a few elderly regimental colonels and one divisional commander'.[7]

The effect of Allenby's actions was reinforced as news of his intentions filtered down to the rank and file. This new style of leadership, which included sharing his general objectives with all his men, was to produce positive results in the days immediately preceding the third Battle of Gaza. Noel Drury, a junior officer in the Royal Dublin Fusiliers, described the new mood among the troops:

> Everybody is in a great state of delight at getting a move on at last and, specially, as we know beforehand the general outline of the scheme. Why does no other commander realize that the men are capable of taking an intelligent interest in things, and that if they know what is going on, are much more likely to hit on the right solution when things don't go exactly to plan? Thank goodness, Allenby has some common sense and understands his Tommy Atkins.[8]

On the other hand, there was a danger that his appearances at the front would become a little too regular for the comfort of at least some of his troops. According to Wavell, 'so sudden and frequent became his appearances that corps staffs suborned a signal officer at GHQ to broadcast a warning whenever the chief set out from camp. The warning was conveyed by the letters "B.L.", the interpretation of which was "Bull loose"!'[9]

Allenby's decisions were based on firm foundations: he not only maintained close contact with his troops but took a deep interest in the physical landscape in which the campaign was to take place. A colleague reported that

> his interest in everything appertaining to Egypt or Syria which might affect the troops or the campaign was insatiable. Whether it was a fly expert from the British Museum, a railway engineer, an expert on

town planning or a naturalist who could tell him something about the flora or fauna of the country, he had them all up and sucked their brains of anything they could tell him.[10]

There was also evidence of a welcome new flexibility in his approach to battle tactics. In the weeks since the British defeat at the second Battle of Gaza in April, Eastern Force planners had been working on a new plan of attack. Under the new leadership of Sir Philip Chetwode – and with strong support from Brigadier-General Guy Dawnay, his principal staff officer and a brilliant strategist – the options were carefully considered and an elaborate evaluation of the whole situation was prepared.[11]

The possibility of repeating the essential features of the plan used in the second Battle of Gaza was reviewed and quickly dismissed. A direct attack on the town of Gaza had obvious advantages, given the easy access to supplies and communications that would be afforded by the Qantara railway nearby. Naval support could also be relied on to reinforce an artillery bombardment of Turkish entrenchments around Gaza. However, Chetwode's staff believed that the enemy defences at Gaza were now too strong to be broken easily by direct attack. Superior British forces had made little impression on Turkish positions during the second battle and even with substantial reinforcements it would be no easy task to break the line. The absence of water supplies in the immediate proximity of Gaza also enhanced the Turkish position, while the strength of the enemy force there depended on various unquantifiable external factors, including the level of activity on the Caucasus and Mesopotamian fronts and the capacity of the Palestine railway to resupply it effectively.

Some later commentators have suggested that this was too conservative an assessment and that the stronger force led by General Allenby could have quickly pierced the line at Gaza, capturing large numbers of enemy troops before they escaped northwards. Even if a decision between the two main options was more finely balanced than it seemed at the time, it was hardly surprising that the British rejected another direct attack. They had already been defeated at Gaza twice; a third attempt using essentially the same failed approach was too risky and would be difficult psychologically for the men to accept. The series of failed Allied frontal attacks on German lines in France also reinforced the general staff's conviction that a third direct assault in the same place would be unwise.

It was evident to Chetwode that a new approach was needed. The possibility of indirect attack on the Turkish defences had been under discussion for some time but it was only when communications had been developed that it became a realistic option. This alternative plan, which depended on secrecy and deception, rested on an assessment of the relative weakness of the extreme left of the Turkish line in comparison with the sectors that lay closer to Gaza. Located about ten miles north-west of Beersheba, the left flank was based on Kauwukah (at the end of the Hareira–Sheria line). It had an open flank and was less well developed than other Turkish defences in the area. It was also less well positioned: an opposing force advancing from the north-west would approach on higher ground than the defending Turkish forces. A complicating factor was the small gap between the Turkish left and the defending enemy force at the town of Beersheba, which would have to be taken before the main attack could be launched. Although in 1914 Beersheba had been 'a poor little Arab town', the arrival of the Turkish railway had led to the construction of 'good store buildings at the station', followed by 'a square of pretentious houses . . . containing even a German beer garden'.[12] In addition, it had water and other supplies that would be invaluable to an invading army. However, it would have to be taken rapidly if there was to be any chance of capturing intact the water supplies on which future British operations would depend.

Once Beersheba was taken, the attacking force would be deployed on the high ground to the north and north-west of the town, and from there a rapid advance would be undertaken against the Turkish left-flank defences with the aim of rolling up the enemy line towards Gaza. The cavalry would strike northwards to intercept Turkish forces evacuating Gaza and to secure new sources of water. The main factor crucial to the success of this new plan was the need for the enemy to 'believe until the last moment that a renewed offensive on the Gaza front was contemplated'.[13] Chetwode estimated that the plan would require the deployment of seven infantry divisions and three mounted divisions. These estimates were made against a background of further increases in Turkish troop strength in the area. By July 1917 the Turkish force consisted of six infantry divisions and one cavalry division, which had at their disposal 46,000 rifles, 2,800 sabres, 200 guns and 250 machine guns.

On his arrival General Allenby reviewed Chetwode's plans and endorsed the approach he had adopted. Allenby later acknowledged that his 'plan of operations was based on [Chetwode's] appreciation of the situation and on the scheme he put forward to me on my arrival in Egypt . . . To his strategical foresight and tactical skill the success of the campaign [was] largely due.'[14] The new commander-in-chief affirmed the need for more troops and, on 12 July, sent a telegraph to the War Office specifying his requirements as Chetwode had calculated them. The major items on the list were two additional infantry divisions and more artillery and anti-aircraft guns.

Despite Robertson's reservations about investing more resources in this theatre, the military authorities honoured the commitments given earlier and, with the exception of several artillery pieces, Allenby's needs were fully met. The 10th Division arrived from Salonika and a new division, the 75th, was created in Egypt from various British and Indian units. This substantial increase in the number of British troops massed on the Egyptian border prompted a major reorganization of the entire force. Eastern Force was abolished and replaced by three corps. General Chauvel led the Desert Mounted Column, which consisted of the Anzac, Australian and Mounted Divisions. The XX Army Corps, under the command of General Chetwode, consisted of the 10th, 53rd, 60th and 74th Divisions. The third corps – XXI Army Corps, which was led by General Bulfin, a 'stout-hearted warrior' – included the 52nd, 54th and 75th Divisions. In addition, there were a number of infantry and cavalry units under the direct control of general headquarters.

The release of additional resources to the Palestine front reflected the new-found interest of the War Cabinet in securing an early success on this front. The instructions issued by the War Office to Allenby on 10 August 1917 made it clear that the War Cabinet attached the 'highest importance' to the need to 'strike the Turks as hard as possible'.[15] A major British victory in Palestine would help to reinforce morale at home during a period when positive news on the Western Front was in short supply and it was feared that the European War could extend well into 1919. It would also exacerbate the war-weariness of the Turks and place further strains on their alliance with the Germans. Also at issue were Britain's longer term aims of securing her post-war influence in the Middle East, where her main rival was likely to be France rather than Germany or Turkey.

Because of the difficulty of predicting the strength of the Turkish opposition, which depended on how far the situation in Russia would enable the Turkish army to divert troops away from the

Caucasus, the Cabinet did not present Allenby with any specific targets. His instructions were necessarily of a general kind; as the official historian states: '[Allenby] was . . . enjoined to defeat the Turks opposed to him, to follow up his success vigorously, and to continue to press them to the limit of his resources.'[16] In the War Cabinet discussions on the draft instructions, some ministers argued that they did not go far enough, while others thought they might encourage Allenby to overextend himself. In an accompanying letter of 10 August to Allenby, Robertson said that the instructions 'simply amount to doing the best you can with what you have got; to giving the Turk as hard a knock as you can; at the same time avoiding going too far forward and getting into a position from which you can neither advance nor go back'.[17]

Both politicians and military leaders were agreed that resting on the Gaza–Beersheba line after a British victory was not a realistic option. Such a position, in Allenby's opinion, would be difficult to hold. In his view, the 'only line I can hold with reasonable security is the line Jerusalem–Jaffa with my flanks on the Dead Sea and the Mediterranean', and this on the assumption that his establishments were maintained at existing levels.[18] Allenby revealed his plans in some detail in a secret memorandum issued to his corps commanders a few days later, informing them that he intended to launch an attack, which would be concentrated on the enemy's left flank, as soon as seven divisions were ready for action.[19]

The progress of the Arab revolt, which had freed itself from the confines of the Hejaz during this period, was another factor considered by Allenby in making his plans, since it offered him the possibility of diverting Turkish forces away from the Palestine theatre. It was not clear, however, how much impact action by the Arabs could make. The arrival of Lawrence in Cairo on 10 July helped to clarify the issue. Crossing the desert from Aqaba to Cairo – a distance of 100 miles – in forty-nine hours, Lawrence brought with him news of the remarkable Arab achievement in capturing the Red Sea port of Aqaba on 6 July. Lawrence quickly initiated discussions with Allenby on Arab collaboration with the British as both armies worked their way northwards. British support was crucial to the Arab armies, which could make little progress without British money and supplies. Equally, the advance of Feisal's forces through Syria could only be maintained if Allenby broke through the Gaza–Beersheba line and moved forward into Palestine.

Allenby quickly appreciated the future benefits of military collaboration with the Arabs and formed a favourable impression of
Lawrence:

> His exceptional intellectual gifts were developed by mental discipline;
> and the trained mind was quick to decide and to inspire instant action
> in any emergency. Hence his brilliance as a leader in war. Lawrence
> was under my command, but, after acquainting him with my strategi-
> cal plan, I gave him a free hand. His cooperation was marked by the
> utmost loyalty, and I never had anything but praise for his work,
> which, indeed, was invaluable throughout the campaign.[20]

Although he was later to give more attention to his Arab flank,
Allenby's immediate priority was to end the stalemate at Gaza. Under
the plans developed by General Chetwode, the Gaza offensive would
consist of two attacking wings. The main attack against the Turkish
left based at Kauwukah was to be undertaken by XX Corps and the
Desert Mounted Corps (less one mounted division). The secondary
advance on Gaza itself would be carried out by XXI Corps. The gap
in the centre between the two attacking forces, which was some 20
miles long, would be covered by the remaining mounted division. It
was not particularly vulnerable to the enemy because the area was
open and any offensive action would be difficult to sustain.

The initial attack on Beersheba, which would precede these operations, was, however, far from straightforward. Beersheba was 15
miles from the railhead at Shellal and there was no road system
linking it with other towns in the area; mechanized vehicles could
not be used. There was also no water source available nearby; the
attacking forces would have to carry their own food and water. The
striking force, however, could only carry sufficient water supplies to
take them to Beersheba (some 30,000 camels were to be used for this
purpose). For operations beyond this point they would need to use
water drawn from the wells at Beersheba. If the British could not
capture these supplies intact, the whole operation would be doomed
to failure.

The ability of the British to maintain the secrecy vital to the
success of the offensive was seriously impeded by the fact that, for
much of the period of preparation, the Turks retained air superiority
and operated a network of agents in the area. The British intelligence
effort was led by Brigadier-General Gilbert Clayton, who was dir-

ector of intelligence in Egypt, but day-to-day operations at Gaza were the responsibility of Colonel Richard Meinertzhagen, head of military intelligence at GHQ, which was now established near Khan Yunis. Meinertzhagen's record against the Germans in East Africa suggested that he had the imagination and initiative to provide effective intelligence support to Allenby's offensive. He improved the analysis and interpretation of signals intelligence collected by the local listening stations – including one located among the pyramids of Egypt – that intercepted and decoded enemy messages, and identified and exposed the main Turkish spy in Beersheba by convincing the Turks that he was a double agent. (The man was executed on the strength of a false letter of thanks, and enclosed payment for services to British intelligence, which had been intercepted by the Turks.) Meinertzhagen also authorized regular leaflet drops over enemy lines, often accompanied by cigarettes allegedly laced with opium.

The main aim of British intelligence was to persuade the enemy that military activity in the Beersheba area was no more than a feint and that Allenby intended to make the main attack, for the third time, directly against Gaza. The deception extended as far as making an actual attack on the town, but other means were also used in advance of the offensive to disguise Britain's real intentions. At the heart of the deception was a successful operation in which a British staff officer's bloodstained haversack, which contained false information about Allenby's plans, was dropped during a contrived chase in which he was pursued by Turkish cavalry on outpost duty. The haversack was only picked up during the third attempt in which Meinertzhagen himself participated, as he later described:

> . . . near Girheir I found a Turkish patrol who at once gave chase. I galloped away for a mile or so and then they pulled up, so I stopped, dismounted and had a shot at them at about 600 yards. That was too much for them, and they at once resumed the chase, blazing away harmlessly all the time. Now was my chance, and in my effort to mount I loosened my haversack, field-glasses, water-bottle, dropped my rifle – previously stained with some fresh blood from my horse – and, in fact, did everything to make them believe I was hit and that my flight was disorderly . . . I made off, dropping the haversack which contained the rifle and various maps, my lunch, etc. I saw one of them stop and pick up the haversack and rifle, so I now went like the wind for home and so gave the them the slip, well satisfied with what I had

done and that my deception had been successful. If only they act on the contents of the notebook, we shall do great things.[21]

About once every two weeks through the summer months a British reconnaissance force moved in close to the Turkish defences at Beersheba, in order to inculcate in the Turks the belief that British action in this area would be confined to reconnaissance and that the actual assault would take place at Gaza. It was hoped that once the real attack on Beersheba was under way the British would gain an early advantage if their forces were mistaken for another reconnaissance patrol. Such an outcome was unlikely, however, given that the preliminary advance across difficult terrain from Shellal to the Beersheba area – a distance of some 12 miles across open country – was to involve four infantry divisions and two mounted divisions. The advance could hardly escape the enemy's notice, even if movement towards Beersheba was to be delayed until the last possible moment with the aim of concealing the size and real purpose of the force from the Turks. Stores were hidden as far as possible.

The British intelligence service also spread false rumours of a naval landing to the north of Gaza, a story that gained currency because the Royal Navy controlled the sea off Gaza and steps were taken to assemble a mock invasion force. A week before the attack on Beersheba, naval units were to contribute to a sustained bombardment of the Gaza defences and the railway stations on the line to the north. This prolonged attack would inevitably concentrate the Turks' minds on the security of Gaza and while they were distracted the striking force would be moved into position. This would be followed up by an attack by XXI Corps on the Gaza defences as the first stage of the assault on the Turkish left flank. It was hoped that the combined effect of these measures would convince the Turks that the main British attack was to be launched against Gaza.

The chances of the British deception succeeding were greatly enhanced by the changing balance of power in the skies. German dominance of the airspace above the battlefield was brought to an end abruptly by the autumn of 1917 with the arrival of new British aircraft, including the Bristol fighter, which outperformed the opposition. As a result, with much more limited opportunities for regular surveillance, British preparations on the ground escaped the enemy's attention. The combined impact of these reconnaissance and intelligence activities reinforced the Turk's conviction that the main attack would fall once more on Gaza. The deception was to have a 'very important effect on his plans'; according to Dawnay, 'it is pretty clear from captured orders and other evidence that the strength of our attack on the Beersheba front completely surprised the enemy. He thought our main effort was to be made against Gaza.'[22]

★

British preparations for the attack continued throughout the summer months in conditions that were often hard to endure. The effect of uncomfortably high temperatures was exaggerated by the regular arrival of the *khamsin* – the hot desert wind that made life difficult to bear. In these extreme conditions disease inevitably flourished on both sides of the line and 'sand-fly fever', a debilitating illness which left victims exhausted for several days, was commonplace. The Turks' health problems were made worse by serious food shortages and the heavy casualties caused by frequent British artillery bombardments.

Difficulties of transportation resulted in long delays in bringing up new equipment to the Turkish front line. Reinforcements were slow to reach the defending forces, and it was only once the British attack got under way that there was any large movement of Turkish troops through Palestine towards the Gaza–Beersheba line. In the meantime the Turks had to be content with the arrival of the 24th and 48th Divisions in September. They were able however to make further improvements to their defensive lines as a result of advice from the Germans who instructed them on the latest techniques being used in France. In particular, the strength of barbed wire entanglements was increased and more communicating trenches, linking reserve forces with the front line, were built.

Widespread health problems did not, however, seriously interfere with British preparations for the offensive that took place over the summer as individual units were briefed in detail on their particular roles. Troops were progressively withdrawn from the front line in order to undergo training in special camps near the sea, where they received instruction in the principles of mobile warfare and the need to endure long marches with limited water supplies. Intensive training had to be given to units newly arrived from overseas in order to integrate them into existing structures – a process which lasted until October.

Even more significant than the need for training were the

problems facing the military authorities in regard to shortages of transport and water. Complex arrangements had to be made to ensure that the troops could be kept supplied while operating at considerable distances from their original bases for periods of up to a week or more. Apart from any wells that the British might capture intact at Beersheba, there were no other significant water supplies available in the area until Sheria and Hareira had been captured. Priority was therefore given to improving water supplies and storage facilities near to the front line. Transport problems also took up a good deal of time. The use of motor transport was ruled out because of the absence of suitable roads south of the enemy line. (This proved to be the case to the north as well.) With heavy mechanical transport impracticable, Allenby envisaged using a combination of the Holt caterpillar tractor and the camel once the offensive was under way.

The movement of men and machines by rail from the rapidly growing port of Qantara was facilitated by the completion of double track as far as Bir el Mazar, a distance of some 70 miles. The construction of branch lines near the front greatly improved the supply arrangements of the forces that would be attacking Beersheba and enabled operations to be carried out over a wider area. Despite this rapid progress, Allenby was aware of the continuing problem of bringing supplies to the front:

> considerable strain was thrown on the . . . railway . . . during the period of preparation. In addition to the normal requirements of the force, a number of siege and heavy batteries, besides other artillery and units, had to be moved to the front, and large depots of supplies, ammunition and stores accumulated at the various railheads.[23]

The protracted process of assembling, equipping and training the invasion force meant that Allenby's preferred date for the attack, September – when advantage could be taken of a relatively narrow interval between the heat of summer and the onset of the winter rains in November – could no longer be maintained. The earliest date that an assault could be launched with a full complement of forces was the latter part of October and Allenby decided on delay even though he ran the risk of encountering adverse weather conditions.

This delay was accepted in London despite the fact that the political need for a major victory in Palestine was increasing, with the occupation of Jerusalem the major prize. On 5 October, Robertson sent Allenby a telegram informing him that the War Cabinet had again discussed the military situation in Palestine. It was clear on the desirability of eliminating Turkey from the war 'at a blow'.[24] This could be achieved, the Cabinet believed, by a heavy defeat of Turkish forces on the Gaza line and a rapid advance northwards as far as a line from Jaffa to Jerusalem, which the Allies would occupy. This defeat, it was thought, would be sufficient to induce Turkey to break with her allies. To achieve these objectives, however, so Allenby told Robertson, a total of twenty Allied divisions would be needed. The War Office had expected to secure its aims from existing resources in Palestine and quickly informed Allenby that the prospects of achieving a threefold increase in his forces were virtually non-existent.

The need to demonstrate early progress in the Middle East led to a revival of Cabinet discussions of the Alexandretta project – an Allied amphibious landing on Turkish territory in the Gulf of Iskanderun with the aim of cutting enemy supply lines to the east. But the necessary commitment of resources – six divisions and a million tons of shipping – was enormous when compared with the risks involved and the uncertainty of the outcome. And at a time when demands on Allied shipping resources – still depleted as a result of the U-boat campaign – were at a premium, this project could not command sufficient priority. Even so, it became the subject of an unsuccessful ruse to persuade the Turks that a landing on the north coast of Syria would be made. False intelligence about preparations being made in Cyprus was widely circulated. But the deception did not continue for long as the Turkish air force soon established that there was no substance to these rumours.

Growing evidence of the British military build-up at the Palestine border reached Turkish headquarters early in the autumn and had the effect of undermining their plans to mount an offensive to recapture Baghdad. Due to be launched by the enemy divisions concentrated at Aleppo over the summer months – the so-called Yilderim force – the planned offensive revealed the great gap that continued to exist between Turkish intentions and performance: by September, there were only three divisions available for action and these were all weakened by sickness. As Kress reported:

At this period the army was losing in sick and wounded 3,000 to 4,000 men per month, and about 25 per cent of its strength – 10,000 men – were always in hospital. This lack of men prevented the frequent reliefs of divisions so necessary for rest and training of the troops; the inefficiency of the railway service on the lines of communication resulted in a constant shortage of supplies, and the only sound measure which could have relieved this situation – a withdrawal of the Turkish forces from the Hedjaz – was excluded on political grounds.[25]

The German Asia Corps, which was due to form part of the new force destined for Mesopotamia, had only managed to reach Constantinople and was delayed there for weeks during the summer. Intelligence reports reaching General von Falkenhayn suggested that the Baghdad project would be fraught with difficulties and success was by no means guaranteed. It soon became clear to him that this high-risk project had to be abandoned as the arrival of British reinforcements began to threaten the security of Ottoman Palestine. Recognizing that 'the Palestine front was in a precarious position', he determined that the Turkish forces once destined for Baghdad should be switched to Palestine to ensure that the Gaza–Beersheba line was strong enough to resist an enemy attack.[26] Opposition to his proposals, however, came from Enver and Djemal Pasha. Enver continued to favour the Baghdad option over all others, whilst Djemal, commander of the Fourth Army, though aware of the need for reinforcements in Palestine, was concerned at the increased German influence which would result from the transfer of the Yilderim headquarters to this front. He also feared that the presence of Falkenhayn would reduce his power as 'absolute viceroy'. Early in September Falkenhayn toured the Palestine front and came to the conclusion that a new Turkish offensive could be launched against the enemy's eastern flank with a fair prospect of success. The aim of such an attack would be to disrupt British preparations for a major offensive.

In the light of Falkenhayn's conclusions, in mid-September 1917 the Turkish government decided to give first priority to saving the Palestine front, but it shrank from handing over the whole command to the Yilderim force. Instead the force took control of all Turkish troops to the south of Jerusalem and west of the Dead Sea, whilst Djemal retained control of forces and operations in Syria and the Hejaz. Falkenhayn obtained Enver's agreement to the immediate transfer of the Turkish Seventh Army, then assembling at Aleppo, to the Palestine–Egyptian border. However, conflict within the high command about military priorities had caused long delays, and before most of the reinforcements could reach the area the British attack had begun. Falkenhayn's plans had suffered a further setback earlier that month when a huge explosion at Haidar Pasha station in Constantinople had destroyed large quantities of ammunition and supplies destined for the Yilderim force.

When Beersheba was attacked there were nine Turkish infantry divisions and one cavalry division on the front. The total strength of the defending forces consisted of up to 45,000 rifles, 1,500 sabres and 300 guns. The British view was that although the Turkish defences 'were very strong . . . it was too long a line for the force at von Kress's disposal'.[27] The Eighth Army, commanded by Kress, consisted of XXII Corps, holding the Gaza area, and XX Corps positioned at Sheria. On the Turkish left stood the recently arrived Seventh Army, commanded by Fevzi Pasha, which was still far from complete. It assumed responsibility for III Corps at Beersheba. Fevzi played no active role in command during the early stages of the third Battle of Gaza and the entire front remained under Kress's control.

★

The British offensive was due to begin on 31 October, the earliest date by which preparations could be completed. The date also gave the advantage of a full moon for the complicated night movements necessary to bring the leading troops within striking distance of Beersheba by dawn. Allenby issued his orders on 22 October.[28] The operation would be opened with an attack on Beersheba, but the complex manoeuvres needed to concentrate the Desert Mounted Corps and XX Corps on the right flank, together with their associated lines of communication, had to be carried out first. These operations were to be conducted at the last minute by night with the intention of reducing the risk of detection by the enemy. According to Cyril Falls, the official historian, these first moves 'were the most anxious of all, not by reason of danger from the enemy, for they were beyond reach of his arm, but because they supplied the clue, if the Turks could read it, to the whole programme'.[29] They involved shifting units of the Desert Mounted Corps and XX Corps from the Gaza area progressively south-east towards Beersheba over a period of ten days.

On 27 October, an unexpected Turkish attack on the London Yeomanry of the Eighth Mounted Brigade as it held a low ridge

above the Wadi Hanafish resulted in heavy British casualties, but did
not affect the progress of preparations for the Beersheba attack. F.V.
Blunt, a private in the London Regiment, described how his unit
came under attack as it reached its final place of deployment:

> Here we got our baptism of fire and a taste of fighting wind up. Rifle
> fire opened up and enfiladed us from neighbouring hills. It was a
> rather terrifying experience in the dark hearing bullets whizzing
> about all over the place with no idea from where they came. We had
> one or two casualties and a camel and horse were knocked out close
> to me. The numerous little wadis and gullies made excellent cover and
> we were able to lay down and await the dawn in comparative safety.[30]

By 30 October, the process of concentrating forces prior to attack
had been completed. Three divisions of XX Corps were in position
as follows: the 53rd at Goz el Geleib; the 60th at Esani and the 74th
at Khasif. (The 10th Division was held in reserve at Shellal.) The
Desert Mounted Corps, which had finally reached its positions by
29 October, was based at Asluj (Anzac Mounted Division) and
Khalasa (Australian Mounted Division). These troops were accompanied by transport columns often several miles long, but despite this
the whole operation had been successfully accomplished with the
enemy completely failing to appreciate the scale of the general
movement eastwards that had been made under cover of darkness.
According to the British official history, 'from first to last it was conducted without a hitch . . . the advance was a monument to staff
work and skill in the memorizing of almost featureless country by
guides . . . who carried out hasty reconnaissances.'[31]
    Prior to the attack the Turkish army believed that there were still
six British divisions encamped outside Gaza, whereas in reality there
were three. The Turkish assessment of the position at Beersheba was
equally flawed: they believed that no more than one infantry division
and one cavalry division had been moved to the area. This impression
had been reinforced by the fact that camps opposite Gaza were left
intact after having been evacuated by the British, and the illusion that
they were occupied was maintained by keeping them alight at night
and by other means. The effect of this deception was heightened
when the bombardment of Gaza began on 27 October. But according to the official history, there was another factor at work, as 'it must
be added that the British superiority in numbers was so great that,

despite this dispersion, they were still strong enough on their left to have made their principal effort on that flank'.[32]

In reality the British force now assembled for action against Beersheba was very substantial – it consisted of two mounted divisions and three infantry divisions. Ranged against it, according to official British estimates, were the 40,000 rifles (their maximum strength was later found to amount to no more than 33,000), 1,400 sabres, four batteries and some 50 machine guns of the defending Turkish garrison. According to British calculations, this meant that the Allies had a preponderance in infantry of 2:1; in mounted troops of 8:1; and in guns of 3:2 – the advantage in numbers being necessary to ensure that Beersheba was captured speedily with its water supplies intact. The strength of the town's defences was also uncertain. Beersheba was the base of the Turkish III Corps, commanded by Ismet Bey, which consisted of the 27th Division, together with some units of the 16th and 24th Divisions and of the Third Cavalry Division. In the end, as Wavell put it, it was 'like taking a county cricket eleven to play a village team; but the pitch was a difficult one, and there was much at stake'.[33]

At that time a small white town with 'no vegetation anywhere about and all round just brown and barren', Beersheba is located at the foot of the Judean hills on the Wadi es Saba.[34] It is surrounded by hills to the north, south and east; to the west, the land is flatter and the railway entered the town from this side. Beersheba was defended on all sides. To the north and south the defences, which consisted of trenches without wire, were fairly skeletal. To the south and south-west – a more likely source of enemy attack – the defences were positioned on a series of heights up to four miles from the town. These defences included a series of well-sited redoubts but consisted mainly of a single line of trenches. Concerned though the British were at the relative strength of the enemy and the quality of its defences, they always believed that the natural features of the country posed 'the greatest obstacle and caused most anxiety as the day of battle approached'.[35]

Under the British plan for the capture of the town, two divisions (the 60th and 74th) were to attack these works, which were located between the Khalasa road and the Wadi es Saba. At the same time, the other forces (the Camel Brigade and two battalions of 53rd Division) were to assault Turkish positions north of the wadi. The left flank of the attack was vulnerable to an assault from Turkish forces operating in the Hareira area and the remaining units of the 53rd Division were sent northwards to cover the position. The right flank of the attack was covered by a cavalry regiment. While the infantry attack was engaging the defending Turkish garrison, the Desert Mounted Corps was ordered to advance on the town further east from a position opposite its southern defences – its most vulnerable side. This meant making a night ride of about 25 miles from their bases at Khalasa and Asluj in order to arrive east of Beersheba early in the morning. Their first task was to cut the Hebron road which entered Beersheba from the north-east and then, without delay, to enter the town; with the town taken, they were to seize the water supplies and cut off the Turkish retreat from the west, where the enemy was expected to have engaged with the British infantry.

In secret talks in Cairo in September, it was agreed that a small independent force, commanded by Lieutenant-Colonel Newcombe, would encircle Beersheba in an even wider arc than that planned by the cavalry. He was to cut the Hebron road well to the north of the town and harass any Turkish troops unwise enough to use it either to advance on the town or escape from it. As he passed through the desert to the east he would raise the Bedouin against the Turks as they came under attack from the British. His recent experiences in the Hejaz in support of the Arab revolt ensured that he was well qualified for this new task.

By the early hours of 31 October 1917, with the benefit of the light from a full moon, all the troops involved in the assault on Beersheba were moving towards their allotted stations in preparation for the attack. In the case of the infantry this involved a night march of some eight miles before they were in position 2,500 yards from the enemy's entrenchments south of the town. By 3 a.m. all units of XX Corps were at their stations. The 60th and 74th Divisions shared a front of some 5,000 yards divided equally between them. Two brigades from each division led the attack. Their first target was an outwork, located on a position known as Hill 1070, which barred the way to the enemy's main line of defence. According to an eyewitness report, the advancing regiments, moving into action after a delay of more than six months, 'presented a wonderful sight, a solid square of troops moving in the bright moonlight with a ripple of dust in front like the bow wave of a ship, rising into a great cloud through which the moon shone redly in the rear'.[36]

The attack on Hill 1070 was launched with a heavy bombardment which began at 5.55 a.m. but soon had to be suspended: the shells created a small dust storm that made it difficult to assess the effects of the attack. Shelling was restarted at 7.45 a.m. and within forty-five minutes the 181st Brigade of the 60th Division had attacked and captured the Turkish positions on Hill 1070. This allowed the British artillery time to move up to the Turkish main line. In theory, they were now sufficiently close to be able to cut through the wire defences.

Shelling from these new positions began at 10.30 a.m. and continued until noon, between intervals during which the dust was allowed to clear. There was some uncertainty about whether the artillery had been successful in cutting the wire that protected the Turkish positions, in particular on the front opposite the 74th Division; elsewhere, in the sector occupied by 60th Division, the artillery was believed to have cleared the obstacle sufficiently to enable the infantry to advance. In practice, much of the barbed wire had to be cut by the advancing troops as they came across the obstacle. They were fortunate in other respects since the enemy had largely disappeared by the time they approached the Turkish positions.

The final assault began at 12.15 p.m. Private Blunt of the London Regiment described the experience:

> We were told that we should not go over the top until Hill 1070 was taken. We lay quietly waiting for the time. Was I frightened, I don't know. All I knew was that over the ridge in front of us were the Turkish lines and these had to be taken. We had our tea and rum, cakes, and cold bacon for breakfast. At 12 o'clock we heard that Hill 1070 had been taken and at 12.15 we went over the top. I was in the front of the first assaulting wave . . . We were in a little wadi behind a ridge. It was necessary to get over the ridge, and off the sky line as quickly as possible. Once over the ridge it was a rush down the valley and a charge up the opposite ridge where the Turkish trenches were at the top. Over the ridge I noticed at once that there were scattered groups of machine gunners . . . in emplacements of rocks and shallow trench. They were out there to keep a protecting fire on the Turkish trenches . . . They had been out [in the open] since early morning and had suffered many casualties . . . Once over the ridge we all rushed down the slopes past the machine gunners. Bullets were falling everywhere. Several of our lads were hit . . . In the excitement I did not have the 'wind up' one little bit . . . Every minute I was expecting a

bullet to get me but my good luck stuck to me . . . When we got to the Turkish trenches we jumped straight in and shot or bayoneted or took prisoner all that was there. I was lucky, the section of trench I jumped in was empty.[37]

Despite the intensity of the fighting, success was quickly achieved. By 1.30 p.m. this part of the operation was over: the enemy line from the Khalasa road to the Wadi es Saba was in British hands. The works north of the wadi were the next target for the British infantry. The Camel Brigade (together with two brigades of the 54th Division) was charged with monitoring the position there, but they had been unable to establish whether or not the works were held in strength. Eventually, the reserve brigade of the 74th Division was sent in. They discovered that the entire works were held by no more than a few enemy snipers and British forces were soon in secure possession of them. Casualties in this part of the operation were relatively light, with most losses occurring in the early stages of the operation, when it had been difficult to locate the position of enemy guns accurately.

Attention now focused on the role of the Desert Mounted Corps which was charged with entering the town and capturing it before the Turks had a chance to destroy the precious water supplies under their control. The first cavalry units – from the Anzac Mounted Division – had left Asluj at 6 p.m. on 30 October and proceeded in a north-easterly direction. They were followed by the Australian Mounted Division, which left Khalasa and passed through Asluj. Most of these units turned leftwards at Iswaiwin and proceeded north to a point about six miles due east of Beersheba. At this position, some 25 miles from where their night ride had begun, the hills gave way to an open plain that extended as far as the town. The ride continued until, at 8 a.m. on 31 October, the Anzac Mounted Division had reached the line that extended from Bir el Hamam to Salim Abu Irgeig. The Second Australian Light Horse, on the right, was given the objective of taking Tell es Sakatay, whilst the New Zealand Brigade, on the left, was ordered to capture Tell es Saba. The Australian Mounted Division, which was now stationed behind Khashim Zanna, served as corps reserve.

From General Chauvel's headquarters, which were located on a hill nearby, there was a commanding view of the whole battlefield. Hostilities began at 9 a.m. when units of the Anzac Division attacked the Turkish defences north-east and east of Beersheba. The focus of this action was the heavily defended keep at Tell es Saba, which was positioned on the north side of the Wadi es Saba. It proved to be a formidable obstacle. Heavy Turkish machine-gun fire forced the attacking cavalry to dismount and advance on foot. Hampered by the absence of supporting fire from heavy artillery or tanks to counter the effect of Turkish firepower, the Allied forces were obliged to edge forward towards the target by a protracted movement which meant that the keep did not fall to the New Zealanders until just before 3 p.m. Meanwhile, the Second Australian Light Horse advanced on Tell es Sakatay. The leading troops came under heavy fire from Turkish forces to the north of the Hebron road and were soon forced to dismount. It was not until 1 p.m. that the Australians were in possession of Tell es Sakatay and had secured intact the water source nearby.

By mid-afternoon General Chauvel was becoming increasingly concerned that he would be unable to take Beersheba – and its water wells – by nightfall if he did no more than implement the agreed plan in the limited time available. The agreed next step was to send the First and Third Australian Light Horse Brigades to the north of the town, where they were intended to capture Turkish defensive positions before entering the town. This was unlikely to deliver results in the time still left and, under pressure from Allenby, Chauvel decided to adopt a riskier strategy in order to capture Beersheba that day.

He now ordered the Fourth Australian Light Horse Brigade, a brigade of the Australian Mounted Division which had been held in reserve, to make a direct mounted attack on the town from the east. To escape the attentions of German aircraft the brigade had been dispersed and there was an initial delay as it was rapidly reassembled. Under the command of Brigadier-General William Grant, it left from a point east of Iswaiwin at 4.30 p.m. The Fourth Brigade was supported by other Australian brigades: the Seventh Mounted Brigade on the left and the Fifth Mounted Brigade, previously held in reserve, which was ordered to advance on Beersheba in the rear of the attacking troops. Further east other units (the First and Third Australian Light Horse Brigades) were advancing to a point north of Beersheba. The Fourth Australian Light Horse Brigade led a force of nearly two divisions towards the embattled town.

As these mounted troops left the foothills near Khashim Zanna they advanced on to the plains first at a trot and then at a gallop towards Beersheba, some four miles away. It was known that substantial Turkish trenches protected this side of the town, but their precise location was uncertain. Turkish gunners soon opened up on the cavalry but, spread thinly across a wide area and moving quickly, they proved to be a difficult target. British machine guns supporting the offensive soon silenced the enemy gunners and it was the turn of the Turkish infantry to try to stop the advance in its tracks. Several leading cavalrymen and their horses fell to enemy fire but this failed to slow the momentum of the Allied advance. Most of the fire was wildly inaccurate as the defending troops, taken by surprise by the scale of the British attack, had failed to adjust their rifle sights to the correct distance. Soon the Turkish trench lines were overrun. The British advance continued although the majority of the cavalry dismounted to complete mopping-up operations in the trenches. Leading units of the 11th Australian Light Horse Regiment, as they entered the town, passed columns of Turks retreating from the front line. The Turkish commander Ismet Bey had recognized the impending collapse of Beersheba's defences even before the Turkish army had been shattered by the charge of the Fourth Light Horse Brigade, and he had issued orders for a withdrawal of the garrison to the Wadi es Saba to the north, where he planned to form a rearguard.

The enemy was overwhelmed and demoralized by this attack and it took little effort to persuade them to give up their arms. Even so, the Australian cavalry charge had played an essential part in securing the success of the first stage of the campaign. Its action ensured that the water wells of Beersheba – the foundation of further progress – fell into Allied hands intact. But for this rapid action they could well have been sabotaged by retreating Turkish forces; in the event the Turks had no time. The attack also ensured that Turkish losses were heavier than they might otherwise have been: more than half of the dismounted Turkish troops based in the town were killed or wounded during the battle. In these circumstances, all hope of an orderly withdrawal was lost; most of the Turks were quickly rounded up, although Ismet Bey, the Turkish corps commander, managed to escape capture with a few minutes to spare. He quickly 'gathered a score of men about him, beat off the attacks of some Australian troopers and reached the headquarters of 143rd Regiment [some six miles north-north-west of Beersheba]'.[38]

It was clear that senior Turkish officers had been caught off their guard by the scale and speed of the British advance. The elaborate

British deception had led them to expect the main attack to fall on Gaza and, as a result, they were completely unprepared for the offensive that was actually launched. There is no doubt that if their intelligence-gathering had been more accurate they could have mustered a stronger defence, invoking the support among others of Turkish reserve forces based in the Hareira area. The failure to take effective defensive action, combined with the successful demonstration of the power of British cavalry, undermined Turkish resistance as the critical next phase of the operation was about to begin.

This ineffective response was particularly disappointing to the Turks as there was no doubt, according to the British official historian, that their defences in the Beersheba area 'were excellently sited and deeply dug. With good wire they would have been formidable, but lacking a strong obstacle in front, the [Beersheba] garrison was too weak and too little resolute to make a serious resistance, except at isolated points.'[39] There was general agreement that the enemy rank and file had fought well but Private Blunt of the London Regiment had serious reservations about the quality of their arms: 'their clothing and equipment was most rotten stuff. They had no standard uniform but were rigged up in sundry kinds of cloth. The rifles, ammunition, and any uniforms were all made in Germany. Some of the rifles were 1916, but many were as ancient as 1890.'[40]

Some Turkish officers took the view that the Battle of Beersheba should have been fought on very different lines, allowing the defending forces to retain their mobility in preference to holding the front as a static position. The Turks did not need to fight a decisive battle at Beersheba when the odds were so heavily stacked against them. To avoid a situation in which they were completely surrounded Kress should have ordered them to make a tactical withdrawal. These criticisms of Kress carried weight with Falkenhayn and after a short interval Kress was relieved of his command. The British had succeeded in exposing the left flank of the main Turkish position to a decisive blow. At the same time they had inflicted heavy losses on the enemy: some 2,000 prisoners and 13 guns were taken; at least 500 Turkish soldiers died.

★

In the next stage the British would use XX Corps and the Desert Mounted Corps to attack the left flank of the enemy's front line with the aim of rolling it up towards the Mediterranean. There did, however, need to be a brief interval – probably a couple of days – after the Battle of Beersheba while preparations for the new attack were made. The British position had to be consolidated and the captured water supplies seen to be functioning properly. Before long it was confirmed that the quality and volume of water available in the town was sufficient to sustain the renewed offensive; all that remained to be done was to remove the few live charges that had been put in place to blow up the wells. The new attack now needed to be launched before the Turks could withdraw their left wing or bring fresh troops up to reinforce it.

The date for the attack on the Turkish left was set for 3 or 4 November. In order to distract the Turks from this new offensive the British planned to launch a diversionary assault on the town of Gaza two or three days beforehand. This attack was set for the night of 1 November and was preceded by an artillery bombardment of the Gaza defences, which had begun on 27 October.

The period of preparation prior to this bombardment, during which enemy targets were progressively identified, was described by a British soldier, Hubert Earney, who served in the Eighth British Mountain Howitzer Brigade. He recounted the effect of such activity on those positioned in dugouts nearby:

> The battery opened fire with ranging shots registering targets. A field battery just behind us also opened up, as also did several batteries around. Every time a gun was fired a piece of our dugout would fall in, usually down the back of the neck. Bullets whistled over the top of the dugout and an occasional shrapnel burst unpleasantly near. At noon, all batteries having registered targets the signal for the bombardment was given. *Then* we heard the music of the guns. It was great for us, but I guess not so for 'Johnnie'. We soon heard that he was running and that our infantry were gaining their objectives.[41]

The bombardment gradually increased in intensity and involved naval units as well as land-based artillery. XXI Corps was able to deploy 66 medium guns, two 6-inch guns and 150 other artillery pieces, while the naval force taking part in the bombardment included a cruiser and four monitors. According to Allenby, the navy's gunfire was 'accurate and destructive' and close cooperation was received from the service throughout. In a bombardment which was 'the heaviest carried out in the course of the war outside the

European theatres', some 15,000 rounds were fired on land and at sea prior to the day of the attack.[42] Harry Milson, a lieutenant in the Somerset Light Infantry, described the action:

> Our bombardment continued night and day, sometimes bursting forth in great volume and at other times dying down to a steady pounding . . . every part of the enemy's defences seemed to be systematically pounded; the bursting shells from the big guns threw up great clouds of sand and smoke and also very often – and more to the point – bits of dugouts and objects that might be portions of 'discomfited' Johnnie Turks.[43]

The attack on Gaza by XXI Corps was to take place across a 5,000-yard front from Umbrella Hill to the Mediterranean shore. At this latter point the gap between the opposing forces narrowed to about 1,000 yards; at the other end of the line, at Umbrella Hill, the distance between the two armies stood at 5,000 yards. The extent of the advance also varied considerably. On the extreme left, the British had been ordered to capture Sheikh Hasan, a height overlooking the anchorage for Gaza which stood some 2,500 yards north-west of the town and about 3,000 yards from the starting point. On the British left the advance was to extend for no more than 1,000 yards. The attack involved moving slowly across the sand dunes that stretched from the sea to the cactus that protected the outskirts of the town. In places these dunes were as high as 150 feet; the sand was also 'very deep and extremely tiring to the feet, which sank at each step to the ankles'.[44] Movement across it would be difficult for the infantry and for this reason the attack was set to take place at night. The advancing troops would also have to contend with a strong trench system and redoubts on which the Turks had been able to work for months without serious disturbance.

The Gaza attack, which was to take place in two main phases, began at 10.30 a.m. on 1 November. Carried out by the 54th Division, commanded by Major-General S. W. Hare, it was supported by 156th Brigade (which was part of 52nd Division). The attack opened with an assault on Umbrella Hill, some 2,000 yards south-west of Gaza, by the 52nd Division. Projecting out from the Turkish lines, the hill offered protection to the flanks of Turkish trenches further to the west and for this reason had to be tackled first. It was captured within half an hour but, wishing to convey the impression of an isolated attack and to lull the enemy into a false sense of security, the British delayed before renewing the offensive.

It was not until 3 a.m. on 2 November that the second phase began: a night attack, chosen because of the distance that separated the British front line from the enemy's position. Preceded by a heavy artillery bombardment, the main attack — which included the use of six tanks — began with an advance along the whole line. It took some three and a half hours to capture Sheikh Hasan, which was at the furthest distance from the starting point, and soon every British objective, with the exception of a number of well-protected Turkish rear trenches in the centre, had been achieved. Some 450 Turkish prisoners were taken and many others were killed.

Beyond the immediate capture of a belt of Turkish-held land, the attack had caused the enemy high command to focus attention on Gaza and away from the left flank. Its immediate reaction, as the Allies had hoped, was to order the transfer of a reserve division to Gaza to replace losses sustained in the attack; valuable resources were deployed by the Turks to strengthen defences in case the action was renewed. The attack thus succeeded in its main objective of preventing units being moved from the Gaza area to meet the perceived threat to the Turkish left. The capture of Sheikh Hasan and the south-west defences had far-reaching implications, according to the official history of the campaign, as it 'turned the flank of almost the whole of the prepared defences of the town and seriously menaced the Turkish position'.[45]

Meanwhile, at Beersheba, General Chetwode was reviewing in detail his plans for an attack on the Turkish left. XX Corps would once more operate on the British left. Under the original proposals, the 53rd Division was to attack the Kauwukah trench system from the front, while on the British right the 60th and 74th Divisions would assault the enemy's extreme left from the flank and rear; the 16th Division would serve as a reserve. The 60th and 74th Divisions were to aim for Tell esh Sheria. The Desert Mounted Corps, operating further to the north, was to advance on Tell en Nejile, where it was thought water could be found. The Camel Corps Brigade was allotted the task of maintaining contact between XX Corps and the Desert Mounted Corps. It was also charged with protecting the right of XX Corps but Chetwode realized that the infantry would be needed to help with this task. For this reason, 53rd Division was moved, on 1 November, to Towal Abu Jerwal, a position in the hills six miles north of Beersheba. The 10th Division replaced the 53rd Division in Chetwode's plan of attack.

★

While Chetwode was planning his next moves, the newly arrived German staff of the Yilderim force responded quickly to the news of the loss of Beersheba and ordered its early recapture by the Seventh Army. The enemy employed the whole of his available reserves in an immediate counter-strike, which 'might have saved the situation for him if our commanders had been less resolute – but which actually lost him everything'. Dawnay also believed that 'if the enemy had drawn us into a big fight in the difficult mountainous country north of Beersheba, he might well have saved his situation because it could have ended in our being too weak for the knockout blow we had planned.'[46] Allenby saw it as a 'bold effort to induce me to make essential alterations to my offensive plan, thereby gaining time and disorganizing my arrangements'.[47]

Ordered to support the attack, Kress von Kressenstein, the 'ever bold' commander of the Turkish Eighth Army, moved one of his reserve divisions (the 19th) to reinforce the Seventh Army, which constituted the Turkish left. But though Kress sensed that this flank was vulnerable to attack, neither he nor his colleagues could have had any real understanding of the intended scale or direction of the British offensive. Confusion was created by the activities of the Anzac Mounted Division, which was advancing up the Hebron road in search of new water supplies, while further north Colonel Newcombe's raiding force had taken up a position a few miles south of Hebron. These movements led to Turkish speculation that the British might be planning a cavalry raid on Jerusalem or a wide turning movement north of Beersheba in the direction of the Mediterranean.

In this belief the Turks sent six battalions eastwards from Sheria against Newcombe's force (which consisted of less than 100 men). Although they secured its surrender on 2 November, they had locked up half of their force in the Judean hills, where it took no part in the fighting for a week after the capture of Sheria. Newcombe's activities were a significant factor in the success of Allenby's operations following the capture of Beersheba. Though for a time held as a prisoner of war, Newcombe later escaped and continued to participate in guerrilla attacks against the enemy. Allenby had also been expecting support from the Arabs but the raiding party led by Lawrence had been unable to secure the destruction of one of the railway bridges in the Yarmuk valley. As a result supplies to Turkish forces in Palestine continued uninterrupted.

Also on 2 November, a second Turkish force (consisting of the Third Cavalry Division, the 19th Division and elements of the 24th and 27th Divisions) was assembled with orders to attack the British defending forces to the north of Beersheba and drive them back towards the town. The opposing forces met in combat at Tell el Khuweilfeh, a prominent height held by the Turks about ten miles north of Beersheba which afforded significant access to water supplies. Ordered by General Chauvel, commander of the Desert Mounted Corps, to capture the hill, the Seventh Mounted Brigade was unable to overcome strong Turkish opposition and reinforcements were brought up. The 53rd Division and the First Australian Light Horse Brigade renewed the attack on the following day but they too were unable to dislodge the Turkish forces, which had also been reinforced.

The stalemate continued on 4 and 5 November; the Turks remained secure on Tell el Khuweilfeh, while their efforts to dislodge the Allied cavalry from its position to the east also failed. There is no doubt, according to the official British history, that 'the ground lent itself admirably to the defence, as is proved by the fact that in the whole course of the fighting neither side can be said to have made a single successful attack'.[48] The British had to struggle with the problem of bringing up supplies from Beersheba across difficult terrain, whilst the Anzac Mounted Division failed to uncover any new sources of water and horses had to return to Beersheba to resupply. However, as a result of the fighting in the hills, British forces 'had established themselves in a position of vantage from which to roll up the enemy's flank, and all [Turkey's] efforts had not been able to dislodge them'.[49]

In an attempt to break the deadlock at Khuweilfeh, it was decided that a renewed attack using all available Allied forces should be made at the same time as the main assault on the Turkish left flank by XX Corps and the Desert Mounted Corps. The Turkish position was based on defences in the Sheria area, which extended for 7,000 yards from the Hareira redoubt as far as the Beersheba railway line south of Sheria station. Their principal components were the Rushdi and

Kauwukah trench systems, which were well constructed and heavily protected by barbed wire. Like other parts of the Turkish defensive system, except for those in the Gaza area, the trenches here lacked depth and were vulnerable to an Allied attack in strength. These trenches were subsequently extended a further 6,000 yards east of the railway but did not have the same degree of protection as the rest. XX Corps was positioned to the south-east of these defences and ordered to attack in a north-westerly direction. The 74th Division, located on the right of the attacking forces (its position on the left of the 53rd Division, which was operating in the Khuweilfeh area, had been taken by the Yeomanry Mounted Division), was ordered to attack the extended trench system to the east of the railway and then, once it had reached the railway, support the 60th Division on its left. It was then to capture Sheria, which had its own water supply.

The 60th Division had been ordered to assault the Kauwukah trench system before turning northwards in support of the 74th Division as it attacked Sheria. The whole operation, including the capture of the high ground to the north of Sheria, was to be completed before darkness fell on the first day (6 November). The Desert Mounted Corps was instructed to extend the search for new water supplies beyond those found in Sheria. As soon as the enemy's defences were shattered, the Desert Mounted Corps was to aim for the Huj and Jemmameh area, where there were known to be significant supplies of water. Water shortages were not the only problem facing Allied troops as they advanced northwards, as Private Blunt reported in his diary: 'What a time we had been through during the last ten days. Rations nothing but bully beef, biscuits and jam. No cigarettes. Not one night's proper rest and continually on the march. We had marched and fought from Beersheba to the sea.'[50]

The delayed attack on the Turkish left began at 5 a.m. on 6 November. It was led by the three brigades of the 74th Division, which had to advance for some five miles over open country before they were in striking distance of the Turkish defences. Despite the absence of artillery cover for much of the time and the fact that it faced some of the most determined opposition of the day, the division made steady progress: within four hours it had passed the midway point and by 1.30 p.m. it had achieved all of its initial objectives. It was then ready to begin the advance on Sheria. Meanwhile, Turkish defences to the west, at Kauwukah and Rushdi, had been under heavy artillery attack as leading troops from the 10th and 60th

Divisions advanced towards them. These divisions were to assault the south-east face of the Kauwukah system as soon as the bombardment had proved effective and then take the rest of the system in enfilade. Both systems were in British hands by 4.30 p.m.

In the wake of this success, and following on from the 74th Division, which had started its advance somewhat earlier, the two leading brigades of 60th Division began the march north towards Sheria, whose significance was explained by Guy Dawnay: it was 'the central strong point of the enemy's line and essential to us because of the water there'.[51] However, a decision to postpone the advance soon had to be made when it was discovered that the departing Turks had set fire to a large depot of military stores at Sheria station. With the fire lighting up the whole of the surrounding area, an Allied advance across the Wadi esh Sheria en route to attack the mound of Tell esh Sheria was considered too hazardous. On the left, British troops had almost reached the Hareira redoubts, although these remained in enemy hands. During the course of the attack of 6 November, the British had advanced some nine miles and captured a series of strong enemy works covering a front of some seven miles. About 600 Turkish prisoners were taken.

On the far right of the British line, fighting had also been renewed at Khuweilfeh on 6 November in accordance with earlier plans, in an attempt to break the deadlock of the previous days. Further action was also needed because 'the Turkish forces in the hills represented a potential obstruction. [The Turks] had been pushed back just far enough to prevent the line being enfiladed and rolled up, but they still held positions inconveniently close to the flank of the British attack.'[52] Attack and counter-attack again characterized the fighting in this area. A brigade of the 53rd Division, together with units of the Camel Brigade, began their assault at dawn. They succeeded in taking part of the Khuweilfeh ridge but were only able to hold on to some of their gains in the face of a heavy Turkish counter-attack.

The stand-off continued for much of the following day and the Turks, who were under German pressure to maintain the fight, only abandoned it as part of the general withdrawal of their line to the north. This outcome was no more than a small consolation to the Allied troops who had fought so hard to take the commanding ridge over the previous days. Their fight had, however, not been entirely in vain as the debilitating struggle had used up large numbers of Turkish troops held in reserve. When the British broke through at Sheria, the

1. General Sir Edmund Allenby and Prince Feisal (photographed after the war as respectively Field Marshal and King)

2. Major-General Sir John Maxwell. Over his shoulder can be seen Field Marshal Lord Kitchener

3. Lieutenant–General Sir Archibald Murray (*left*) with another officer

4. Colonel T.E. Lawrence with Colonel Guy Dawnay and Commander David Hogarth

5. T.E. Lawrence as Lawrence of Arabia

6. Field Marshal Sir William Robertson

7. Colonel Mustapha Kemal before he became Atatürk

8. General Erich von Falkenhayn on the platform of Jerusalem station with Djemal Pasha, the Ottoman Governor and Commander-in-Chief of Syria and Palestine

9. General Otto Liman von Sanders

10. (*left, above*) British fortifications at the Suez Canal

11. (*left, below*) A battalion of the Northamptonshire Regiment crossing the Canal

12. (*above*) A dust storm about to strike British aircraft at Gayadah, in 1916

13. The 4th Essex Regiment in line for the first assault on Gaza, on 26 March 1917. Note the lack of cover

14. The Northamptonshires' dugouts on the front line at Gaza, April–June 1917

15. A British Mark II tank in action during the battle for Gaza, 1917

16. A British observation balloon over Sinai

17. A British lorry-mounted anti-aircraft gun in action at Tel el Ajjul

18. The triumphal entry of Lawrence's Arab troops into Aqaba on 6 July 1917. Lawrence himself took this photograph

19. Aqaba Fort from the land side. This photograph was taken by Harry St John Philby

20. A camel ambulance used by men of the Northamptonshire Regiment

21. A dressing station for wounded in the monastery at Kuryet el Enab

22. Junction station, seized on 14 November 1917

23. The Imperial Camel Corps marching into Beersheba on 17 November 1917

24. Jerusalem as it was in 1917

25. General Allenby listening to the Proclamation of Occupation at the base of the Tower of David, Jerusalem, 11 December 1917

26. Allenby leaving Jerusalem by the Jaffa Gate

27. British infantry about to enter Nazareth, 1917

28. The Imperial Camel Corps crossing the Jordan at Hajlah on 25 March 1918, during the Amman raid

29. Lawrence's forces wrecking Ghadir el Haj, on the Hejaz railway, August 1918

30. Sherifian troops pass Turkish prisoners during the capture of Damascus in
October 1918

31. Armoured cars at Aleppo, October 1918

Turks had no reinforcements to bring up and could not make an effective response. On 7 November the British advance continued with little opposition. The attack on Tell esh Sheria, which had been deferred from the previous evening, was successfully made by the 60th Division during the morning of the 7th. The Hareira redoubt also fell to the 10th Division.

In the face of this powerful British advance the Turkish high command had bowed to the inevitable and given orders for a general withdrawal northwards from the Gaza–Beersheba line. When, during the evening of 6 November, XXI Corps, on the far left of the British line, converged on Ali Muntar, the formidable barrier in front of Gaza, it was pushing at an open door. It was in British possession within hours. In the rush to move forwards a Turkish rearguard was left in the Tank and Atawineh redoubts – the only part of the original Gaza–Beersheba line that the enemy retained intact.

★

General Allenby had always been clear that his next move would be the interception of the defeated Turkish army as it withdrew northwards. Mounted troops from Beersheba would cut across the Turkish line of retreat and delay its further withdrawal until the advancing Allied infantry could arrive and complete its final destruction. During the evening of 6 November, once the extent of the infantry's success had been confirmed, the Desert Mounted Corps was ordered to advance through the enemy's 'broken centre' and press on towards Jemmameh and Huj. Lieutenant Noel Drury, Sixth Royal Dublin Fusiliers, who witnessed the corps' departure, described it as a

> thrilling sight, and the whole battle area was just perfect for using cavalry. They swept up the rising ground towards Sheria in a big left-handed sweep, moving in lines of sections at about 250 yards interval between the lines. The frontage was about two miles, and the thunder of the hoofs and glitter of arms was a sight never to be forgotten.[53]

Beyond Huj, the corps was expected to move to the north-west with the aim of cutting off the retreat of Turkish forces between the Wadi esh Sheria and the Mediterranean. But its choice of route to the coast, and the presence of large numbers of enemy troops in the area, ruled out a direct advance from the east. The cavalry would have to funnel through the gap at Sheria at a slower pace before their advance could begin. Once through the gap, which had been created by the earlier infantry action, their route and progress would be heavily influenced by the availability of adequate water supplies. The most obvious route was the one northwards along the railway to Tell en Nejile, then westwards towards El Mejdel, where it was likely that the retreating Turks could be intercepted. A shortage of water along this route, however, ruled it out.

Taking an alternative course, the Anzacs soon captured Ameidat station where they took 400 prisoners, but they could make no further progress owing to the presence of a Turkish rearguard at Tell Abu Dilakh a few miles further north. Meanwhile, the Australian Mounted Division was involved in operations to clear the area immediately beyond Tell esh Sheria. It was not until nightfall on 7 November that it was in a position to move on. There was little doubt, in the words of the British official history, that 'the chances of capturing Turkish prisoners and guns had been greatly diminished by delays at Tell esh Sheria'.[54]

There was more movement in the Gaza area than elsewhere on 7 November. The bombardment of Gaza had continued throughout the day and another attack on the town was ordered for the night of 6/7 November, its aim being to take Outpost Hill and Middlesex Hill on the right and the line from Belah trench to Turtle Hill on the left. Intelligence reports revealed that Turkish military vehicles were on the move north of Gaza but there were no indications yet of a general withdrawal. However, the attack on Outpost Hill and Middlesex Hill, launched at 11.30 p.m. on 6 November, met with little opposition. When these positions were occupied during the early hours of 7 November there was no sign of the enemy. On the left the position was much the same. When the British advanced they found that the Turks had withdrawn from this area as well. The barrier that had held up British forces for some eight months had collapsed without a fight. The experience of Lieutenant Henry Milson of the Somerset Light Infantry was no doubt typical:

A wonderful sight greeted us, we were abreast of Gaza close on our left; the country was interlaced with trenches and dense cactus hedges, also bushes and trees grew plentifully, all affording excellent cover, especially for machine guns, but not a shot was fired at us and we advanced unopposed.[55]

The main Turkish withdrawal had in fact taken place two days earlier, on the night of 5 November, and was completed within twenty-four hours. Refet Bey, commander of XXII Corps, had received reinforcements on two separate occasions within the previous few days, but, by 4 November, local Turkish reserves had been exhausted. The Gaza garrison was faced with the option of encirclement and defeat or rapid withdrawal to the north. Kress obtained authorization for the second option and the whole evacuation was completed rapidly and efficiently, with nothing of real military value being left behind for the British. Kress had nothing but praise for Refet Bey who gave 'fresh proof of his wonderful skill, energy and personal bravery'.[56] The Turkish army planned to regroup and establish itself on the line of the Wadi Hesi, some seven miles to the north; it was partly fortified but its main advantage was the strength of its natural features.

The British soon occupied the northern and eastern defences of Gaza. The 54th Division occupied the town itself, while 162nd Brigade advanced through the gardens and fields to the main road north. According to the official history, little had survived the Allied assault:

> Patrols entered Gaza and found not a single living soul in its streets. It was, indeed, the ghost of a city. But the houses were mere shells; there was hardly one of them that had not been hit by the British artillery, and they had been gutted by the Turks, who had torn up every scrap of cloth to make sandbags and had removed most of the woodwork for the revetment of their trenches.[57]

While other Allied units pressed on northwards, Turkish rearguards continued to fire on Gaza from their positions in nearby trench systems. Leading units of the 52nd Division advanced northwards up the coast road, with its 157th Brigade crossing the Wadi Hesi, near its outlet to the sea, as darkness fell on 7 November. Establishing itself in the face of considerable opposition among the sand dunes on the north bank, it was closely followed by other British units, and before long it became clear that the Turkish army would be unable to establish an effective defensive position on the line of the wadi. The rapid appearance of British forces on the north bank of the wadi was the result of a 'mighty effort' and was 'hugely important'. Though part of Allenby's plan, in Dawnay's words, one had never hoped, except in very sanguine moments, to do it all in one rush. The importance lay in the fact that von Kress had prepared on the Wadi Hesi a position for use in case of accidents, and by establishing ourselves at the mouth of the wadi at once, we were placing ourselves in a position to turn the western flank of the position if he ever succeeded in holding it, and making it very unlikely that he would be able to hold on to it at all. And so it turned out . . .[58]

General Allenby and his staff hoped that the Desert Mounted Corps would make rapid progress to the north-west so that the Turkish forces remaining in the area would be encircled and unable to withdraw further to the north. These forces included the enemy troops fighting the British 52nd Division on the Wadi Hesi and those formerly occupying the Atawineh redoubt as a rearguard. The Turks, who understood the objectives of this part of the British plan, resisted strongly, and, as a result, the Desert Mounted Corps made no more than steady progress. Lack of water was another constraint, although many units pressed on regardless: the Dorset Yeomanry, for example, covered 60 miles in fifty-four hours without water for their horses, although the record was held by horses of the Lincolnshire Yeomanry, which survived without water for eighty-four hours.[59] British reinforcements were called up in order to increase the pace of the advance and avoid giving the enemy time to prepare a line of defence. Those added included the Yeomanry Mounted Division and the Camel Corps, which had been involved in the pursuit of enemy troops following the end of the battles around Khuweilfeh. The Anzacs finally reached Jemmameh by mid-afternoon on 8 November; the Australian Mounted Division and 60th Division reached Huj later the same day, following a notable encounter with the enemy not far short of their destination.

At about 2.00 p.m. the progress of leading units of the British 60th Division was brought to a halt by heavy artillery fire near Huj. Several enemy artillery batteries together with an escort of machine guns and infantry troops had been located on a ridge in order to protect the withdrawal of the Turkish Eighth Army headquarters. The use of infantry to attack this position was quickly ruled out and it was agreed that the Warwickshire Yeomanry should lead the assault. The attacking force consisted of one and a half squadrons of the Warwickshire Yeomanry, together with one and a half squadrons of the Worcestershire Yeomanry.

The attack was mounted without covering fire because the required supporting units were not immediately available. However, the yeomanry's advance towards the Turkish guns was protected by an intervening ridge until they were within about 300 yards of the enemy's gun position. With their swords drawn – for the first time in this campaign – 120 officers and men emerged in a column of half squadrons to face the flanks of the enemy guns, which were protected by an infantry escort. The leading squadron of the Worcestershire Yeomanry led the attack on the enemy infantry, which was quickly dispersed. They then turned and made a flank attack on the Turkish artillery positions. Lieutenant Mercer, who participated in the charge and was the only officer to survive uninjured, described the action:

Machine guns and rifles opened up on us the moment we topped the rise behind which we had formed up. I remember thinking that the sound of crackling bullets was just like a hailstorm on an iron-roofed building, so you may guess what the fusilade was . . . A whole heap of men and horses went down twenty or thirty yards from the muzzles of the guns. The squadron broke into a few scattered horsemen at the guns and then seemed to melt away completely. For a time I, at any rate, had the impression that I was the only man left alive. I was amazed to discover we were the victors.[60]

The effect of the charge on the German and Turkish gun detachments, according to Captain Alan Williams of the Warwickshire Yeomanry, had been devastating:

They had served their guns until our advanced line was within 20 yards and then threw themselves under their guns. Few remained standing and, where they did, were instantly sabred. Others running away from the guns, threw themselves on the ground on being overtaken and thus saved themselves, for it was found almost impossible to sabre a man lying down at the pace we were travelling.[61]

At the same time as the main body of the Worcestershires made a flank attack on the enemy batteries, the leading squadron of the Warwickshires, with the remaining units of the Worcestershires, attacked the batteries (and their covering machine guns) from the front. The remaining Warwickshire units were used to round up Turkish troops already to be seen escaping from the battlefield.

The yeomanry won a famous victory at Huj and 'for sheer bravery [it] remains unmatched'.[62] The Turks had been quickly overwhelmed by the speed and determination of the charge. Losses on both sides were, not surprisingly, high – Turkish losses included 11 guns and four machine guns as well as 70 prisoners taken by the British; among those killed were most of the Austrian and German gunners who manned the batteries. Inevitably, the British also suffered heavy losses in an operation in which they were fully exposed to enemy fire and supporting arms were largely absent: all three squadron commanders were killed, together with six other officers; 26 men were killed and 70 wounded. In the words of the British official history, the charge 'must ever remain a monument to extreme resolution and to that spirit of self-sacrifice which is the only beauty redeeming ugly war'.[63] The British had taken high risks – admittedly against a force that was in the process of disintegration – and the gamble had paid off; as Captain Williams recorded: 'undoubtedly, the flash of the swords and the great pace which we came at them completely demoralized the [German and Austrian] gunners, and although a few got away, they would never wait again for a cavalry charge.'[64] The way was now open for an attack on the flank of the retreating Turkish forces, although the Allies did not have the units immediately available to take advantage of this opportunity.

★

Meanwhile, on the far left of the British advance, the opposing forces met in battle on the banks of the Wadi Hesi. Lying some seven miles north of Gaza, it ran parallel to the Wadi Ghazze and was the last of the major watercourses along the Palestine coast. Troops of the 52nd Division had begun crossing the wadi during the morning of 8 November and had come to a temporary halt in the sand dunes to the north, facing in the direction of Askelon. To their right was a Turkish-held ridge – named by the British Sausage ridge – which extended for three miles from Burberah to Deir Sineid. Protecting their withdrawal from the Gaza area by road and rail, the ridge was held by the Turks in strength.

The first attack on the ridge was carried out by the 155th Brigade during the afternoon of 8 November but had to be abandoned when a Turkish flank attack was made on the British left. As reinforcements arrived, the British attack was renewed. On four occasions the British captured part of the ridge before being pushed back. By

9 p.m. the ridge was finally in British hands. Here as elsewhere, the Turkish rearguard had fought with considerable determination. Combined with the effect of a general water shortage in the battle zone, the defence was sufficient to slow down the progress of the British advance and allow the great majority of the retreating Turkish units to escape northwards.

This is not to suggest that the retreat was entirely orderly, despite the well-disciplined rearguard actions that had prevented defeat turning into disaster. The Turkish army had been badly shaken by its major reverse at the third Battle of Gaza which had given the Allies entry into Palestine for the first time. The relentless pursuit by British ground forces, combined with constant air attacks, had brought chaos to their retreat northwards. At some point the Turkish units would need to regroup and reorganize before they could fight again. They would also have to travel some distance beyond the Wadi Hesi before encountering the next natural defensive line which could be employed to turn the tide of events. This was the Nahr Sukhereir, a river some 15 miles further on, which Allenby's staff expected to form the next Turkish objective: in this belief, on 9 November, mounted troops were ordered to take the line from Et Tineh to Beit Duras – a position from which they would be able to turn the Nahr Sukhereir line.

The Anzacs led the renewed British cavalry drive northwards on the morning of 9 November; however, other mounted troops, including the Australian Mounted Division and the Yeomanry Division, and their horses, needed rest and water before they could move off again. The Anzac Mounted Division, which was already prepared for further action, advanced initially to El Mejdel, a large village near the coast some 13 miles north-east of Gaza, then proceeded to Beit Duras and Esdud before nightfall. It was a sign of the continuing disarray in the Turkish forces that the British encountered less opposition than on previous days and larger numbers of enemy troops were taken prisoner. According to the British official history, the Australians found the roads 'bestrewn with the debris of a defeated army . . . Those captured on this date were either the weaklings always to be straggling at the tail of a big retreat or else bodies of transport in which the galled and starving beasts would respond no longer to the flogging of their drivers.'[65]

The British advance continued northwards, its pace now significantly slower than that of the previous few days. It was becoming increasingly difficult to supply the advancing forces as they moved further and further ahead of the standard-gauge Sinai railway; the Turkish metre-gauge lines in Palestine were short of rolling stock and, initially, were of limited use to the Allies. As the army advanced northwards, the Royal Navy was able to unload supplies at various points on the coast as they came under British control, but the effect was limited. The weather was also a constraint on rapid progress as heat and wind took their toll. At the same time there was a general strengthening of the enemy's resistance along the line of the Wadi Sukhereir, with their forces concentrated around El Kustineh.

Despite these problems the Anzacs established a bridgehead over the Nahr Sukhereir on 10 November and managed to expand it during the following day. The Australian Mounted Division, which had left Huj after dark on 9–10 November, advanced on the right of the Anzacs at Arak el Menshiye and Faluje. The right flank was strengthened by the arrival of the Yeomanry Division on the same day (10 November). They were soon ordered to join the Anzacs as the bridgehead was being enlarged. Two divisions of XXI Corps – the 52nd and the 75th – operated in support of the Desert Mounted Corps and, by 10 November, had advanced to the line Beit Duras–Esdud. Owing to continuing supply problems other units of XXI Corps – the 54th Division and the Imperial Service Cavalry Brigade – remained stalled at Gaza. The 53rd Division, XX Corps, was still in the hills north of Beersheba, while the 60th Division had progressed no farther than Huj; the 10th and 74th Divisions were held at Karm.

As the momentum of the British cavalry advance proved difficult to maintain, it became clear that a large proportion of the Turkish force had escaped northwards, avoiding the British pincers. Although the progress of the Allied mounted troops was constrained by water supply problems and other factors, the fighting qualities of the Turkish soldier did not desert him. As a result, the Allies were simply not quick enough to encircle their adversaries, who avoided complete defeat at this stage largely owing to the 'unexpected courage and even fanaticism' with which their individual units had fought.[66] However, General Falkenhayn was sufficiently alarmed by the rapid decline in Turkish fortunes to order the Seventh Army to launch a counter-attack. From their base in the Judean hills, they were in striking distance of the flank and rear of the British forces advancing north-westwards across the plain. Launched from the Hebron area on 10 November, in the direction of Arak el Menshiye, the attack made little impression because the Turkish army was in such poor shape; the attacking army retired to the north-east, extending the line to Beit Jibrin.

As the Allied advance lost pace, so the Turkish Eighth Army, recovering its composure, also prepared to make a stand. The Turkish units positioned along the Nahr Sukhereir were expected to hold their ground in order to give more time for the main defences to be prepared. At this point the Turks' aim was to protect their lines of communication to Jerusalem and in particular the point – Junction station – at which the Jerusalem branch joined the main railway line. This junction was protected by a new line of defence that was established along the Wadi Surar and Nahr Rubin. No more than about 20,000 Turkish troops manned this line, which extended for almost 20 miles in a northerly direction. Although it lay rather too close to the main Turkish communication routes to the north, the new line was strengthened by the fact that it linked together a series of villages with good defensive positions, typically built on small hillsides, surrounded by cactus. In this sector there were two villages – Qatra and El Maghar – built on heights that underpinned the enemy's whole position. The formation of a new front line was a major Turkish achievement. Despite the heavy losses in men and matériel sustained since the evacuation of Gaza, the Turks had skilfully avoided the Allied net. The opposing forces were no longer advancing on parallel lines; the Turks had moved ahead and the two armies were face to face once more.

General Allenby was prepared to attack as soon as possible. The capture of the station would have the effect of splitting the Turkish forces in two. The Seventh Army in the Judean hills would be remote from the main lines of communication running through coastal Palestine. Its units 'were weak in numbers, disorganized and short of transports'.[67] Falkenhayn would be forced to use them in a diversionary attack on the British right in order to reduce pressure on the Turkish Eighth Army, the main focus of Allenby's immediate plans. The Seventh Army could be dealt with at a later date. Allenby's staff made plans to turn the enemy's right flank on the coast, a line that ran north to south from El Kubeibe to Beit Jibrin. The cavalry would turn the Turkish right, while the infantry was to attack the right centre. But first the British would need to position themselves correctly for the attack.

Progress was not easily won as the whole front moved forward on

12 November: to the east, the Australian Mounted Division was driven back as it tried to advance towards Tell es Safi. To the west the 52nd Division only prevailed after a difficult engagement at Burkah, to the north of the Nahr Sukhereir, which cleared the way for an attack on the enemy's main position, beginning on 13 November. The plan was for the cavalry – the Australian Mounted Division and the Desert Mounted Corps – to attack Turkish positions to the south of the road from Gaza to Junction station. The XXI Corps, which consisted of the 75th and 52nd Divisions, was to advance up the Gaza road towards Junction station and the railway to the north, making its way between the Gaza road and the village of Qatra. The Yeomanry Division and the Cavalry Brigade were positioned to the left of XXI Corps during the attack. After Junction station the cavalry would resume their advance northwards.

The attack began as planned at 7 a.m. on 13 November and, initially, good progress was made. The 75th Division advanced up the Gaza road and captured Tell el Turmus and Kustineh, while the 52nd Division took Beshshit. Yebnah fell to the Yeomanry Division. But progress was soon halted as the 52nd Division reached the obstacles of Qatra and El Maghar. The offensive was also in trouble elsewhere. Stronger Turkish resistance was evident at Mesmiyeh as the 75th Division tried to push forward. The progress of the yeomanry also came to a halt as Turkish resistance paid dividends at Zernuqa and El Kubeibe. But for the moment the main obstacle to further progress was the El Maghar ridge. It was decided that the Bucks and the Dorset Yeomanry should attack the ridge, while the Lowlanders of the 52nd Division would make a further attempt on Qatra and El Maghar.

At 3 p.m. on 13 November, the two cavalry regiments emerged from their cover in the Wadi Janus in a column of squadrons. At that point they had 3,000 yards to cover before reaching their goal – the ridge at El Maghar. Highly effective covering fire was provided by light guns and six machine guns, but their entire route was exposed to enemy fire. Soon a field artillery brigade of the 52nd joined in, directing some destructive firepower on to Turkish positions on the ridge. The advance began as a trot but ended at a gallop. Except for one unit, they charged up the hillside and seized their objectives on the crest of the ridge. A squadron of the Dorset Yeomanry on the left of the British line was forced to dismount and fight its way up the hill on foot.

Once in possession of the ridge the successful regiments deployed several machine guns against the Turks as they withdrew, increasing the enemy's already heavy casualties. The difficulty of the terrain and the condition of the horses ruled out a pursuit. The British quickly established a strong defensive position against possible counter-attacks. Although a key section of the ridge had been taken, fighting in this area was not successfully concluded until other British troops had captured the village of El Maghar. It finally fell at about 5 p.m.

This determined and courageous action of the yeomanry was to pay handsome dividends. The British took over a thousand prisoners and several hundred were killed. They also captured two field guns and 14 machine guns. The losses of the yeomanry included 16 killed and 113 wounded in addition to the destruction of 265 horses. More important, the charge helped to break the spirit of the Turkish defenders, who retreated to the east and north. The process was completed by the heavy losses inflicted on the Turks elsewhere in the line. The 155th Brigade took Qatra as well as El Maghar after fierce fighting which cost the Turks more than 2,000 casualties. By this time Mesmiyeh had also fallen to the 75th Division and the way was open, as the Turks retreated, to capture Junction station.

It fell to units of the 75th Division, supported by several armoured cars, to capture Junction station during the course of the following morning (14 November), breaking the railway link between Jerusalem and the outside world. The station provided the Allies with valuable facilities, including a steam pumping plant and, for the first time, plentiful supplies of water. The next priority was to cut the road to Jerusalem which lay to the north of the railway. This would sever the only communication with the holy city apart from the road northwards to Ramleh. There is no other way through the mountains from the west except by footpath and mule track.

The Australian Mounted Division captured Et Tineh, while further north the New Zealand Mounted Brigade fought off a vigorous counter-attack. The mounted troops pressed forward, reinforcing the wedge that had been driven between the Turkish Seventh and Eighth Armies. On 15 November, the Anzac Mounted Division advanced northwards and soon occupied Ramleh and Ludd, some five miles from Junction station. On the same day, the Australian Mounted Division and the 75th Division advanced eastwards from the station in the direction of Latron. A Turkish rearguard, positioned on a ridge above the village of Abu Shusheh, blocked the Vale of

Ajalon, one of the main entry points to the Judean hills and on the right flank as the British advanced on Ramleh. The enemy was removed by the 6th Brigade of the Yeomanry Division after a fine cavalry charge which resulted in heavy Turkish casualties. The action 'was even more daring than that of Maghar owing to the rocky ground, but the effect of that action had been to make the Turks less ready to face a cavalry charge; consequently their shooting was wild, and [British] casualties very low.'[68]

On the coast, the New Zealand Brigade took possession of Jaffa, the seaport of Jerusalem, on 16 November without any enemy resistance. It was, in Dawnay's words, a 'small town on high ground over the sea – rather like a southern French, or still more, southern Spanish town. Not very eastern – and to a cursory look not very interesting. But it is inhabited – not cleared like Gaza, for the Turks never expected to lose it.'[69] The Turkish Eighth Army had already withdrawn to a new defensive line behind the River Auja. The retreating Seventh Army had also recognized that this phase of the campaign had come to a natural end and it sought the protection of the Judean hills in the Jerusalem area.

These defensive movements marked the end of the ten-day pursuit (7–16 November) following the third Battle of Gaza. The British had advanced some 60 miles on their right and 40 on their left, driving an enemy force of ten divisions from an entrenched position that it had held for six months. According to Dawnay, it was recognized at headquarters that 'the pursuit has about reached the limit of what is possible'.[70] The advance was achieved at relatively heavy cost to both sides. The British suffered more than 6,000 casualties, while Turkish losses included more than 10,000 men taken as prisoners, in addition to 80 guns and more than 100 machine guns. At the same time, despite poor morale and a breakdown in organization, the Turks had managed to escape the closing net with most of their forces intact.

The outcome of the operation could have been very different if the mobility of the British cavalry had not been impeded by water shortages and adverse weather conditions. British progress was also hindered by the determined action of Turkish rearguards, although this factor was less important than the lack of water in slowing the British advance. Despite their narrow escape from encirclement, the Turkish position had deteriorated markedly during the final few days. Apart from the loss of southern Palestine, the two Turkish armies had been split – with no road to connect them in the area – and could be tackled individually by British forces. The Turkish Seventh Army in the Judean hills also faced increased supply problems. It was now deprived of access to the Palestine railway and all future supplies would have to be brought to the area by road. The nearest rail access still under Turkish control was near Nablus on the Palestine railway, which was some 40 miles from Jerusalem.

It was in these apparently more favourable circumstances that Allenby had to consider whether to proceed immediately with the next phase of the campaign – the capture of the holy city of Jerusalem.

# 6

# *The Fall of Jerusalem*

Now that the Allied pursuit of the Turks up the Plain of Philistra had come to a natural end, General Allenby had to decide his next step. His original plan, after Jaffa had been captured, was to suspend further operations until his supply lines and communications had caught up with the rapid British advance. He wanted to ensure he was in a position to sustain his whole army at the front without difficulty before moving on. Units also needed to be restored to full strength and the troops given a period of rest after two weeks of hard campaigning when water and rations had been in short supply. As Private Blunt of the London Regiment commented: 'Owing to casualties the battalion is now only just over half strength. Everyone seems just beat and worn out. I am as weak as a kitten, feeling done up all over. My face is covered in septic sores and my feet are all blistered.'[1]

However, powerful political and military pressures suggested that the immediate suspension of offensive operations would be unwise. In the end there was no more than a day's break in operations (on 17 November) before Allenby decided to press on to Jerusalem. In ordering an immediate renewal of hostilities the British would be able to take advantage of the fact that the Turkish Seventh Army would have had no time to regroup after its long retreat and its troops would be tired and demoralized. Its new base in the Judean hills was potentially strong but there would have been no opportunity to organize proper defences. Allenby was concerned that 'if we had given the Turks time to organize a defence we should never have stormed the heights.'[2]

At the same time, Allenby believed that it should be possible to contain the Turkish Eighth Army on the coastal plain while this new advance to Jerusalem took place. He accepted that there was, however, a risk of a Turkish counter-attack at Jaffa and Ludd.[3] He was also aware that the War Cabinet had expressed concern at the risk of operating in the rugged and difficult terrain that separated the Allies from their goal of Jerusalem and, given that Allied troops were tired and their ranks depleted after the Gaza campaign, had advised extreme caution. As well as the hazard of winter rains that were due at any moment and could make a difficult route impassable, he was reminded of the possibility that a substantial part of his force could be withdrawn early in 1918 to meet manpower demands on the Western Front. Lloyd George's earlier requirement that Jerusalem be captured before Christmas 1917 had been tempered by a recognition of the potentially dangerous circumstances in which Allenby's troops now found themselves.

Allenby's revised plans envisaged the creation of a new defensive line in the Plain of Philistra which would serve to protect the main Allied communications to the south. It would be located opposite the recently established Turkish line of defence based on the Nahr el Auja, a river some four miles north-east of Jaffa. This defensive role was allotted to the Anzac Division with support from the 54th Division. The main operation, which involved the bulk of his forces, consisted of an advance eastwards into the Judean hills towards Jerusalem. As Allenby wished to avoid fighting in the vicinity of Jerusalem – with the risk of damage to the holy city and the resulting propaganda advantage that would be handed to the enemy – he planned an encircling movement that would be much more difficult to execute than a direct attack. Once British units were within striking distance of the city they were to advance to the north-east, cutting Turkish communications by pivoting on the right and swinging to the left across the road between Nablus and Jerusalem. As essential supplies dried up, the enemy garrison would be forced to surrender or withdraw.

In these operations, units of XXI Corps were to play a leading part. The 75th Division (which consisted of West Country territorials) would advance up the main road from Jaffa to Jerusalem – the only one in the whole area with a metalled surface – as far as Kuryet el Enab. The 52nd Division (Lowland Scottish) would advance on its immediate left. To the left of the 52nd Division was the Yeomanry

Mounted Division, which was ordered to advance on Bireh, ten miles to the north of Jerusalem, via Beit Ur el Foka. It would be joined by the 75th Division which was ordered to turn north-east to Bireh as it approached Jerusalem. The combined force would then cut the Nablus–Jerusalem road. This would disrupt the Turks' main line of supply and force the enemy to evacuate the city.

The advance eastwards into the hills towards Jerusalem began on 18 November. The Australian Mounted Division was responsible for clearing the enemy from Latron, on the Jaffa–Jerusalem road, before the 75th Division prepared to move off. The Yeomanry Mounted Division began its advance towards Bireh. The two infantry divisions prepared to follow them: the 52nd Division started from Ludd and Ramleh, while the 75th began its advance from a position near Latron. Their move into the Judean hills began on 19 November, the same day that saw the outbreak of the heavy winter rains. The 75th Division advanced through Latron towards the villages of Saris and Kuryet el Enab, where the Turks had damaged the road in several places.

The 52nd Division and the Yeomanry Division had a much more difficult task. They soon found that the routes they had been ordered to follow were no more than unmade tracks that were often steep and difficult for all but mule transport to negotiate; vehicles and guns could go no further and had to be returned to their starting points. As Guy Dawnay described it, the landscape was typically 'very rough and rugged . . . Great hills overhanging deep valleys 1,500 or 2,000 feet almost sheer down in many places. Hill villages perched as in Italy on the tops of conical mountains. No roads – or only one, that to Jerusalem.'[4] The deteriorating weather added to British problems: troops were equipped for the extreme heat of Sinai and Gaza earlier in the year, rather than the cold and wet winter conditions that they now had to face. There was no early relief to the suffering of the rank and file as winter clothing was slow to arrive because of continuing transport bottlenecks.

Despite these constraints, however, some progress was made on the ground and during the course of 19 November the leading brigade of 52nd Division reached Beit Likia, while the Yeomanry advanced to Beit Ur el Tahta. By 20 November, the 75th Division had reached the villages of Saris and Kuryet el Enab. The Turks were strongly entrenched in ridges above these settlements and proved to be difficult to dislodge. The Turkish position at Saris fell during the after-

noon but strong resistance was maintained on the ridge at Kuryet el
Enab. On this occasion, for once, bad weather came to the aid of the
British. Thick fog obscured the view of the Turkish gunners, giving
the three British battalions the opportunity to charge the enemy
positions without effective challenge. The result was that the entire
ridge had been taken by the early evening, thus reopening the road
towards Jerusalem. By this point, according to the official history, it
was

> pretty certain that the enemy meant to defend Jerusalem. Only small
> rearguard detachments had yet been encountered, and the great diffi-
> culty found in dislodging them from positions so admirably suited to
> their tactics augured ill for the moment drawing nigh when the Turks
> should be met with in strength.[5]

The advance also continued on other parts of the front line. The
52nd made useful progress, but further to its left the Yeomanry
Division was unable to reach Bireh, where it was charged with
cutting the vital Nablus road. Instructed to capture Zeitun ridge to
the west of Bireh, which was held by a determined enemy force of
3,000 troops and several artillery batteries, the yeomanry was initially
unable to dislodge them. (It did in fact take it briefly on 21
November but was soon forced to relinquish it.) At this point for the
first time, Falkenhayn's strategy had been revealed. He left small rearguards to delay the progress of the Allied advance and thus gave the
Turkish Seventh Army additional time to organize the defences surrounding Jerusalem.

Meanwhile, the 75th Division continued its advance, turning
north-east on 21 November towards Bireh and moving across the
front of the 52nd Division on its left. The progress of the 75th
Division was brought to a rapid halt when it discovered that its route
to Bireh was completely blocked at Biddu. Here they encountered
the dominating hill of Nebi Samweil, often described as the 'key to
Jerusalem', which provided uninterrupted views of the city. The hill
was taken by the 234th Brigade during the late evening, but the 52nd
and 75th Divisions could make no further progress. Their attack on
El Jib, the next important height beyond Nebi Samweil, on 22–24
November, was unsuccessful. Without substantial reinforcements,
and in the absence of artillery support because of the lack of roads in
the area north-west of Jerusalem, it was likely to stay beyond their

reach. The Turkish defensive positions were held in strength and could not be dislodged by infantry action alone. General Allenby recognized that there was nothing to be gained by prolonging the fighting and, on 24 November, he ordered it to be broken off. The existing battle line was to be held and consolidated until fresh troops could be brought forward to renew the offensive.

The Turks made a concerted effort to recapture the Nebi Samweil height during the period 27–30 November but they were repulsed. Its defence was a brilliant feat of arms. Some 750 Turkish prisoners were taken during these few days. Fresh British forces now needed to be brought up to replace weary front-line troops who had been campaigning for three weeks in strenuous conditions. The first campaign to capture Jerusalem had stalled in face of the difficult terrain northwest of the capital where the British were unsupported by artillery; the Turks on the other hand had more flexibility because the Jerusalem to Nablus road remained under their control. The British action, however – generally characterized, in the words of the official history, by 'boldness' and 'determination' – was not entirely without benefit as it had left them in a stronger position than if they had delayed an attack until the Turks had dug themselves in. Allenby was quite clear about the gains that had so far been secured:

> The narrow passes from the plain to the plateau of the Judean range have seldom been forced, and have been fatal to many invading armies. Had the attempt not been made at once, or had it been pressed with less determination, the enemy would have had time to reinforce his defences in the passes lower down, and the conquest of the plateau would then have been slow, costly, and precarious. As it was, positions had been won from which the final attack could be prepared and delivered with good prospects of success.[6]

In the meantime, there had been far less action on the coastal plain and it was only on the day that the first Battle of Jerusalem ended, 24 November, that the Anzacs were ordered to advance across the River Auja and establish a bridgehead. The aim was to keep the defending Turkish Eighth Army on its guard and to discourage the possible transfer of troops from the coast to the Jerusalem area. Following a successful action by the New Zealand Mounted Brigade, two battalions of the 54th Division held two small bridgeheads on the northern banks of the wadi for a brief period. The occupation was, however, short-lived as the British infantry was forced to withdraw when the Turks attacked in overwhelming strength on 25 November.

★

Following this action there was a lull in the fighting on both fronts while the British made preparations for a second attack on Turkish forces in the area. In better weather conditions, existing roads and tracks were improved and new ones constructed to enable heavy and field artillery to be placed in position and ammunition and supplies brought up. The water supply was also developed. The British front-line forces needed both renewal and reinforcement and Allenby decided that the effectiveness of his front-line troops would be enhanced if he were to exchange his forces in the Judean hills with those on the coast. Under these plans XX Corps would leave its coastal bases and move inland, while units of XXI Corps would move in the opposite direction. XX Corps, under Chetwode, assumed its new duties on 28 November.

It was inevitable that the Turks would seek to capitalize on this time of uncertainty and instability. Over the period of a week they launched a series of attacks designed to test the resilience of the British position, in particular exploiting the gap of some five miles that existed between the right of the line in the plain and the left of the force in the hills. Using the 'shock tactics' employed by German troops on the Western Front, the Turks achieved a series of short-lived successes at the end of November and early in December. However, as British reinforcements arrived, lost ground was recovered and gaps in the line were soon closed. By 3 December the Turks had abandoned their action.

By 7 December, the exchange of British forces had been completed and XX Corps was prepared to make a second attempt to overcome the Turkish defences that protected Jerusalem. The Turkish Seventh Army, which consisted of some 16,000 troops, remained strongly entrenched in the hills to the west of Jerusalem. However, its morale had been seriously damaged by a succession of setbacks and defeats and it was not clear how much more resistance it would offer before withdrawing. The renewed attack was led by General Chetwode, commander of XX Corps, who adopted a very different plan from that of his predecessor. The original plan, to pivot on the right of the British line with the left swinging across the Nablus road, had entailed crossing rugged country with poor access.

It failed because rapid movement had been impossible and wheeled transport, including artillery, could not be deployed. The Turks, on the other hand, could use the Jerusalem–Nablus road to bring up reinforcements quickly to meet any British advance.

As outlined by Chetwode at a conference on 3 December, which was attended by his divisional commanders, the new plan sought to address the weaknesses inherent in the original attack. Chetwode decided to pivot at Nebi Samweil on the left, with his right advancing up the Enab–Jerusalem road and past the western suburbs before cutting the Nablus road immediately to the north of the city. This plan, unlike its predecessor, would enable the British to deploy sufficient artillery against the Turkish defences by using the Jaffa road for this purpose, one of the few routes in the area that had the capacity to handle it. The main attack would be carried out by the 60th and 74th Divisions. To protect their right flank, two brigades of the 53rd Division were to advance up the Hebron road towards Bethlehem, moving round the eastern suburbs of Jerusalem and cutting the city's road links with Jericho.

During the four days before the attack the main units moved into position. The 10th Division was to operate on a wider front than had originally been envisaged. This gave the 74th Division the opportunity to work in support of the 60th Division at Nebi Samweil. Starting from a point south of the Enab–Jerusalem road, the 60th Division was to advance with its left flank on this road and its right almost touching the Hebron road, making use of the 10th Australian Light Horse Regiment and the Worcestershire Yeomanry to maintain contact with the 53rd Division. The 53rd was expected to be close to the Bethlehem defences before the attack began.

The British advance on Jerusalem began during the night of 7 December when the 179th Brigade of the 60th Division took the high ground south of Ain Karim. Private Wilson, 179th Machine Gun Corps, recorded his movements at the start of the operation:

> We are moving tomorrow morning [7 December] for the Jerusalem operations. Apparently the place is to be ours by Sunday . . . We started off from Enab at nine in the morning . . . We were ordered to dump our packs, including bivvies and blankets, so we knew we were in for something hefty . . . we soon discovered why we had dumped our packs. We could never have got through with those burdens on our backs. The distance on the map which we went that night was

roughly two miles as the crow flies. Not being crows, however, we had to do the journey as the donkey walks and found it a very different matter. Up hill and down ravine, winding about along ridges, and down precipitous hill paths, the whole way literally strewn with stones and boulders, it took us seven hours without a stop to traverse that two miles, 'as the crow flies'.[7]

The main attack followed at dawn in conditions that were less than favourable: it was cold, there was persistent heavy rain and visibility was restricted because of mist. These latter two factors slowed the pace of the advance, although the Allies were faced with a less energetic Turkish defence than they had experienced on other occasions since entering Palestine. On the Allied left, however, the 74th Division was delayed by enfilade fire from Turkish positions on Nebi Samweil. The heaviest fighting took place on the front covered by the 60th Division, which eventually prevailed against the enemy, capturing the main Turkish defences west of Jerusalem shortly after dawn. These defences, which in places were carved out of rock, should have been difficult to overcome. However, as Wavell explained, 'the Londoners [of the 60th Division] attacked with their usual dash, and the Turks defended with less than their usual tenacity'.[8] As a result of the adverse weather conditions, the 60th Division had lost touch with the 53rd Division on its right. With its right flank unprotected, the 60th Division was exposed to attack.

During the course of the afternoon, offensive operations were suspended to enable the British to regroup. According to the same British private, conditions for the advancing troops remained difficult in the hours leading up to the Turkish evacuation of Jerusalem:

Our quarters for the next twenty-four hours were against a ledge of rock surmounted by a stone wall which proved effective cover for shrapnel. This ledge of rock was near the top of the ravine on the side of it opposite the road . . . All the morning Johnnie kept shelling the road; but his range was inaccurate, and every shell fell into the ravine. Our little mountain guns were also busy speaking back. Towards evening a party was sent down to the village, who brought back water and some most welcome blankets and bits of carpet. Under the wall we kipped for the night, preserving some small warmth beneath these scant coverings . . . About ten o'clock over came about half a dozen more shells into the ravine. These, had we known it, were Johnnie's parting shots.[9]

The British had intended to renew their advance towards the Nablus road the next day, but by then it was evident that the city was about to fall into their hands. The impact of the British attack – particularly the apparent loss of their main defences – had been sufficient to convince the Turks that their position was untenable. This was underlined by the fact that panic had spread among several Turkish units after the loss of the defensive works. As explained by Kress, the British secured the city by a 'lucky chance':

> The capture of a small sector of the Turkish front-line trench by a British patrol on the night of 7 December was magnified by a false report into the loss of the whole of the western defences. Ali Fuad, the commander, having received orders from the army group to withdraw on Jericho in case of the loss of Jerusalem, feared to execute a counter-attack lest he should be unable after it to carry out these orders, and therefore evacuated the holy city forthwith.[10]

The Turkish retreat from Jerusalem began during the evening of 8 December, not long after the British had suspended operations for the day. The entire city was vacated within a few hours, the Turkish governor being the last official to leave (in a cart commandeered from an American resident). By the early hours of 9 December the city was in the hands of the civic authorities. Public order was largely maintained and only a few isolated examples of looting were reported before the British arrived. Four hundred years of Ottoman occupation had come to an abrupt end. The transfer of power was completed during the course of the day. Early in the morning, the mayor came out of the city carrying a white flag but he had some difficulty in handing the keys over to a representative of the victorious army. Having been refused by some cooks of a London regiment who had lost their way and by several other individuals, he finally succeeded in making contact with the commanding officer of 303 Brigade, Royal Field Artillery (60th Division). Lieutenant-Colonel Bayley described their meeting:

> At the top of the hill I came to houses on the outskirts of the town, still no sniping. Suddenly ahead I spotted a white flag and to my utter astonishment it appeared through my glasses that numbers of persons surrounded it and that three were coming towards me . . . Well, I beckoned the leading one and he came up to me . . . He said the

Turks . . . had bolted in the night and that the mayor of the town was at the flag . . . I walked on to him and there he was with three chairs in a row on the road. I sat down with the mayor on one side and his chief of police on the other, when the mayor formally said that he wished to hand over the city to the British authorities as the Turks had fled, so I accepted the city . . . [11]

While formal arrangements for the handover were being made and the arrival of a British general officer was awaited, Bayley's troops occupied key buildings, including the post office. In the meantime, as Bayley recorded, 'I got all my guns up and pointed their muzzles to the north and east over the city just to let them know that the British had arrived'.[12] At around noon, in a short surrender ceremony outside the city gates, the Mayor of Jerusalem handed the city keys over to Major-General Shea, commander of the 60th Division, who accepted them on behalf of Allenby. The first occupying troops arrived later in the day. One of them described their reception:

We entered Jerusalem about four o'clock, our division being the first within the city. The people received us with a heartiness quieted by a real sense of the greatness of the event. They did not shout much, but on their faces there was a great welcome. The departing Turks had looted them as thoroughly as haste would permit, so it is not exactly surprising that their affection for us should be very fresh and strong.[13]

Meanwhile, mopping-up operations continued. During the course of 9 December, Jerusalem was encircled by Allied forces as the key units moved up to secure their final positions. Although most of the Turkish defenders had slipped away under cover of darkness during the previous night, the enemy briefly retained its hold on the nearby Mount of Olives. The 60th Division ejected this enemy rear-guard during a brief but fierce engagement on the afternoon of 10 December that cost 70 lives.

On 11 December, two days after the official surrender, General Allenby made his entry into Jerusalem. It was exactly six weeks since he had launched his attack on Beersheba. Emphasizing his respect for Jerusalem as a religious centre – it was sacred to three of the world's religions – Allenby entered the city on foot, passing through the Jaffa Gate. Accompanied by French and Italian representatives, he was followed by Sir Philip Chetwode, commander of XX Corps, and some of his staff officers. Also present in the procession was T.E. Lawrence, who said that 'it was impressive in its way – no show but an accompaniment of machine guns & anti-aircraft fire, with aeroplanes circling over us continually. Jerusalem has not been taken for so long: nor has it ever fallen so tamely before.'[14]

Allenby proceeded through the streets towards the citadel, where he read a short proclamation and met various notables. The streets were lined with men of the 60th Division and other units, who according to Guy Dawnay 'had a touch of colour added to them by the light blue of the French and the cocked hats à la Napoleon of the carabinieri'.[15] The ceremony ended when the procession returned to the Jaffa Gate. Allenby described the event in a letter to his wife:

> Today I entered Jerusalem, on foot, with the French and Italian commanders . . . of the detachments in my army; and the attachés, and a few staff officers. We entered at the Jaffa Gate; and, from the steps of the citadel, hard by, issued a proclamation in many languages to the assembled multitude. Great enthusiasm – real or feigned – was shown. Then I received many notables and heads of all the churches, of which there are many . . . After this, we reformed our procession and returned to our horses.[16]

★

The capture of Jerusalem was the logical conclusion of an offensive, designed and launched by Allenby and his staff, that had finally forced open the door to Palestine at the third attempt and then initiated a relatively brief war of movement. The enemy had been driven from the heart of territories it had ruled for centuries in a matter of five weeks (instead of the six months originally estimated by British military planners). The fact that superior British forces were unable to cut off the retreating Turkish forces in their entirety was explained partly by the supply constraints – particularly lack of water – that they had to face. The advance was slowed at various points to enable men and horses to be refreshed; even so, there was a tendency for British forces to outrun their supply lines, which were still under construction. The troops also faced remarkable variations in weather conditions. Almost unbearable heat lasted until late November but within a few days there had been a substantial drop in temperature and the onset of heavy rains.

These factors affected the course of the campaign but not its final outcome. Allenby's drive and determination had produced a much needed victory for the Allies within the timescale demanded by the British prime minister. This was reflected in reactions to the victory in Allied capitals, where there were public celebrations for the first time since the war began. A War Cabinet telegram summed up the general mood: 'the capture of Jerusalem . . . is an event of historic and world-wide significance and has given the greatest pleasure to the British and other Allied peoples.'[17]

Although there is little doubt that, in Wavell's words, 'the occupation of Jerusalem itself had no special strategical importance, its moral significance was great'.[18] It was a heavy blow to Turkish prestige, particularly following their expulsion from two other holy places – Mecca and Baghdad – during the course of the war. On the other hand, the victory was not simply a victory for Christian interests. The holy places of Jerusalem were now in the hands of an occupying power that was more likely to adopt an even-handed approach to the varying religious claims on the city.

Beyond the symbolism of the event, the Allied capture of Jerusalem had wider strategic consequences that were to help to determine the subsequent course of the war in the Middle East. One of the intended effects of the Palestine operations was to draw off Turkish reserves destined for other campaigns. The British advance had forced the Turks to deploy troops from other theatres, thus ensuring that the British capture of Baghdad was secure and the progress of the offensive across Mesopotamia could continue unimpeded. The Turkish position in the area was further weakened by the steady progress of the Arab revolt, which was to gain further encouragement from Turkey's defeat at Jerusalem. Added to this were the heavy losses sustained by the Turks during a campaign which had resulted in the defeat of eleven divisions. In total, the Turks suffered 28,443 casualties compared with the British losses of 18,928 men. In addition, according to Allenby, some 12,000 Turkish troops had been taken prisoner and 100 guns and scores of machine guns had been lost to the British. They had also lost 'more than 20 aeroplanes and 20 million rounds of small arms ammunition'.[19]

As a result of the Palestine operations, the Turkish army had been split in two, although, as already indicated, their supply lines had not been cut off. One part of the army had retired northwards and had come to a halt on the hills overlooking the plain lying north of Jaffa and Ramleh. This force consisted of five divisions, four of which had been badly shaken in the recent retreat. Opposite the Turks the XXI Corps held a line which started at the Nahr el Auja, three miles north of Jaffa, crossed the Turkish railway from Ludd to Jiljulieh at a point five miles north of Ludd and thence ran in a south-easterly direction to Midieh. Other surviving parts of the enemy force had retired in an easterly direction to Jerusalem, where the remains of six divisions had been concentrated. The British XX Corps, having forced the enemy to evacuate Jerusalem, held a line across the roads leading from Jerusalem to Jericho and Nablus, four miles east and north of the city and then westwards through the hills past Beit Ur el Foka to Suffa. The two wings of the Turkish army were separated by an area dominated by a series of spurs running westwards, with rocky valleys between them. There were no roads capable of taking military vehicles or artillery, ruling out the possibility of a large-scale British operation in the area. The only lateral communication available to the Turks lay some 30 miles to the north.

Various factors, including the continuation of winter weather and the need to develop lines of communication, militated against an early renewal of a full-scale British offensive, although pressure to do so was soon to be applied from London. But before the British could rest for the winter, further action was needed to secure their positions in the Jaffa area and in front of Jerusalem. It was essential in both areas that the distance between the Turkish army and these two key centres was increased. Accordingly the British conducted two separate operations to advance their line, reflecting the fact that the two defending Turkish armies were still isolated from one another. The XX Corps was ordered to move to a line from Beitin to Nalin. This involved an advance on a 12-mile front to a depth of six miles immediately north of Jerusalem. On the left the XXI Corps was to advance to a line running from Kibbeh to El Jelil, which passed through Rantieh, Mulebbis and Sheikh el Ballutah. Once successfully completed, the latter operation would increase the distance of the enemy from Jaffa to eight miles.

The XXI Corps, which formed the British left on the coast, began moving its units into position from 7 December, with the aim of enhancing the security of the port of Jaffa which, now in Allied hands, would become an increasingly important centre for the landing and distribution of military supplies. The three divisions of XXI Corps – 52nd, 54th and 75th – were assembled from left to right and ordered to advance northwards. If they succeeded, they would move the Turkish army well out of artillery range of Jaffa. A major obstacle to the British operation was the River Auja, a significant natural barrier that entered the sea some four miles north of Jaffa. Turkish troops occupied the northern bank of the Auja and controlled the main crossing points, including a ford at the mouth of the river. The Turks were assisted by the fact that all approaches to the river were overlooked from Sheikh Muannis and Khurbet Hadrah. At these places two spurs running from north to south terminated abruptly in a steep slope some 500 yards from the river. However, security was lax and it was decided to take advantage of apparent Turkish shortcomings by launching a surprise attack. The main difficulty lay in concealing the collection and preparation of rafts and bridging material. However, the preparations were completed without attracting the enemy's attention. Heavy rain fell on 19 and 20 December and raised the water level of the Auja, causing the Turks to believe that there would be no early British attempt to cross it in these conditions.

The operation was in fact timed for the following night and despite the less favourable conditions the 52nd Division crossed the river in three columns without difficulty. The left column, fording the river near its mouth, at this point four feet deep, captured Tell el Rekkeit, 4,000 yards north of the river mouth. The centre and right crossed the river on rafts. They rushed Sheikh Muannis and Khurbet Hadrah at the point of the bayonet. By dawn a line from Khurbet Hadrah to Tell el Rekkeit had been consolidated, and the enemy was deprived of all observation from the north over the valley of the Nahr el Auja. The successful crossing of the river reflected, according to Allenby, 'great credit on the 52nd (Lowland) Division'. This difficult operation, which required considerable preparation, was complicated by the 'sodden state of the ground and the swollen state of the river'.[20] Despite these difficulties, the whole of the division had crossed the river during the hours of darkness. Even more remarkable was the fact that the enemy was taken completely by surprise and that 'all resistance was overcome with the bayonet without a shot being fired'.[21] Over 300 Turkish troops and 10 machine guns were captured during the operation.

Once temporary bridges had been built and the artillery could cross the river, the 52nd Division was ready to move on. On 23 December, the advance continued up the coast for a further five miles as the 52nd and 54th Divisions ejected the enemy from key defensive positions. Supported by British warships, the left of the 52nd Division reached Arsuf, a coastal settlement eight miles north of Jaffa. With the port now safe from further Turkish attack the objective of the operation had been secured. As the British official history described it:

> The passage of the Auja has always been regarded as one of the most remarkable feats of the Palestine campaign . . . its chief merits were its boldness – justifiable against troops known to be sluggish and slack in outpost work and already shaken by defeat – its planning, the skill of the engineers; the promptitude with which unexpected difficulties in the bridging of the river were met; finally, the combined discipline and dash of the infantry which carried out the operation without a shot being fired and won the works on the right bank with the bayonet.[22]

Allenby also planned to strengthen his position in the Jerusalem area, where fighting had effectively been suspended since 12 December. In the words of the British official history, the Turks were 'breathless after their defeat and hasty withdrawal. The British were not yet ready for the effort which would be needed to win more elbow room round Jerusalem.'[23] Allenby's main concern was that the city still lay within easy reach of Turkish artillery, with the attendant risk that the enemy might attempt to recapture it. His response was to plan a renewal of offensive action on 24 December, aiming to reach a line running from Beitin (Bethel) to Nalin. Three divisions were ordered to advance towards it: the 60th Division would advance up the Jerusalem to Nablus road to the ridge on which stood the Turkish defensive line from Bireh to Ramallah. Here they would join with the 74th Division, which was to advance eastwards from Beit Ur el Foka, and together move northwards towards the Bireh–Ramallah line. The 53rd Division on the British right and the 10th Division on the left were ordered to protect the flanks.

These plans, which had already been delayed by bad weather, were postponed again when British intelligence learned from a decoded radio signal that the Turks were planning a counter-attack on Jerusalem. Using troops newly arrived from the north, an attack was to be launched from the north and the east with the aim of recapturing the city. The British responded by ordering the 74th and 10th Divisions on the British left to advance as originally planned. The

53rd and 60th Divisions on the British right were to maintain their defensive positions in the face of a Turkish assault. The enemy operation, launched during the night of 26/27 December, was staged with great determination, but did not amount to much, although it persisted until the afternoon of the second day. The action was focused on Tell el Ful, a hill east of the Nablus road, some three miles north of the city, where the 60th Division successfully resisted a succession of strong Turkish attacks. At only one point did the enemy succeed in reaching the main line of defence. He was driven out at once by local reserves and in all these assaults lost heavily.

Meanwhile, early on 27 December, the 74th and 10th Divisions began their attack and during the day advanced some 4,000 yards on a six-mile front. They made sufficient progress to bring the Turkish counter-attack on Jerusalem to an end. This was the signal to launch, on 28 December, a general British advance which continued for three days. On the right, the 60th Division – supported by the 53rd Division – advanced to El Jib, Er Ram and Rafat, which fell after heavy fighting. Beitunia fell to the 74th Division, while the 10th Division also made progress as it moved eastwards. The Allied advance continued over the next three days until 30 December, when resistance was brought to an end. A front 12 miles wide had been pushed forward to a depth varying from six miles on the right to three miles on the left. This advance had to overcome not only a determined and obstinate resistance but also great natural difficulties before guns could be brought up in support of the infantry. For the Turks the attempt to recapture Jerusalem had been a complete failure and had cost the lives of over 1,000 of their soldiers. In addition, the British took some 750 Turkish prisoners, 24 machine guns and three automatic rifles.

The holy city and the Allied lines surrounding it were now secure and operations were temporarily suspended. But persistent winter rains meant that there was little opportunity for British troops to recuperate in comfort. Nor was there to be any early relief from these adverse conditions: communications and supplies had to be brought up, in line with the rapid northwards advance of the previous few weeks. Any further advance northwards was out of the question for the time being. Besides the construction of new roads and the improvement of communications in the forward areas, stores of supplies and ammunition had to be accumulated – a task made difficult by the distance between the front and the existing railhead at

Ramleh, and rendered still more difficult by frequent spells of bad weather. Moreover before a further advance could be made, it would be necessary to drive the enemy across the River Jordan to ensure that the British right flank was fully secure.

British control of the Jordan crossings would have a number of other advantages. Control of the Dead Sea would be obtained; the enemy would be prevented from raiding the area to the west of the Dead Sea; while a point of departure would be gained for further operations eastwards, in conjunction with Arab forces based in Aqaba, aimed at interrupting the enemy's line of communications to the Hejaz. An operation across the Jordan would almost certainly allow direct contact to be made for the first time with Feisal's army.

# 7

# *The Arab Advance*

THE TURKISH-OCCUPIED port of Aqaba had fallen to tribesmen led by Lawrence and Auda, the Howeitat leader, on 6 July 1917. Following this unexpected news discussions had been held by General Allenby in Cairo within a few days that acknowledged the potential benefits of military collaboration between British and Arab forces. Lawrence had already formed his view of how the Arabs might collaborate with the British army as it advanced through Palestine, envisaging their main role as the staging of guerrilla attacks on the Hejaz and Palestine railways, cutting sections of track and destroying important bridges. In his view the disruption of communications in the area around Deraa, the junction of the Palestine and Hejaz railways, was of particular importance.

Lawrence arrived in Cairo from Aqaba on 10 July, and in due course met Allenby for the first time. One of Allenby's biographers describes the meeting in some detail. Uncertain about the reception he would receive, Lawrence

> strode into 'the Bull's' extremely orderly office in Arab dress, his sandals slip-slopping on the well-polished floor. It was, as Lawrence himself afterwards agreed, a somewhat comic affair. Allenby was extremely large and, to all appearances, more than conventional: Lawrence was rather small, and could hardly have appeared more unconventional.[1]

Lawrence dominated the meeting, outlining his strategy of spreading the revolt northwards to Damascus, and reducing Turkish front-line strength by forcing them to guard every mile of the Hejaz railway rather than by mounting conventional operations at Medina and elsewhere. Allenby listened carefully but said very little. Stressing the contribution the Arabs could make to a British advance, Lawrence maintained that the government's aim of capturing Jerusalem by December would be much more likely to be achieved if the Arabs were able to disrupt vital lines of communication well behind enemy lines.

Lawrence then made a long string of requests for money and supplies in support of the Arab revolt, to which Allenby merely replied: 'Well, I will do for you what I can.'[2] Though Lawrence gained a high opinion of Allenby at this time, partly as a result of the latter's positive attitude to the Arab cause, Allenby, initially reserved, soon came round to Lawrence. Impressed by the Aqaba operation, and attaching more importance to the Arab revolt than had his predecessor Murray, the commander-in-chief realized that Lawrence could be of considerable use to him. For the time being, he decided to back him and, wherever possible, to give him what he asked. Allenby also decided to promote Lawrence to the rank of major and recommend him for the Order of the Bath. By promoting him and making him responsible in future to the commander-in-chief himself, he had recognized Lawrence's role in the Arab campaign and freed him from the control of his British superior officers in the Hejaz. Allenby also took the opportunity to integrate Feisal's forces at Aqaba into his own command structure rather than leaving them in the hands of Sherif Hussein and Sir Reginald Wingate, the Egyptian High Commissioner.

Following subsequent discussions with Allenby, more detailed plans were prepared for Arab activity east of the Jordan which would assist a British advance in Palestine by disrupting Turkish communications. Guerilla raids would focus on the railway lines running north, south and west of Deraa, aiming to cut the track at various points and demolish major bridges. From their base at Aqaba, the Arabs would also occupy the hill country east and south-east of the Dead Sea, to the west of the Hejaz railway. Lawrence did not rule out the possibility of a general attack on Deraa if its railway link with Palestine could be broken. Such an operation, he believed, if successful, would lead to other locally inspired risings in the area. The retention of the Aqaba base (and access to the route to the interior of Syria) was essential, he maintained, to the Arabs' northward progress, as was the furnishing of adequate funding and supplies by the British.

Arab progress was equally dependent on Allenby's success in making a major push through Palestine. Unless there was continuing British military pressure to the west of the Jordan, the Turks would be able to amass sufficient forces to suppress the Arab revolt in Syria.

Allenby's response to Lawrence's plans, even though he did not think they would be fully achieved, was favourable, as he confirmed in a telegram to Sir William Robertson on 16 July:

> There is no doubt that Turkish railway communications south of Aleppo would be seriously disorganized even by the partial success of Lawrence's scheme, whilst its complete success would effectively destroy [the Turks'] only main artery of communication between the north Syria and Palestine and Hedjaz fronts . . .[3]

Allenby realized that the capture of Aqaba altered the conditions of the desert war. Not only could Arab raids on the Hejaz railway be extended, but in the event of a general British offensive, the tribes of eastern Syria could be enlisted for operations against Turkish railway communications with Palestine, disrupting vital points on the railway such as Deraa which were beyond British reach.

With the arrival of Allenby and the capture of Aqaba, staff at general headquarters fell in behind the Arab revolt. As a consequence the Hejaz became a much less significant factor in the war. Local fighting continued on a limited scale, but the main unresolved issue was the future of Medina, which was still under siege. The advantages of leaving the situation as it was soon became clear: the transfer of Turkish forces manning the defences at Medina to the Palestine front would have been a very unwelcome development, as would the wholesale capture of enemy forces in the province, which would have reduced the debilitating burden on the Turkish army of maintaining significant forces so far from home. The best policy from the British perspective was 'to allow the railway just, but only just, to remain working and never to frighten the enemy so seriously as to induce him to evacuate Medina'.[4] This was not an explicit policy in 1917 but the principle was widely accepted. In the spring of 1918, on receipt of news that the Turkish army was considering the final evacuation of the Hejaz, the railway was destroyed near Maan so that the Turks were unable to withdraw from Medina whether they wished to or not.

With Aqaba serving as a base for operations Arab forces would inevitably be brought more directly in touch with the British, from whom they were now separated only by the Sinai desert. It was a development Allenby welcomed and encouraged. In order to forge closer collaboration – and to reduce Hussein's influence – it was decided that Emir Feisal should become, in effect, an army commander under the direction of Allenby, responsible for the conduct of Arab operations north of Maan. While Allenby was assessing the potential benefits of success, the Turks were considering the implications of failure and what action they could take to rectify it. Well aware of the threat posed to their security by the creation of a substantial Arab base at Aqaba they began to make preparations to recapture it by forming a camp at Abu el Lissan (on the most accessible route between Aqaba and Maan).

Progress in Cairo was matched by rapid developments at Aqaba; within a few weeks of the enemy's enforced departure it was barely recognizable as a Turkish base. A regular shuttle was operated by British warships between Wejh and Aqaba, transporting Arab soldiers and supplies northwards, and in late August Feisal himself and his senior commanders arrived within days of each other. Among Feisal's adjutants was Jafar Pasha, who had volunteered for service with Feisal a few months earlier, when still based at Wejh. Jafar Pasha had served as an officer in the Turkish army and had been given the task of training the Senussi in their fight against the British in the Western Desert. Captured in December 1915 and imprisoned in Cairo, he was induced by the news that Djemal Pasha had executed some of his friends in Syria to volunteer for service with the Arabs in the Hejaz. A valuable addition to Feisal's resources, he was, in the words of Basil Liddell Hart, a 'Baghdadi Arab of marked capacity and even greater capaciousness. He spoke eight languages and had been trained in the German army.'[5] Feisal's force of 2,000 regulars now assembling in Aqaba needed training and discipline. Known as the Northern Army, it was fortunate in having

> in Feisal an inspiring leader who held together discordant elements by his prestige, charm and tact; in Jafar a soldier of its own race experienced in the employment of modern weapons; in Lawrence a bold and inventive partisan; in Joyce a tireless and efficient organizer.[6]

The troops arriving from Wejh were supplemented by growing numbers of Arab volunteers who flooded in from the surrounding areas. Aqaba was protected by British warships and by four aircraft based at El Arish. These aircraft operated from a temporary landing strip in the Sinai desert some 50 miles north-west of Aqaba. Towards the end of August 1917, the four planes were used in raids against Turkish positions at Maan, Fuweila and Abu el Lissan. These attacks did sufficient damage to reduce the risk of an immediate Turkish attack on Aqaba, although enemy action since its capture had been confined to minor attacks on Arab outposts. It was essential for the Arabs to maintain control of the route from Aqaba through the Wadi Itm as this provided them with their most direct access to the north.

A full-scale Turkish assault still remained a possibility but the limited availability of water between Abu el Lissan and Aqaba was a problem in any attack. The uncertainty of Bedouin loyalties was a further obstacle to Turkish plans which had to be overcome before Aqaba could be reconquered. The Turkish commander-in-chief could not risk arriving here with less than 2,000 men – the number possessed by Jafar – and the fighting quality of the opposition, so long as it was not shown by premature action to be bad, had to be assumed by the Turks to be good.

Although Jafar's regulars were not yet ready to fight the Turks in a set-piece engagement, Lawrence had not ruled out early offensive action of a more unconventional kind. Neither was he inclined to wait until Allenby had initiated the third Battle of Gaza, which began on 31 October 1917. Indeed he believed that an aggressive Arab stance towards the Turks was likelier than inaction to enhance the security of Aqaba. His initiative took the form of guerilla raids against a 70-mile stretch of the Hejaz railway between Maan and Mudawara. He reported that there were 'seven waterless stations here, and I have hope that with the Stokes and Lewis guns we may be able to do something fairly serious to the line . . . As soon as the railway attack is beginning a force of "regulars" will enter the Shobek-Kerak hills and try to occupy them.'[7] The capture of this area to the north-west of Maan together with attacks on the railway on an extended front was likely to force the withdrawal of the Turkish garrison at Fuweila. This, in turn, would ensure that Aqaba was safe from attack.

Lawrence himself took part in these raids. On 7 September 1917, he left Aqaba with the aim of attacking Mudawara station, an important local target which held the only substantial water supply to cover 150 miles of line south of Maan. On this occasion, for various reasons, he was unable to raise sufficient local tribesmen willing to support him and was forced to abandon the raid and return to Aqaba. On 17 September he set out with a smaller force intending to make a second attempt, but soon decided that Mudawara station was beyond his reach. Instead, operating from an isolated location, he held up a Turkish train, which he came to regard as one of his 'notable exploits'. According to Lawrence,

> it had two locomotives, and we gutted one with an electric mine. This rather jumbled up the trucks, which were full of Turks shooting at us. We had a Lewis, and flung bullets through the sides. So they hopped out and took cover behind the embankment, and shot at us between the wheels, at 50 yards. Then we tried a Stokes gun, and two beautiful shots dropped in the middle of them. They couldn't stand that . . . and bolted away to the east across a hundred yard belt of open sand into some scrub. Unfortunately for them the Lewis covered the open stretch. The whole job took ten minutes, and they lost seventy killed, thirty wounded, eighty prisoners and about twenty-five got away. Of my hundred Howeitat and two British NCOs there was one (Arab) killed, and four (Arabs) wounded.[8]

A further raiding party, also led by Lawrence, left Aqaba on 27 September and did major damage to another Turkish railway engine.

Lawrence's raids were rare examples of Arab military success, although it is not clear how many Turkish troops they managed to divert from the Aqaba mission. In any case, the build-up of Turkish forces at Maan continued and it could only be a matter of time before they launched an attack on Aqaba. Feisal's main base was ill-equipped to respond to this challenge: it had more tribesmen volunteers than it could afford to support, as the volume of supplies sent from Egypt was still inadequate; his army moreover was inexperienced and untrained. To strengthen his position, Feisal called on his brother, Emir Zeid, and his army to join him at Aqaba. The leaders of the Arab revolt came under further pressure when they were informed of British plans for a major offensive in Palestine, aimed at capturing Jerusalem by Christmas. The Arabs had little hope of matching British progress northwards, and unless the Wadi Itm could be secured, their own advance northwards would incur enormous risks. To these difficulties must be added the consequences of a failed British offensive. It could have left Feisal's revolt isolated and vulnerable to a devastating Turkish counter-attack.

On the other hand, if Allenby's offensive were successful, it might lead to a general Turkish withdrawal. In these circumstances, it was essential that the Arabs were in a position to exploit a potentially beneficial situation. Lawrence identified Deraa, 'the junction of the Jerusalem–Haifa–Damascus–Medina railways, the navel of the Turkish armies in Syria', as the key target, 'where our weight and tactics would be least expected and most damaging'.[9] It was an area where Arab tribesmen were ready and willing to fight in support of the revolt. A successful Arab attack on Deraa would disrupt the flow of essential supplies to the Turkish armies in Palestine and would provide substantial support for the British as they progressed north-wards. However, Lawrence's optimism was tempered by realism. If Allenby's advance were to stall and the Arabs were forced to retreat, the local population could be vulnerable to severe reprisals once the enemy had reoccupied the area.

Lawrence concluded that the risk of failure was too great, and that an alternative approach must be found. He decided, therefore, to lead a small raiding party in an attempt to destroy one of the strategi-cally important bridges in the Yarmuk gorge that carried the railway from Deraa into Palestine. The attack would be timed to coincide with the opening stages of Allenby's assault on the Gaza–Beersheba line and, if successful, would hinder a Turkish retreat by preventing the enemy being resupplied. Allenby, who approved the plan, requested that the bridge be destroyed during the period 5–8 November.

This extraordinarily difficult venture, beginning with a 400-mile camel ride northwards from Aqaba, failed by a small margin. The expedition left the Red Sea base on 24 October, but soon ran into difficulties. Local tribesmen were unenthusiastic about the plan and by the time the group departed from Azrak, a desert oasis and the final assembly point for the expedition, the bridges accessible to an Arab assault had been reduced to one. This was the Tell el Shebab which, according to Lawrence, was a 'splendid bridge to destroy'.[10] Even this option was ruled out when, on 7 November, the explosives they were carrying were abandoned during a firefight with Turkish guards in the Yarmuk area. The raiding party escaped without loss, but Lawrence inevitably felt a strong sense of disappointment: 'Our minds were sick with failure, and our bodies tired after nearly a hundred miles over bad country in bad conditions, between sunset and sunset, without halt or food.'[11] Although they hoped to return to the same target later, the opportunity never recurred: 'If the Turks have not increased their guard we can do it later: but I am very sick at losing it so stupidly. The Bedu cannot take the bridge, but can reach it: the Indians can take it, but cannot reach it!'[12]

To compensate for this setback, Lawrence quickly devised an alternative plan – blowing up a train on the Hejaz line between Deraa and Amman. This operation succeeded – he destroyed two engines and some hundred Turks – but it did nothing directly to affect the working of the Damascus–Palestine line, which continued without interruption to deliver supplies to the two armies fighting the British.

Despite the failure of the Yarmuk raid, the Arabs had succeeded in tying down large numbers of Turkish troops east of the Jordan while Allenby advanced through Palestine. These troops would otherwise have reinforced the enemy units that were under pressure in Jerusalem in the face of Allenby's advance. The official history estimates that, before Allenby's final offensive, the Arab campaign had killed, wounded, captured or contained well over 25,000 enemy troops.[13] This figure is similar to the combined ration strength of the Hejaz expeditionary force and the two composite forces with headquarters at Tebuk and Maan, but does not include Turkish forces held in reserve further north in case they were needed against the Arabs. The maintenance of these front-line forces in the south, and of supplies to them, made heavy demands on railway plant and rolling stock and on reserves of food and stores at Damascus, a great proportion of which would otherwise have been available for the Palestine front.

★

After the abortive Yarmuk raid, Lawrence decided to remain in the north until the outcome of Allenby's Palestine offensive was clear. He therefore made his base in the desert at Azrak, some 200 miles northeast of Aqaba. Feisal and his army subsequently joined Lawrence at Azrak, turning an old Arab oasis and fort into their headquarters. From here efforts were made to extend the base of support of the Arab revolt throughout Syria in a campaign in which Lawrence was closely involved. Taken prisoner by the Turks at Deraa during a journey of reconnaissance, he was savagely beaten before being freed and returning to Aqaba.

Arriving there on 3 December, more determined than ever to secure Arab independence, Lawrence sent a message to Cairo expressing a wish for high-level discussions on future military collaboration between the Arabs and the British. Within days, he was in British-occupied Jerusalem, locked in meetings with General Allenby and his staff about the future course of the war and the prospects for the close coordination of Arab and British military efforts. Allenby's plans for 1918 had not yet been finalized but it was clear that he would not be able to renew his advance before February 1918. His first moves were likely to include the capture of Jericho, an advance to the east across the River Jordan to Es Salt and the expulsion of the enemy from the northern shores of the Dead Sea. A large-scale offensive to the north would not take place until later in the year.

The Arab revolt had already made a real contribution to the campaign against the Turks, and Allenby needed little convincing that more might be done as the enemy was pursued northwards. His head of intelligence, Brigadier Clayton, had however made an assessment of the impact of the Arab revolt which was to be highly influential on the course of discussions in Jerusalem. Apart from the direct military losses cited above, the revolt, particularly in its disruption of the Hejaz railway, had caused serious damage to the economic infrastructure. The extension of the Arab revolt northwards, as now proposed by Allenby, was certain to result in further economic disruption. Lawrence was asked by the British high command to obtain Feisal's consent to an advance northwards from Aqaba, through the highlands and on to the southern shores of the Dead Sea, which would include the seizing of the small towns of Shobek, Tafila and Kerak. The effect of this new campaign, if successful, would be to disrupt supplies of grain and timber to the Turkish army. Not only would the plan deprive the Turkish engineers of regular supplies of wood, the fuel essential to running the Hejaz railway, it would also facilitate a plan for British and Arab regular forces to come together at Madeba, north-east of the Dead Sea. If all these plans were successful, the Arabs would shift their base from Aqaba to Jericho.

During Lawrence's absence in Jerusalem, the Arab regulars had secured the area immediately surrounding Aqaba. They were commanded by Maulud el Mukhlus, a former Turkish officer captured by the British in the Mesopotamian campaign, who was described by Liddell Hart as 'a real fighting soldier and the first regular soldier to join Feisal'.[14] Forces under the Emir Zeid, Feisal's younger half-brother, who had been put in overall charge of the Dead Sea campaign, captured Tafila at the turn of the year. Despite this success, Zeid was unable to manage conflicts between two of the tribes under his command – the Abu Tayi Howeitat and the Motalga horse – and was forced to send the smaller group, the Abu Tayi, away.

Meanwhile the Turks were making plans to recover Tafila. Although the town itself was small and unimportant, the Turks could not contemplate losing control of an area vital for corn and other products. They were even prepared to divert resources from the Palestine front to recover it. Under the command of Hamid Fakhri Pasha a force was assembled in the Amman area, consisting of three battalions of the 48th Division (totalling 900 men), 100 cavalry, two mountain guns and 27 machine guns, and then moved down to Kerak, where it was joined by officials intended to re-establish Tafila's civil administration. Leaving Kerak on 23 January on the final leg of the journey to Tafila, on the following day it defeated an Arab detachment positioned on the Wadi Hasa, which represented the last expected barrier to the recapture of Tafila.

Lawrence prepared to meet the Turks in a conventional battle. On 26 January, the leading units of Turkish cavalry were thrown back by the combined efforts of the Motalga horse, supported by the inhabitants of Tafila. The Arabs withdrew to a point where the main Turkish column was expected to emerge from a track through the hill from Kerak on to a plateau in front of the village. The Turks deployed their forces on low ridges to the left and right of the northerly point at which they had entered the plateau. Opposite the Turks, on the southern side of the plateau, Lawrence assembled his central reserve, positioning his main firing line on a 60-foot ridge in front of the village. An attack on the Turkish-held western ridge by the combined force of villagers and Motalga horse was soon repelled and the Arabs retreated southwards and joined the southern reserve, which now amounted to 520 men.

Lawrence then organized another attack. Rasim Bey, an Arab regular officer, led 80 mounted men behind the Turkish left on the eastern ridge, while a hundred villagers from El Eime, armed with three machine guns, carried out a parallel manoeuvre on the western ridge. Advancing under cover towards the Turkish rear they were not spotted by enemy reconnaissance aircraft until it was too late. Before long the Turkish positions were under attack from three sides: already facing heavy fire from the central reserve, their flanks were now attacked from the rear. The El Eime villagers launched a surprise attack on the western ridge and despite their advantage in men and guns the Turks were forced to abandon their positions.

At this point, Rasim launched his attack on the ridges to the rear and to the east, while Lawrence unleashed his central reserve, moving rapidly across the plateau to attack the enemy centre which soon buckled under the pressure. As the advancing Arabs mixed with troops retreating from the two ridges, the escape route back to Kerak soon became jammed. The Turkish troops caught in the centre were cut down by the Arabs. Some 300 enemy soldiers were killed, including Hamid Fakhri Pasha, the Turkish commander; 250 were taken prisoner. Turkish casualties would have been much higher had it not been for an effective rearguard action by their cavalry and the close proximity of the Wadi Hasa, a natural barrier that limited the extent of the Arab action. Arab losses were minimal, with 25 dead and 40 wounded.

The action provided compelling evidence that Lawrence, the master of guerilla warfare, could also handle a conventional battle with great skill. The War Office recognized his achievement and Allenby later presented him with the Distinguished Service Order for his victory at Tafila. On 28 January, this phase of the campaign was concluded when a small Arab force under Abdullah el Feir left the highlands and captured the Dead Sea port of El Mezraa, one of the centres for the transport of grain and wood produced in the Hauran area south and east of the Dead Sea. Seven boats were anchored in port and all were scuttled. A large supply of grain was lost and 60 Turkish prisoners were taken.

Lawrence was anxious to maintain the momentum of the Arab offensive beyond Tafila, hoping to take control of the northern end of the Dead Sea. Following a reconnaissance in that direction in mid-February, he concluded that 'each step of our road to join the British to the north of the Dead Sea was possible for us: and most of them easy. The weather was so fine that we might reasonably begin at once: and we could hope to finish in a month.'[15] Unfortunately, Zeid lacked the will or the means to advance further as he had distributed all the available British money to members of his force in payment for their past services. But staying where they were was not an option: without further movement, the Arabs were likely to face an attack from the Turks and the possible loss of many of their recent territorial gains. It was in these unpromising circumstances that Lawrence returned, in late February 1918, to EEF headquarters.

★

Lawrence arrived at GHQ at a time when discussions on future British strategy for the whole theatre were reaching a definitive conclusion. Although news of the steady progress of the Arab revolt was welcomed in London, it was not regarded as a substitute for the early renewal of action on the main Palestine front. Allenby was, therefore, soon under pressure to indicate when he planned to initiate further offensive action. Practical problems of resupplying British forces after the capture of Jerusalem were not expected to delay action for too long. Lloyd George was greatly encouraged by the positive results of the Jerusalem campaign, which had been a rare example of success in a costly world war that was now entering its fifth year. He wrote to Robertson on 11 December, the day on which Allenby entered Jerusalem:

> The Cabinet ought at the earliest possible moment to decide whether the advance in Palestine should be exploited. It is quite clear that the information which had been given to us about the number of troops available in that theatre was utterly wrong, and that the more recent information . . . as to the complete breakdown of the Turkish transport is nearer the mark.[16]

Within days the Prime Minister was asking for estimates of the number of troops that could be released for other theatres of war if British forces were able to capture Aleppo in northern Syria and thus bring the campaign in the Middle East to a close. He believed that if Allenby were to advance immediately from Jerusalem a string of further British military successes in the Middle East could produce a much bigger prize: Turkey's complete withdrawal from the war at an early date and the consequent break-up of the enemy coalition. It might also enable British forces to make direct contact with their Russian and Romanian allies and open the way to launching an attack on the Central Powers from the rear.

However, in pressing for immediate action, the Prime Minister underestimated the problems Allenby faced, including adverse weather conditions, overextended lines of supply and exhausted troops. General Allenby had been quick to point out that the offensive could not be renewed until British forces had been reorganized and refreshed after the last few weeks' gruelling campaign. He also needed to ensure that his supply lines were in better shape before putting even more distance between his troops and their principal sources of supply which were still based in Egypt. Progress in constructing the standard-gauge railway was another constraint on early action, as was the continuance of the rainy season, which lasted until the end of January.

Initially, Allenby planned to advance his right to the Wadi el Auja, a river that runs into the Jordan some ten miles north of the Dead Sea. During the remainder of the rainy season, he would send units against the Hejaz railway and the 20,000 defending Turkish troops south of Amman. Later he planned to advance leftwards to Tul Keram, as the basis for a push northwards in cooperation with naval units. This tentative approach had little in common with the bold action called for by the Prime Minister. The disaster of the third Battle of Ypres (July–November 1917), in which the Allies had made no progress, had convinced Lloyd George that the only way to break the stalemate and make early gains was to mount new offensives against Germany's allies in the Near East. Britain, as Turkey's sole surviving military opponent, had a special responsibility to take effective action. A rapid advance to Aleppo, disrupting Turkey's links with Mesopotamia, could well knock Turkey out of the war. If this plan proved too ambitious, Lloyd George wanted, as a minimum, to free the whole of Palestine from Turkish occupation.

Allenby was asked to give an indication of the force levels associated with each option. Under plans already formulated Allenby informed Sir William Robertson on 19 December that he expected to reach a line running from Nazareth to Haifa by July 1918, if he were able to advance without serious Turkish opposition.[17] This plan, so Allenby reported to Robertson, should secure the British conquest and retention of Palestine, whilst the alternative policy of a further advance northwards to Aleppo – Lloyd George's preferred option – would, in Allenby's view, require as many as sixteen additional infantry divisions, as well as more mounted troops, if success was to be assured.

Concurrent developments in Europe did not seem particularly favourable to an increase in the scale of military action in Palestine early in 1918. The armistice on the Eastern Front freed large numbers of German troops who were transferred to France in preparation for a major assault against the Allied line. The German army was under pressure to make the most of a final window of opportunity before the American army arrived in strength in the summer of 1918. There was a strong body of opinion in London which argued that the security of the Western Front was paramount and that every available soldier should be thrown into the fight against the Germans. On all other fronts, including Palestine, Allied forces should be put on the defensive and their surplus troops transferred to France. It would be disastrous if the Germans broke the Allied line in Europe and the early arrival of reinforcements would help to prevent that. In a memorandum to the War Cabinet of 28 December 1917, Robertson pointed to the grave risk involved in increasing British commitments in a secondary theatre at a moment when all the omens pointed to a major new German offensive on the Western Front. He also identified a further argument against investing more resources in Palestine: 'It would seem to be very difficult for Turkey to shake off the German grip – even if she wished to do so.'[18]

Against this, the 'Easterners' who shared Lloyd George's views argued that the Allied defences could withstand a new German onslaught and that no significant transfers of troops from one theatre to another were necessary at that time. This group believed that the Allied line in France would hold until numbers were reinforced by the arrival of more American troops. This belief in the effectiveness of the defence was well supported by the history of trench warfare on the Western Front and the failure of earlier Allied offensives, which had enjoyed much greater superiority in numbers than the Germans were able to achieve in 1918. In their view, Palestine offered a real opportunity for a decisive victory against Turkey and her removal from the war. With the withdrawal of Bulgaria, which was war-weary and likely to follow suit, this would in turn open up a new route to Austria and, ultimately, Germany – although not one that could be exploited very rapidly.

Throughout this period of debate, Allenby maintained his own cautious view that it would be advisable to deal with Turkish forces on the Medina railway before moving north. When he came under further pressure from London early in the New Year, Allenby elaborated his plans. He believed that it would be prudent to consolidate on his present line, secure his eastern flank as far as the Jordan and capture Jericho before considering any move to the north.

At the end of 1917 Lloyd George tried to resolve this deadlock by consulting the permanent military advisers of the Allied Supreme War Council at Versailles and asking them to 'report on the military and strategical position' in the Turkish theatre. Their report, which represented a great victory for the 'Easterners', was based on the assumption that Turkey, in the words of the British official history, 'was the weakest point in the hostile coalition and should be the object of attack'.[19] The military advisers' recommendation, issued on 21 January 1918, was that the Allies should stand on the defensive on the Western Front, Italy and the Balkans, while undertaking 'a decisive offensive against Turkey with a view to the annihilation of the Turkish armies and the collapse of Turkish resistance'.[20] Sir William Robertson reacted immediately, as he reported in a letter of 24 January to General Haig:

> I have told the War Cabinet they cannot take on Palestine & I shall stick to my guns and clear out if I am overruled. It is of no earthly use filling a post & having one's advice overruled. From a rational point of view it is *wrong* I think.[21]

Despite Robertson's opposition, Lloyd George, with the support of his closest allies, dispatched General Jan Smuts to Egypt early in February 1918. Instructed to consult with Allenby, Rear-Admiral Jackson, who commanded naval forces off the Palestine coast, and Major-General W. Gillman, chief of staff of the Mesopotamian Expeditionary Force, Smuts was required to identify 'the best method of coordinating British efforts in the Middle East and of employing British resources for the elimination of Turkey from the war'.[22] He was specifically requested to establish the additional resources necessary to secure this objective.

It did not take Smuts long to complete his consultations. Reporting back to London in a telegram dated 15 February, he ruled out the possibility of Britain resuming offensive action simultaneously in both Palestine and Mesopotamia as neither force was strong enough without reinforcement to be certain of success. Believing that the decisive battles with Turkey should take place in northern Palestine, Smuts, in a final report to the British government dated 1 March 1918, recommended that British forces in Mesopotamia should go on the defensive since they would find it more difficult to capture Aleppo – the ultimate objective agreed by the Allies – than Allenby's forces based in Palestine. The Mesopotamian force was at a greater distance from Aleppo than Allenby's army; its right flank was vulnerable if it advanced beyond the Mosul area, and railway communications needed greater investment. With military operations in Mesopotamia effectively suspended, two of its six infantry divisions and a cavalry brigade, together with an Indian cavalry division from France, could be transferred to Palestine. This represented a substantial enhancement of Allenby's current force of eight infantry divisions and three mounted divisions.

Smuts's recommendations were based on plans for a future offensive already being developed by Allenby. An essential first step was to secure the British right flank by advancing eastwards and occupying the Jordan valley. This would allow Allenby to cut the Hejaz railway in the Amman area and finally destroy the main lifeline sustaining the Turkish troops who were still occupying the besieged city of Medina and operating between there and Maan. These developments would give further encouragement to the progress of the Arab movement, which could play an important role in supporting the main British thrust to the north. This thrust was to be based on a renewal of the coastal advance which, as the next stage, would involve the occupation of the Plain of Esdraelon and the securing of a line from Tiberias to Haifa. The main advance would then continue along the coast, taking Tyre and Sidon before reaching Beirut as its final objective. The right flank of the advancing column would be protected by the Judean hills. Further to the right, smaller columns would be ordered to advance up the Yarmuk valley and by road to Jericho.

With these enhanced levels of manpower potentially available, the main constraint in Allenby's mind was the speed with which the standard-gauge railway could be driven forward along the coast. The plan Allenby was developing still assumed that priority would be given to an early advance to the River Jordan, from which the Allies would seek to destroy a significant section of the Hejaz railway, thus isolating the substantial Turkish forces operating between Medina and Maan. The second phase – an advance northwards by the main force – would be closely linked to the progress in constructing the standard-gauge Sinai railway which Allenby envisaged extending as far as Haifa and possibly even to Beirut. The existing metre-gauge line from Haifa to Deraa would support a smaller Allied group that would advance eastwards on Deraa and then on to Damascus.

In its original form the scheme was inextricably linked in Allenby's mind with the progress of the railway. While the scheme was feasible – and secured War Office endorsement – it had, in the words of the official history, serious weaknesses: 'it was stiff and mechanical, and it made transport master instead of servant';[23] it was also likely to be painfully slow. Fortunately, with the start of the German army's March offensive, events on the Western Front were to take a decisive turn and the push to the north was postponed until the autumn. During the intervening months Allenby was substantially to modify his plans, coming up with a more imaginative and flexible scheme that did justice to his abilities and was to achieve the desired results within days rather than the probable weeks or months of the original plan.

Lloyd George had already agreed the Allied strategy for the first part of 1918 early in February, at a meeting of the Supreme War Council at Versailles. The key to the plan was a renewal of the offensive in Palestine with the aim of forcing Turkey out of the war at the earliest opportunity. On the Western Front the Allies would continue to remain on the defensive, although the French were cautious enough to insist that no white troops should be transferred from France to Palestine for the new offensive. During the course of the meeting, Robertson broke ranks with the Prime Minister, saying that the proposed offensive against Turkey was not a practical plan, and that to attempt it would be very 'dangerous and detrimental to our prospects of winning the war'.[24] Robertson was rebuked by Lloyd George and it was clear that his days as Chief of the Imperial General Staff were numbered, though disagreements over plans for a strategic reserve rather than the Palestine issue were to lead to his dismissal shortly afterwards.

★

Allenby had planned to give effect to the Supreme War Council's decision by starting the first stage of his main coastal offensive to the north in April. The earlier occupation of the Jordan valley would enable him to sever the Hejaz railway, the last remaining physical link between Turkish-occupied Medina and the outside world. The operation would also have the benefit of disrupting Turkish supply routes across the Dead Sea. Allenby took the view that before the country round Jericho could be used as a base for operations against Amman, a further local advance northwards was necessary to gain sufficient space to neutralize the impact of any enemy irruption from that direction. Allenby had intended to carry out this advance to the north simultaneously with the advance eastwards to the River Jordan. It became clear, however, that if this was to be carried into effect the operations against Jericho would have to be postponed for a considerable time to enable preparations for the northern advance to be completed. He therefore decided to carry out the advance to the Jordan as a separate, self-contained enterprise, the limits of the advance being the River Jordan to the east and the Wadi el Auja to the north.

The operation, which began on 19 February 1918, was led by the 60th Division, which was ordered to advance from its base east of Jerusalem directly on Jericho. The Anzac Mounted Division, which was attached to the 60th Division for this operation, was ordered to attack and turn the Turkish left. By entering the Jordan valley near Nebi Musa and driving a wedge between the Turkish forces and Jericho, the Anzacs would cut off the enemy's retreat from the town. The advance of 60th Division towards the Jordan valley however was slow, impeded more by the difficulty of the terrain than any opposition offered by the enemy. The eastern flank of the Judean hills was not intended for rapid movement: it falls away sharply to the valley below and its dominant features are narrow gorges and inaccessible ridges. Wavell described it as 'one of the most desolate yet impressive parts of the earth'.[25] On no previous occasion during the campaign had such hard terrain been encountered. It was to take a field artillery battery thirty-six hours to reach Nebi Musa – the distance covered, as the crow flies, being only eight miles. Between Jerusalem and the top of the scarp above the Jordan valley the ground falls over 2,000 feet in 12 miles. There can be 'few countries in the world where hills of insignificant height give so strong an impression of savage and melancholy grandeur'.[26]

It was ideal terrain for a defending army and active Turkish machine-gunners slowed down British progress even further. The Turks also delayed the Anzacs' progress, withdrawing across the Jordan during the night of 20/21 February and thus avoiding attempts to entrap them. The only enemy forces then remaining on the western bank of the Jordan formed a strong bridgehead at Ghoraniyeh (on the main road from Jerusalem to Jericho and Es Salt). The way was now open for the seizure of Jericho, which was captured by the Allies on the morning of 21 February.

Although the occupation of Jericho ended the danger of a Turkish attack on Jerusalem from the east, it did not provide a secure base from which to mount new operations against the Hejaz railway and beyond. According to the British official history, Allenby's advance to the edge of the escarpment above the Jordan valley 'had made the British right flank secure, but it had not won a frontage wide enough to allow operations to be carried out east of Jordan'.[27] Before any such operation could be undertaken it was essential first to cross the Wadi el Auja and secure the high ground on the north bank of the river. It was also necessary to cover the approaches to the Jordan valley by the Beisan–Jericho road and to advance sufficiently far northwards on either side of the road from Jerusalem to Nablus to deny the enemy the use of any of the tracks and roads leading to the lower Jordan valley. Once this had been accomplished any troops the Turks might determine to transfer from the west to the east bank of the Jordan would have to make a considerable detour to the north. A further advance northwards would drive the Turks from the Judean hills and the valley and increase the distance between them and the new centre of operations. If successful, it would enhance Allenby's control of entry to the Jordan and a British advance towards Amman would be much less vulnerable to a flank attack if this initial operation was successful. This push forwards was intended to extend as far north as the hills of Samaria, which was a more favourable environment as a base for occupying troops than the Judean range.

This general advance involved troops of both XX and XXI Corps. On the right of XX Corps, positioned in the Jordan valley, was the 60th Division which was ordered to push the enemy back beyond the River Auja and secure a commanding position near Abu Tellul and Musallabeh. This would give the British access to an invaluable water supply as well as control of the Beisan–Jericho road: an important access route for the Turkish forces moving into the valley from the north. To the left of the 60th Division, other units of XX Corps – the 53rd, 74th and 10th Divisions – were to advance on both sides of the Nablus road, proceeding as far as a line running from Kefr Malik to Nebi Saleh. In a parallel operation, XXI Corps was to move its right forward to a line from the Wadi Deir Ballut to Ras el Ain, an old Crusader stronghold. The joint advance by XX and XXI Corps, which began on 8 March 1918, lasted for no more than four days. They moved forward on a front of 26 miles up to a maximum depth of seven miles. As a consequence of this movement, XXI Corps was placed in a much better position for a further advance. The Turks, as Allenby wrote, put up strong resistance – 'cheered, no doubt, by the Russian peace' – but were unable to prevent the Allies achieving their objectives, despite the fact that reinforcements from the Seventh Army had been poured in.[28]

★

Organizing the Turkish response was one of the first acts of General Otto Liman von Sanders who succeeded General von Falkenhayn in command of the Turkish Seventh and Eighth Armies in Palestine on 1 March 1918. Falkenhayn's departure reflected great concern in Berlin at the loss of Jerusalem and the need for a new commander who could stem the British advance. At the same time Kress von Kressenstein was superseded as commander of the Turkish Eighth Army by Djevad Pasha, while Djemal, 'the autocrat of Syria', had also been recalled to Constantinople.

By all accounts Liman was a 'corpulent and charming gentleman' who had extensive local contacts, both Arab and Turk. Liman knew Feisal from pre-war days when he was head of a German military mission sent to Constantinople to help in the task of modernizing the Turkish army. He had been based in the Ottoman empire for most of the war – it was he who had successfully organized the defence of Gallipoli in 1915 – and had a better understanding of the psychology of his military allies than most of his colleagues. According to Wavell, he had less 'brilliance in manoeuvre than Falkenhayn, but was a staunch fighter on the defensive'.[29] He was also more sensitive to local circumstances than his predecessor: he well understood the resentment which the German-dominated staff appointed by Falkenhayn had created among the Turkish officer corps and realized that a very different mix – with Turkish officers as the principal element – would be needed to restore confidence in the staff. By replacing most of the German staff with Turkish officers, Liman alleviated much of the friction between German and Turk that had existed since the outbreak of war. Allenby later wrote, in a private letter of June 1918, that he 'should not be surprised if Liman von Sanders has a crack at me before the autumn. He appears to have a better understanding of the Turks, and to be less unpopular, than . . . Falkenhayn. Him, they hated.'[30]

Although more strongly supported by his immediate staff than his predecessor, in other respects Liman suffered severe handicaps. There were three Turkish armies in Palestine but only the Seventh and Eighth Armies were fully under his control. The left of the Turkish line in the Jordan valley was manned by the Fourth Army, which was not under his direct command. This army (under the command of Djemal the Lesser) was required to supply the Sixth Army, which operated in Mesopotamia under the direct orders of Turkish GHQ. Outside the Palestine theatre, and responsible for the defence of the coast from northern Lebanon round to the Gulf of Iskanderun and beyond, was the Second Army, whose headquarters were at Aleppo and which also reported direct to GHQ. The Second Army was therefore based immediately to the rear of the Seventh and Eighth Armies and their separation in the command structure was, in Liman von Sanders' view, 'inappropriate'. In addition, his relations with the Turkish military authorities became increasingly difficult as they consistently failed to produce the reinforcements and supplies he urgently needed for the Palestine front. To this difficulty must be added Enver Pasha's inclination to interfere in matters of detail which he should have left to the commander of the Yilderim group; he even attempted to supervise the administration of the German troops serving on the Turkish fronts, an interference which led to a more than usually acrimonious controversy between him and Liman von Sanders.[31]

★

The successful completion of the initial operations in the northern end of the Jordan valley cleared the way for the first British raid on Amman, late in March 1918. Its first objective was the small town of Es Salt, which would help to protect its flank; it was then expected to aim for important targets on the Hejaz railway south of Amman. One of the main purposes of the raid was to support the progress of the Arab revolt, which was advancing northwards in parallel to the British, who were far to their left. Since the capture of Aqaba, the Arabs had advanced south-east of the Dead Sea, capturing Shobek and Tafila in turn. When a Turkish detachment tried to recapture Tafila in January 1918, it was heavily defeated and in response Falkenhayn had concentrated a new force at Qatrani, on the Hejaz railway halfway between Maan and Amman. This force succeeded in retaking Tafila and then driving the Arabs back to Shobek in March 1918. Lawrence's view was that Kerak and Tafila 'were not worth losing a man over; indeed, if the Turks moved there, and kept a main force there, they would weaken either the garrison of Maan or the garrison of Amman, and make our real work easier.'[32]

Allenby's immediate reason for attacking Amman, which was some 30 miles north-east of Jericho, was to compel the Turks to recall the large force which had occupied Tafila in March. However, there would be insufficient time for the returning force to help with the defence of Amman, and resistance to the British attack was expected to be light. By cutting the railway near Amman and capturing a key tunnel and viaduct, he would isolate the enemy forces to the south and reduce pressure on the Arab forces operating in the Maan area. It might, in addition, compel the enemy to call on the garrison of Maan for support. If this were the case, Feisal would have the opportunity to attack Maan, the most important station between Deraa and Medina, with some chance of success.

This prospective operation underlined the extent of military cooperation between the Arabs and the British and offered the hope that the two armies might soon establish direct contact. The nature of that cooperation had been thrown into question, however, by the publication of the Balfour Declaration in London in November 1917. The declaration, which was not officially published in the Middle East at the time although its contents were soon to be known to Arab leaders, stated that the British government would view favourably the establishment of a Jewish national home in Palestine. Though made subject to a proviso that such a development did not affect the rights of Arabs already living there, the declaration and its condition have never been reconciled. Given the task of ensuring that the British action did not affect Feisal's commitment to the war effort Lawrence was at pains to assure the authorities that 'the Arab attitude shall be sympathetic, for the duration of the war at least.'[33]

The continuing military involvement of the Arabs was a significant element in the whole campaign, particularly as major objectives appeared to be within their grasp. The capture of Maan, if achieved by the Arabs, was expected to bring the southern phase of the Arab campaign to an end. Direct assistance to Arab forces operating in the Hejaz would, it was hoped, help them to force the surrender of Medina. In Dawnay's view, 'the difficulty of bringing the operations in the Hejaz to a definite end appears largely to be due to the volatile character of the Arabs and to the difficulty of concentrating their efforts'.[34] Success at Maan would also enable the Arabs to play their full part in the campaign further north. Arab regular forces would move to new bases to the north-east of the Dead Sea where they would be in a position to contribute to Allenby's planned offensive, undertaking as one of their tasks the cutting of the Hejaz railway in Palestine, in the rear of the Turks, probably near Deraa. Allenby suggested that the Arabs might take Deraa – to which Lawrence agreed as long as the Imperial Camel Brigade was made available to them as shock troops.

The Arab role was never completely carried out, partly because they were unable to take Maan; partly because the British were unable to establish themselves in Es Salt. The extent of Feisal's military opportunities would depend on the amount of damage the British could do to the Hejaz railway further north. Near Amman the railway crossed a viaduct and passed through a tunnel. If these could be destroyed it would be some weeks before traffic could be resumed. Allenby, therefore, had few doubts about the value of

> a raid on Amman, with the object of destroying the viaduct and tunnel and, if it should be found impossible, to damage the railway as much as possible. Even if traffic was only interrupted for a short time, the mere threat of repetition of the raid would compel the enemy to maintain a considerable force to cover Amman. The troops available to operate against the Arabs would be reduced and possibly the enemy might transfer a portion of his reserves from the west to the east of the Jordan, thereby weakening his power to make or meet any attack on the main front.[35]

But Allenby's action had a wider strategic purpose. He always intended to make his next major advance northwards along the Mediterranean coastal route and he sought to weaken the potential opposition in that area well before operations were due to start. The more Turkish troops that could be drawn away eastwards across the Jordan the better. Significant British action in the Amman area might also help to conceal Allenby's real intentions by persuading the Turks that he intended to attack the vital railway junction at Deraa with the British forces located east of the Jordan. It represented an additional pressure on the Turkish high command to shift some of its forces eastwards from the coastal plain. Once the Amman raid had been successfully completed Allenby's immediate plan was to resume the advance on Nablus and Tul Keram.

The raid on Amman, which began as the force assembled on the western banks of the Jordan on 21 March 1918 – the same day as the Germans launched their great offensive on the Western Front – involved the 60th Division, the Anzac Mounted Division, the Imperial Camel Brigade and other units. They were led by Major-General Sir John Shea, commander of the 60th Division. From the beginning the operation was hampered by bad weather: it took the force two days to cross the Jordan river, which had been swollen by heavy rains. The attempt to bridge the river at Ghoraniyeh failed owing to the strength of the current, which defeated all attempts to cross either by swimming or by means of rafts and pontoons. However, at Hajlah swimmers succeeded in reaching the opposite bank and within a few hours a temporary bridge had been built. But, according to the official history, the damage had already been done: 'through no fault of their own, there had been a delay of twenty-four hours, which by giving the enemy time to take measures for the defence of Amman seriously prejudiced the success of the enter-prise.'[36]

Once the main force had crossed the river, it had to face the diffi-cult obstacle of the mountains of Moab as it moved eastwards towards Es Salt. The British plan was for the 60th Division (supported by a mounted brigade on its left) to advance through the hills at Shunet Nimrin and up the main road to Es Salt (which continued towards Amman). On reaching Amman the railway was to be destroyed and the viaduct and tunnel demolished. This achieved, the mounted troops were to withdraw on the 60th Division, the whole force then returning to the relative safety of the bridgeheads at the Jordan. The remaining mounted troops were to reach the plateau by a more southerly route and then proceed direct to Amman. The troops that took Es Salt – the 60th Division and the First Australian Light Horse – were to remain there and, if necessary, operate in support of the troops closing in on Amman.

After the difficulties of crossing the river had been overcome, the 60th Division made good progress on 24 March, capturing the Turkish position at Shunet Nimrin which covered the entrance to the pass leading to Es Salt, and advancing towards Es Salt before darkness. It was occupied on the following day. The mounted troops, who soon found that they could not use wheeled vehicles, made slower progress. Camels were employed to transport essential supplies but they had great difficulty in moving easily across the wet and slippery rocky surface. The delay enabled the enemy to bring up reinforcements. Before Amman could be attacked in strength, some 4,000 Turks, sup-ported by 15 guns, moved into position near Amman, covering the viaduct and tunnel, while another 2,000 men were moving on Es Salt from the north. To have attempted to drive the enemy from its posi-tions without artillery support would have entailed very heavy losses.

Initial attacks were therefore confined to the outskirts of Amman, and five miles of railway line, including several large culverts, and the points and crossings at Alanda station, south of Amman, were destroyed. To the north of the town a two-arch bridge was blown up and, in total, nearly 1,000 Turkish prisoners were taken (against total British losses – killed, wounded and missing – of 1,348). Meanwhile, after two night marches in driving rain, the mounted force reached Ain es Sir, some six miles west of Amman, during the early hours of 26 March. The journey had taken its toll and men and horses were exhausted. The attack on Amman was postponed for a day. Two infantry battalions based at Es Salt were ordered to join the mounted troops before Amman, but they were delayed near Suweileh. By this time the Turks were well aware of British intentions and the various delays had given them the opportunity to reinforce the Amman garrison. Some 15,000 additional troops, together with 15 guns, had reached Amman before the British assault began on 27 March.

The British attacks continued for four days and after a while, though handicapped by the absence of adequate artillery support, began to make an impact on the strongly entrenched Turkish forces. According to Liman's own account, 'the Turkish commanders at Amman were on the point of retiring and were only restrained by urgent and explicit orders from von Sanders that the position was to be retained to the last.'[37] The strategically important tunnel and viaduct remained in Turkish hands and, with little hope of further progress being made, the British decided to withdraw from the Amman area during the night of 30/31 March. With Turkish reinforcements closing in on Es Salt from the north the withdrawal promised to be difficult, but the enemy was successfully kept at a distance as the British returned across the Jordan. The river remained a serious obstacle to the returning troops, having risen by nine feet as a result of the continuous rain of the previous days. Despite this additional problem, the entire British force (except for some troops that were ordered to hold a bridgehead on the east bank at Ghoraniyeh) had managed to cross the river by 2 April.

Despite the difficulties it faced, the expedition had at least secured some of its aims. As Allenby had hoped, the Turkish army abandoned its plans to maintain a permanent presence at Tafila and also withdrew part of its garrison at Maan, sending them northwards to reinforce the troops engaging the enemy. Taking advantage of this opportunity, Feisal commenced operations against Maan. Three mobile columns were dispatched: two were sent to cut the railway north and south of Maan. The southern force attacked Ghadir el Haj station, ten miles south of Maan, and destroyed a substantial length of track. To the north of the town, a section of track near Jerdun was also destroyed. At these places 270 Turks and three machine guns were captured. The third force was sent to attack the main Turkish defences at Maan. On 13 April, the Arabs captured Senna, a Turkish post 4,000 yards south-west of Maan station, and, four days later, the station was entered and 100 prisoners taken. However, the attackers were unable to make any impression on the strong Turkish position 400 yards to the north of the station, despite support from RFC bombers. The Arabs were forced to withdraw with heavy losses and a stalemate developed.

In the meantime another Arab column attacked the Hejaz line at various points between Batn el Ghul and Kalaat et Mudawara, 42 miles south of Maan. By 25 April, as a result of this operation, the line between Maan and Mudawara was extensively damaged. The Arabs now had the opportunity to prevent the Turks repairing the line, ensuring that 'railway communication between Medina and the north should now permanently cease, a result which would entail the withdrawal of all Turks south of Maan into Medina and other isolated stations where they could be closely invested and eventually starved out'.[38]

Most significant, perhaps, in the longer term was the impact of the Amman raid on the distribution of Turkish troops. As a result of the operation, the Turks decided to enhance their defensive capability east of the Jordan by a permanent increase in the number of troops based in the area. This was achieved, as Allenby had hoped, by a reduction in the Turkish presence on the coastal plain, where he had planned soon to launch his major offensive.

Despite these important gains, the principal short-term British objectives of the raid had not been achieved. In particular, the Allies had not been able to capture or destroy the Amman viaduct or cause serious damage to the Hejaz railway elsewhere. The Turks certainly viewed the British withdrawal as a rare success, the first significant achievement since their victory at the second Battle of Gaza in April 1917. It produced a significant boost to Turkish morale. The rank and file – together with their German allies – had fought with great determination and had not allowed recent setbacks to affect their performance. The Turkish defenders were also encouraged by the regular arrival of fresh troops from the north. Continuing rainy weather had delayed the British crossing of the Jordan, which had given the Turks at least a day extra to prepare their defences in the Amman area. These adverse conditions also made it virtually impossible for artillery units or light armoured cars to reach the battle area, although a few eventually did so.

★

The Turks were not the only adversary whose actions delayed Allenby's progress in Palestine. The 'long gathering storm broke in France' on 21 March 1918, when the Germans launched a massive assault against Allied positions on the Western Front. This development was to have a direct effect on the timing of Allenby's future plans, although it had no immediate impact on the decision to go ahead with his first raid against Amman. Except for this operation, the British War Cabinet had within days decided to postpone further offensive action against Turkey and to put British troops in Palestine on the defensive. Surplus troops were needed urgently to shore up Allied defences on the Western Front where the British line had been broken. These decisions were conveyed to General Allenby on 27 March, but the first impact on troop dispositions came even earlier. On 23 March, only two days after the start of the German attack, Allenby was ordered to replace one of his British divisions by the Seventh Indian Division and to prepare the British division for early embarkation to France. On 9 April, the Germans launched a second great offensive on the Lys which made rapid progress; demands for reinforcements from Palestine were again increased as a result.

By mid-April, two British divisions – the 52nd and 74th – had been dispatched from Egypt, eventually to be replaced by two Indian divisions – the Third and Seventh – which had previously operated in Mesopotamia. The 52nd and 74th Divisions were followed to France by a long list of other units that had served in Egypt and Palestine. Those also sent in April included nine yeomanry regiments, ten British infantry battalions, and five and a half siege batteries. During May, fourteen more British battalions were sent to the Western Front. The yeomanry regiments were quickly replaced by Indian cavalry units, which had served in France, but replacements for the twenty-four British infantry battalions took much longer to arrive. Moreover, in place of battle-hardened troops the EEF had to assimilate units which had had no experience on the battlefield and in many cases were not even properly trained. The scale of the replacements meant that the whole Palestine force would have to be reorganized and redistributed before it could be used in battle.

Allenby soon realized that his plans for a major offensive would have to be delayed further while his new forces were organized and trained to an acceptable standard. Since this was likely to take several months, Allenby decided in the meantime to mount one or two smaller operations which escaped the War Office ban on offensive action and which were designed to improve the relative strength of the British position. On 9 April, an operation intended to advance the right of XXI Corps in the Judean foothills was launched. It made less progress than expected because the enemy discovered details of the British plan of attack and also because their machine-gun defences made an advance on the ground difficult to achieve. By the time the operation had been concluded, on 11 April, the British had sustained significant losses and gained little new ground.

This was followed by a British demonstration in force in the Jordan valley undertaken with the aim of persuading the enemy that a new advance on Amman was taking place. Allenby wished to reinforce the efforts of the Arab forces which had been in action against the Hejaz railway in the Maan area since the beginning of April, and he hoped by this means to divert Turkish reinforcements from Maan. The action extended for some 70 miles between Maan and Mudawara and resulted in the destruction of several stations and long sections of track. The fighting came to a head on 17 April but continued until the end of the month.

Allenby's plans for a second major raid across the Jordan had much more strategic significance for the conduct of the rest of the war in the region than had the first. Wishing to reinforce in his opponent's minds a belief that it was his intention to attack the railway junction at Deraa as he advanced northwards, he aimed to draw Turkish troops away from the coastal plain where he really intended to attack. The Turks had already decided to take this perceived threat seriously and, apart from bringing more troops into the area, they had launched, on 11 April, a pre-emptive strike on British positions in the Jordan valley. Heavy Turkish attacks on Ghoraniyeh and El Musallabeh were repelled, with the enemy withdrawing to Shunet Nimrin. Allenby, according to his own account of the campaign, then 'determined to seize the first opportunity to cut off and destroy the enemy's force at

Shunet Nimrin and, if successful, to hold Es Salt till the Arabs could advance and relieve my troops. This would have denied the enemy the use of the harvest.'[39] Arab support had been offered to the British by envoys of the Beni Sakhr tribe but there turned out to be little substance to it.

The second British offensive east of the Jordan began on 30 April 1918. The objective of the raid was to use mounted troops to capture Es Salt. This would cut Turkish communications with the force occupying the stronghold of Shunet Nimrin, which would then be attacked by British infantry. If these operations were successful they would enable the British, with Arab support, to establish a permanent presence in the Es Salt area. This would be a much more acceptable alternative to their continuing occupation of the Jordan valley where the summer heat and disease made conditions intolerable.

Allenby had originally intended to begin this operation in mid-May once the reorganization of his cavalry following the arrival of replacement Indian units was complete. But pressure from his Arab allies dictated an earlier start. By the latter part of April, fighting men of the Beni Sakhr tribe had assembled about 20 miles south of Es Salt and were ready to support the British action. However, their supplies were short and they could not remain in their present position beyond 4 May. Allenby believed that these tribesmen could play a valuable role in cutting off the Turkish troops based at Nimrin by barring the track which gave them access to Amman. Meanwhile British troops would take control of the main route from Nimrin, which led directly to Es Salt: the only track that afforded access to wheeled transport. By the combined action of British and Arab forces the Turkish force at Nimrin would be surrounded and could then be attacked and captured. Allenby decided that it would be worthwhile to bring forward his plans so that he could work in cooperation with the Arabs.

The Allied force assembled at the bridgehead on the Jordan during the night of 29 April. Commanded by General Chauvel, who headed the Desert Mounted Corps (in recent succession to General Chetwode), the force consisted of the Anzacs, the Australian Mounted Division, the 60th Division and the Imperial Service Cavalry and Infantry Brigades. Beginning at dawn on 30 April, two brigades of the 60th Division, supported on their right by the New Zealand Mounted Brigade, launched a direct attack on Shunet Nimrin, where most of the enemy's strength was concentrated. The operation came as a complete surprise to the Turks, according to Liman von Sanders, 'so secretly and ably had their preparations been carried out that even the most important were hidden from our aviators and from ground observation'.[40]

The British assault had pre-empted a Turkish attack on British advanced positions at Musallabeh, just west of the Jordan. East of the Jordan the Turks had some 8,000 men in total, organized as VIII Corps under the command of Colonel Ali Fuad Bey. From these troops the British advance soon faced heavy opposition and stalled before the enemy's second-line works. While this attack was in progress the Australian Mounted Division advanced up the Jordan valley. The Fourth Australian Light Horse, which led the advance, was ordered to proceed some 16 miles north of Ghoraniyeh bridge with the aim of taking the Jisr ed Damieh bridge. If the crossing proved too heavily defended they were to block the route from the bridge to Es Salt. The purpose of this action was to prevent the Turks from bringing in reinforcements from the west bank as they had done during the course of the first Amman raid in March. The Fourth Australian Light Horse Brigade reached Jisr ed Damieh at 5.30 p.m. on 30 April and took control of the track leading to Es Salt, although it was unable to take the bridge itself which was strongly held by the enemy. The brigade took up positions on the track over a distance of eight miles, from Nahr ez Zerka in the north towards Red Hill in the south.

Other Australian units were also ordered to turn eastwards towards Es Salt as they marched up the valley. The Third Australian Light Horse Brigade had turned right at Jisr ed Damieh and moved up the track towards Es Salt. The Fifth Mounted Brigade of the Australian Division turned towards Es Salt at Um esh Shert ford, some seven miles north of the Ghoraniyeh bridge. It was to be followed by the First and Second Australian Light Horse Brigades, Anzac Division, later in the day. The Third Australian Light Horse Brigade made the most rapid progress and during the evening captured Es Salt in a fast and effective operation. The three remaining brigades arrived the following morning (1 May) and the whole town was surrounded and sealed off. The Fifth Mounted Brigade was not required for this operation and was dispatched down the main road to Nimrin. It would approach the Turkish positions from the rear, while the 60th Division renewed the attack from the front.

Although British prospects seemed promising for a while, the whole operation was shortly to end in failure. At the same time as the

Fifth Mounted Division was moving off, the Fourth Australian Light Horse Brigade found itself under surprise enemy attack at three separate points. A Turkish force, consisting of the 24th Division and the Third Cavalry Division, had been rapidly assembled. Some enemy units were to cross the Jordan using a temporary pontoon bridge at Mafid Jozele, a little north of Red Hill. They advanced against Red Hill and moved into the gap between the British left and the hill. Turkish troops from the Nahr ez Zerka were to envelop the British right, while other units from Jisr ed Damieh attacked the British centre.

The British line could not be maintained under the weight of the Turkish attack and the Fourth Brigade was forced back against the Moab hills. It managed to prevent itself being trapped there (although it lost nine guns in the process) and took the only route open to the south. Supported by reinforcements brought up from the south, it established a new line about a mile to the north of the Um esh Shert track (which was the only route to Es Salt still open). The fighting elsewhere offered no encouragement to the British. The renewed infantry assault on Nimrin made no further progress, while the Fifth Mounted Division had not arrived from Es Salt, having been held up in the hills en route.

Progress was also affected by the fact that the promised Arab support never materialized. The route from Nimrin to Amman, which they had offered to close, remained open and, unknown to the British, had been upgraded. This enabled the flow of Turkish reinforcements and supplies to be maintained even when the main supply route had been blocked. The position there continued unchanged on 2 and 3 May, but at Es Salt the British came under severe pressure on virtually all sides. Their escape route back to the valley was highly vulnerable and was likely to be cut by the Turkish army unless they withdrew soon. Liman von Sanders explained the position from his perspective as follows:

> In the evening I issued an order to H.Q. Fourth Army and to the Third Cavalry Division to penetrate into the town *from the north* by means of a night attack . . . The northerly direction was chosen because the ground there facilitated an advance, and also in order to enable the British to retreat from Es Salt to the south-west . . . in my opinion there was no doubt that our weak and thoroughly exhausted troops were not in a fit state to fight a desperate battle, such as must

inevitably ensue if the British saw their line of defence was directly threatened. It would have led to a defeat for us.[41]

In these circumstances, Allenby had no choice but to withdraw British forces from Es Salt and orders to this effect were issued during the afternoon of 3 May. The British left under cover of darkness and escaped into the valley using the Um esh Shert track. Within a day they had reached the safety of the Ghoraniyeh bridgehead and crossed the Jordan during the evening of 4 May. They brought with them nearly 1,000 Turkish prisoners. The numbers of British killed and wounded – some 1,500 in total – were not unduly heavy and were certainly more than matched by those of the enemy.

While the raid had clearly not achieved its immediate objectives, it was successful in convincing the enemy that his left flank would be the main focus of future British offensive activity. The raid had undoubtedly rendered the enemy fearful of further operations east of the Jordan. In the words of the British official history, it was 'to have in the months to come a very important effect: to concentrate the attention of the enemy command on the Jordan valley and thereby to assist materially in the final British offensive'.[42] As a consequence, the Turks felt compelled to maintain considerable forces in the Amman and Shunet Nimrin areas, reducing the forces available to meet the Arab threat further south.

By this time as much as a third of the Turkish army was based in the region to the east of the River Jordan and Allenby wanted to foster the enemy's sense of insecurity by retaining a strong British physical presence there during the summer months. This unwelcome task was allocated to the Desert Mounted Corps, which had two of its four divisions in the valley for a month at a time, while the other two divisions were resting in the hills. It was to continue until the final British offensive was launched in September 1918.

# 8

# *Time to Recoup*

T HE DEFEAT OF the second Es Salt operation to the east of the
River Jordan, early in May 1918, marked the beginning of a
four-month lull in major operations, although there were several
British raids against enemy positions during the hot summer months:
small actions typically designed to improve Allied positions on the
coastal plain or in the foothills. There was also a single Turkish offensive during this period: an attack in the Jordan valley, launched in
mid-July, which sought to undermine British control of the area and
which, if successful, would have made a renewed offensive east of the
Jordan virtually impossible.

The focus of the attack was the British salient east of the Jordan
that extended to the north of the Wadi Auja. Led by German battalions – but with little effective support from the Turks – the attack
foundered because of the strength of the Australian defence. In
Wavell's words, the failed operation 'was a valuable indication to
Allenby both of the continued sensitiveness of the enemy higher
command to the threat of a move east of Jordan and of the decline in
the morale of the Turks'.[1] The failure of the operation sent a similar
message to the Turks – or rather to their more perceptive commander, for as Liman later said: 'nothing showed me more clearly the
decline in the fighting capacity of the Turkish troops than the events
of the 14 July. The incidents which occurred would have been
impossible with any of the troops under my command in the early
years of the war.'[2]

Within days of the start of the German offensive on the Western
Front which broke the long-standing stalemate in France, Allenby

received a War Office telegram on 27 March 1918 cancelling the
instructions he had previously received to take the offensive in accordance with the plans developed by General Smuts. He was warned that
'a defensive attitude must be adopted in Palestine' for the time being.[3]
The main British preoccupation during this period was not, therefore, immediate action against the enemy but ensuring that Allenby's
forces were properly trained and organized for the next great offensive. With the dispatch of British troops from Palestine to the
Western Front – some 60,000 officers and men were sent to France in
1918 – and the arrival of Indian troops to replace them, Allenby had
to concentrate his efforts on major changes in organization. As
Lawrence explained, when these 'drafts came he [Allenby] would
reorganize or rebuild his army on the Indian model, and perhaps,
after the summer, might be again in fighting trim; but for the
moment this was too far to foresee: we [the Arabs] must, like him,
just hold on and wait.'[4]

The scale of the task facing Allenby was indicated by the fact that
only one of the infantry divisions remaining in Palestine – the 54th –
would be composed entirely of British troops. The organization of
the other British divisions that would continue to fight there – the
10th, 53rd, 60th, 75th – was modified to reflect the structures used in
India. Each division would consist of nine Indian battalions and
three British. Most of the replacement troops, who came from India
direct, were found to be of variable quality and were largely unsupported by specialist forces. They also had to accustom themselves to
the new and very different physical conditions. A massive training
programme was instituted and largely completed before the next
major offensive started. However, the last of the new battalions to
arrive in Egypt had little time for training and many British officers
believed that the changes had seriously weakened the efficiency of
the infantry.

On the other hand, the changes that Allenby was forced to make
to the mounted arm seem to have had a more beneficial impact. The
Desert Mounted Corps underwent far-reaching restructuring during
this period and was, according to the official history, 'a more formidable weapon after the reorganization than before it'.[5] The Yeomanry
Division, the Fifth Mounted Brigade and the Imperial Camel Corps
were disbanded. Two new divisions – the Fourth and Fifth – were
formed from newly transferred Indian units, which had arrived in
Palestine in sufficient time to acclimatize themselves to the new con-

ditions, and the remaining yeomanry regiments. The Fifth Division also included the former Imperial Service Cavalry Brigade which became the 15th (Imperial Service) Brigade. In the Australian Mounted Division the Fifth Australian Light Horse Brigade, replacing the Fifth Mounted Brigade, was formed from the Australian battalions of the Camel Corps. This division adopted the sword during the course of the summer. After the changes the Desert Mounted Corps consisted of four divisions: Fourth Division, Fifth Division, Australian Mounted Division and Anzac Division.

The changes had increased the number of mounted divisions from three to four. Three of them − rather than one − were cavalry divisions armed and trained in shock tactics in pursuit. Other sources also added to the potential strength of Allenby's forces. One of the consequences of the Balfour Declaration of November 1917 was the arrival of the 38th, 39th and 40th Royal Fusiliers − battalions of Jewish volunteers recruited from England, America and the Middle East. Although the creation of these units had initially been opposed by the War Office on the grounds that it would exacerbate tensions with Arabs in Palestine, the War Cabinet subsequently agreed to the plan. The French contingent was also strengthened by the arrival of Armenian refugees although their military value was questionable.

Until the September offensive was launched, the mounted troops (at first, almost exclusively Australian divisions) were mainly responsible in turns for protecting the British bridgehead over the Jordan which, according to the official historian, 'was the most ungrateful task which any troops in Palestine were set to perform during the hot season'.[6] As Wavell described it:

> the Jordan valley in summer was a horrible place. The daily temperature was over 100 degrees, the atmosphere, at more than a thousand feet below sea level, humid and oppressive; the hot winds, or the least movement of troops or transport, sent choking clouds of dust along the valley; scorpions, huge spiders, centipedes and flies were the principal representatives of animal life.[7]

According to Lieutenant Robert Wilson, a volunteer in the Berkshire Yeomanry who was based there,

> the summer of 1918 proved our greatest ordeal . . . It was generally accepted that no white man had ever before lived through a summer

there and even the flies died of the heat. The Turks cheered us up by
dropping leaflets telling us that, 'Flies die in July, men in August, and
we will come and bury you in September.'[8]

To these climatic problems was added the ever-present danger of
disease: malaria among the troops often reached epidemic proportions and was only gradually brought under control by a preventative
campaign carried out by British medical staff.

Despite the real dangers of serving in the Jordan valley, Allied
troops based there, as elsewhere in the Palestine theatre, were well fed
and supplied. Substantial resources had been devoted to improving
the capacity of the Sinai railway. By mid-1918, the track had been
doubled as far as Rafa, giving the railway the capacity to transport
2,000 tons of supplies a day to Palestine. A continuing British presence on the Jordan was in any case an essential part of British strategy
even if the cost was high. It was indispensable, in Allenby's view, 'to
control the [Jordan crossings] and to secure command of the Dead
Sea. Otherwise my Arab allies on the Hejaz railway would be abandoned to the Turks.'[9]

The impact on the Arabs of the delay in starting a major new
offensive was problematic in both political and military terms. Unless
the Allies could restart the war of movement, the military stalemate at
Maan would continue. There was a danger that the Turks would
divert troops away from the Palestine front in order to deal with this
problem while the lull in fighting continued. More important,
according to Lawrence, there was a real fear that the momentum of
the revolt would be lost: 'we on the Arab front had been exciting
Eastern Syria, since 1916, for a revolt near Damascus, and our
material was now ready and afoot. To hold it still in that excited
readiness during another year risked our over-passing the crisis
ineffectually.'[10]

To this anxiety was added growing Arab concern at the political
shape of the post-war Middle East and the extent to which their
objectives had been compromised by the Sykes–Picot agreement and
the Balfour Declaration. The combined effect of these undertakings
was to deny Arab claims to full independence in all parts of the
region except the Arabian peninsula. The Arab alliance with Britain
amounted to little more than a wish to be on the winning side, with
the risk that they would have very little to show for it. With a long
military standstill in prospect in Palestine and east of the Jordan, there

was a danger that belief in an ultimate British victory would diminish and that separate peace terms might be agreed between the Arabs and Turks.

To avoid this possibility Lawrence developed plans for a new Arab military initiative east of the Jordan. An Arab force, supported by a gift of 2,000 camels from the Egyptian Expeditionary Force, would launch a long-distance mounted raid against Deraa or Damascus. This would force the Turks to withdraw one or two divisions from Palestine and would enable Allenby to make a northwards advance earlier than might otherwise have been possible. Plans for this offensive however took more time to develop than Lawrence expected and were soon overtaken by events in Palestine. The reorganization and training of Allenby's new troops progressed more rapidly than he had estimated and, by mid-June, his staff were planning to go on to the attack in September.

★

By July 1918 it was clear that the German spring offensive in France, which had forced the postponement of offensive plans on the Palestine front, had failed; the opposing sides had returned again to a continuation of the trench warfare that had dominated the Western Front for nearly four years. With the prospect of the war in Europe continuing well into 1919, Lloyd George was anxious to make visible progress on the Palestine front. His suggestion that British troops be transferred from France to Palestine for a winter campaign (1918–19) was ruled out on practical grounds; Allenby would have to push forward with the troops already under his command and hope that they were sufficient.

The enemy forces ranged against him on the coastal plain were already much reduced thanks to the success of his campaign to convince the Turks that they faced the threat of a major offensive east of the Jordan. The Turks had in any case failed to use the respite from the fighting to reinforce their line in Palestine. Their real political priorities lay elsewhere, in the Caucasus. Encouraged by the terms of the Treaty of Brest-Litovsk, of March 1918, which ended the war on the Eastern Front and gave the Turks assurances about Russian intentions to evacuate the Anatolian provinces still in their possession, as well as territory lost in the Russo-Turkish war of 1877–8, the Turkish government embarked on a series of territorial conquests in the Caucasus. Taking advantage of the collapse of Imperial Russia, she revived her old pan-Turkish ambitions and began to move into northern Persia. In the first stage, Erzerum was retaken from the Russians on 24 March 1918, followed by Van on 5 April. Later conquests included Batum, Kars and Tiflis, which were all former Ottoman possessions. Although such acquisitions had a huge emotional appeal they gave Turkey little strategic advantage compared with the benefits of a military success in Palestine.

Those enemy troops that remained in Palestine were generally in poor shape as Turkey entered its fifth year at war. After a succession of defeats following the fall of Gaza, morale was low and desertion commonplace. These problems were compounded by the fact that food and clothing were often in short supply as a result of disruptions to the lines of communication. Like his British counterparts, Liman was also under pressure to provide troops for other theatres as priorities changed. He resisted these demands as far as possible but did not always succeed. On 11 June, he received an order to withdraw the last German reinforcements to arrive in Palestine – the 11th reserve Jäger Battalion and, according to Liman, 'the backbone of future operations'.[11] He protested to Constantinople and threatened to resign – in his view the leakage of troops to the Caucasus would be fatal to the Turkish cause: 'they will lose the whole of Arabia together with Palestine and Syria, as a result of extravagant enterprises in Trans-Caucasia'[12] – but he was unable to secure the reversal of his instructions.

Continuing tension between Turkish and German troops was also helping to undermine the Turkish army as an effective fighting force. But Turkey suffered from a more fundamental problem: according to the official history of the war, 'she no longer had her heart in the struggle and had begun to neglect the Palestine front.'[13] At the time of the renewed British offensive there were some 100,000 Turkish soldiers south of Damascus, but their front-line strength was considerably less: 32,000 infantry, 4,000 cavalry and 402 guns. (The comparable British figures, which gave Allenby a two to one advantage, were 57,000 infantry, 12,000 cavalry and 540 guns. The quality of his mounted troops was 'considerably superior'.)[14]

In response to Allenby's strategy – and in particular to the perceived distribution of his forces – Liman's troops were spread thinly over an extended front of 75 miles running from Amman to the Mediterranean. The Turkish position was particularly weak west of the Jordan and Liman took immediate action on his arrival to strengthen both flanks by a redistribution of his forces. Turkish defences in this area were not in any case strong enough to withstand a sustained assault by an enemy that was well supplied with artillery pieces. Without adequate barbed-wire protection, such defences were unlikely to detain the British for long. A confidential German assessment of the Turkish predicament, dated 18 January 1918, was highly pessimistic, referring to the 'deplorable condition' of the Turkish army and to the fact that it could only be restored as an effective fighting machine by the dispatch of more German and Austrian troops.[15] It speculated on the possibility that the British could defeat their opponents and reach Damascus or even Aleppo during the course of 1918. To prevent this, the German paper argued that 'our military policy in Palestine must be to avoid pitched battles and fight a long series of delaying but indecisive actions.' This plan would run the risk of widespread desertions by further damaging Turkish morale, but was, it concluded, 'the only one open to us'.[16]

These problems were compounded by the difficulty of retaining troops who were determined to desert rather than face an extended period in the trenches of northern Palestine. According to Liman von Sanders, large numbers of Turkish troops had escaped to local towns such as El Afule and even to Damascus: at El Afule station no less than '700 men were found who had gradually collected there and apparently taken root. The most striking incident was the discovery of a company at Damascus which had risen to 1,200 of all ranks by gathering in reinforcements of every kind.'[17] Although this unit's existence was not recorded for the purposes of pay, it 'merely demanded and had always received the necessary food, etc., from the distributing office of the depot'.[18] It must have been assumed that the company, which had seen no service for months, was under the protection of a higher formation.

Despite all these difficulties, during the lull in the fighting from May 1918 the Turkish army, like the British, took the opportunity to reorganize its forces in Palestine. The surviving troops were sorted into three armies under the overall command of Liman von Sanders, who was based at Nazareth: the Seventh and Eighth Armies held a defensive line west of the Jordan, while the Fourth Army was positioned east of the Jordan. The Eighth Army, whose headquarters were at Tul Keram, held a line running eastwards from the Mediterranean shore for about 20 miles into the hills at Furkhah. Commanded by Djevad Pasha (who had succeeded Kress von Kressenstein), the

Eighth Army consisted of the XXII Corps (7th, 20th and 46th Divisions) and the Asiatic Corps (16th and 19th Divisions, 701st, 702nd and 703rd German Battalions). The Seventh Army, whose headquarters were at Nablus, continued the Turkish line eastwards from Furkhah to the River Jordan. Like the Eighth Army, the Seventh covered a front of about 20 miles, its main strength being in the area through which the Jerusalem–Nablus road passed. Commanded by General Mustapha Kemal Pasha, who succeeded General Fevzi in August 1918 and later became Turkish president, it consisted of the III Corps (1st and 11th Divisions) and XXIII Corps (26th and 53rd Divisions).

In the words of the British official history, Kemal was 'the greatest soldier and man that Turkey had produced in recent years'. He was a 'pan-Turk but was wise enough to see that, while the war lasted, the retention of Palestine was a necessity'.[19] He was, however, 'horrified' by what he found on his arrival in August and recognized at once that an army consisting of undernourished troops, and which had more deserters than men under arms, was unlikely to be able to hold on to Palestine for very much longer. With the exception of a small reserve, the Turkish Seventh and Eighth Armies were enclosed in an area that was rectangular in shape: 45 miles in length and only 12 miles in depth. The remainder of the Turkish line was held by the Fourth Army located in the Jordan valley and the hills of Moab to the east of the river. Commanded by Djemal the Lesser, the Fourth Army, which had its headquarters in Amman, consisted of the II Corps (24th Division and 3rd Cavalry Division) and VIII Corps (48th and Composite Divisions).

Liman quickly formed the view that the Turkish troops based east of the Jordan had an impossible task and he proposed that all Turkish forces south of the Dead Sea should be withdrawn:

> from the military point of view it was hard to understand how the whole Hedjaz railway could be held under conditions then prevailing . . . If the decision had depended on the military point of view alone, the Turkish line of defence east of Jordan should have been withdrawn long before, at any rate as far as the Kalaat el Hesa sector on the southern edge of the Dead Sea. It was quite impractical for the large area as far as Medina to be retained, long after the whole country west and south-west of the Dead Sea had fallen into the hands of the enemy and proved in the long run to be hopeless.[20]

Despite the difficulties of maintaining Turkish troops east of the Jordan, their presence in the region to the north of the Dead Sea was essential if communications between the Yilderim group and Damascus and beyond were to be maintained. The railway from Damascus ran south to Deraa before turning west into Palestine. It was the weakest point in the Turkish front line and 'it was by playing upon von Sanders' fears for his left that [Allenby] was able to effect his great concentration against the other flank with such amazing secrecy and success'.[21] Liman had considered – and rejected – the possibility of abandoning the Hejaz railway and withdrawing his entire force to a shorter line running from Haifa to the Yarmuk valley. He rejected it primarily because he did not think the move was feasible given the present condition of his troops. In his view there was 'more chance of success in holding the positions to the last than in attempting a lengthy retreat with troops whose morale was already shaken'.[22]

★

Allenby's strategy for the concluding operation of the Palestine campaign was his own, in contrast to his first major offensive in the autumn of 1917, which had been heavily influenced by the views of Whitehall staff. His planned attack, which he scheduled for mid-September before the first winter rains arrived, was based on key assumptions about the superiority of British troops in terms of numbers, quality and training. He believed that a rapid victory using his existing resources was possible if an imaginative plan of attack was developed. One of his objectives was to establish a direct link with Feisal's army as the latter advanced northwards:

> I was anxious to gain touch with the Arab forces east of the Dead Sea, but the experience, gained in the raids which I had undertaken against Amman and Es Salt in March and May, had proved that the communications of a force in the hills of Moab were liable to interruption, as long as the enemy was able to transfer troops from the west to the east bank of the Jordan. This he was in a position to do, if he controlled the crossing at Jisr ed Damieh.
>
> The defeat of the VIIth and VIIIth Turkish armies, west of the Jordan, would enable me to control this crossing. Moreover, the destruction of these armies . . . would leave the IVth Army isolated, if it continued to occupy the country south and west of Amman. I determined, therefore, to strike my blow west of the Jordan.[23]

Allenby soon realized how vulnerable the Turks would be if their lines of communication were to be severed at a limited number of strategic points. The Turkish Seventh and Eighth Armies were supported by the railway line that turned westwards into Palestine at Deraa junction, while the Hejaz line, which continued south, supported the Fourth Army. After it left Deraa, the main railway route through Palestine crossed the Jordan at Jisr el Mejamie. It then ran in parallel to (and north of) the Turkish front line, linking Beisan, in the valley of Jezreel, with El Afule, in the Plain of Esdraelon, where there was a branch line to Haifa. At this point the main line turned south through the foothills of Samaria to Messudieh junction, where it turned westwards until reaching the coastal plain at Tul Keram. Here it changed direction and turned south, soon crossing the lines of the opposing armies. It was clear that the early capture of Messudieh, El Afule, Beisan and Deraa during a new offensive would block the escape routes of the three retreating Turkish armies.

The plan Allenby was developing involved a rapid advance by British mounted troops once the enemy front line had been breached by the infantry. The capture of El Afule and Beisan would make escape for the Seventh and Eighth Armies extremely difficult and both towns were within a day's ride of the British front line. Most of the route, which was 60 miles long in the case of Beisan, involved crossing the open coastal plain (Plain of Sharon) until the mountainous offshoot of the Judean hills was reached. The hills of Samaria enclose the coastal plain and end in Mount Carmel at Haifa. This physical barrier presented no great difficulties for mounted troops as two routes led from the Plain of Sharon to the Plain of Esdraelon. The route through the mountains did, however, provide the enemy with many good opportunities to mount an effective defence. It was essential, therefore, that the cavalry crossed these hills before the Turkish army could deploy troops there. Deraa was, of course, beyond the immediate range of the British cavalry but Allenby still intended to take action to persuade the Turks that a major British attack was planned in the area. In this way he hoped to ensure that large numbers of Turkish troops were held there to meet this perceived threat. To maintain the Turks' sense of insecurity, he envisaged involving Arab forces in the operation whose main objective would be to disrupt communications in the Deraa area rather than to occupy the town itself.

In mid-July, Allenby informed the War Office that he hoped to resume offensive operations during the latter part of 1918, with the aim of securing a line from Nablus to Tul Keram, extending to the mouth of the Nahr Iskanderun. With the loan of troops from France, so he informed Sir Henry Wilson, who had succeeded Robertson as Chief of the Imperial General Staff in February 1918, it was possible that he could make further progress, reaching a line from Tiberias to Acre before the campaigning season came to an end. A prompt offer of winter reinforcements from Wilson was withdrawn with equal speed. The War Office was also sceptical of a plan that did not involve the capture of Deraa or give Britain control of the Hejaz railway. Under these circumstances, Sir Henry believed that maintaining the present policy of active defence was the most prudent option. Allenby took a more robust view of the situation and, with accumulating evidence of the weakness of the enemy, came to the conclusion that he could secure a decisive victory within his existing resources.

Allenby's plan of attack went through several drafts over the summer months and was substantially different in its final form. His original proposal involved an infantry attack on the Turkish line across an eight-mile front near the coast, which was to be followed by a rapid cavalry advance as soon as that front was broken. The mounted troops would advance as far as Messudieh junction. This plan would involve turning the flank of the Turkish Eighth Army and threatening the Seventh Army's line of retreat through Nablus. As more evidence emerged of the size and condition of the enemy forces, Allenby believed that his offensive could be much more ambitious in its scope and overall objectives. He was aware that his initial plan did not cast the net wide enough to be certain of catching the bulk of the retreating Turkish troops. The enemy's condition, he now thought, was sufficiently weak to offer him the chance of encircling and destroying its entire remaining forces in Palestine in a single operation. This could be achieved if his mounted troops were given a more ambitious role – and more distant objectives – in the offensive. If they could penetrate further behind enemy lines before turning eastwards, they would be in a position to capture El Afule and Beisan, which were well beyond the rear of the defending Turkish armies. El Afule was just under seven miles south of Nazareth, which was the location of Yilderim's headquarters. Allenby was to send a detachment there to capture Liman and his staff.

Under this revised plan it was hoped that the cavalry would move through the hill passes between the plains of Sharon and Esdraelon before the Turks could block them completely. Allenby believed that this could be done if the advancing cavalry moved quickly enough, although there was clearly an element of risk. The plan was based on the assumption that the movement of enemy reserves from Haifa or Nazareth to the Turkish right flank would be too slow to interfere with the great turning movement of the British cavalry. The whole operation depended on the success of a surprise British attack on the coastal plain breaking through the Turkish defences. A rapid breach in the Turkish line should be made by British infantry, which would be concentrated in overwhelming strength at a specific point. Once the line had been broken, cavalry units would pour through and advance rapidly northwards before turning to the east. It was not intended that they should engage the enemy until they reached the rear of the Turkish defending armies. If this approach was to be successfully adopted, it would mean that other parts of the British line would have to be held by relatively few troops. It was also vital that the enemy remained in the dark about where the real blow was intended to fall as otherwise reinforcements could be mobilized to defend a particular sector in depth. Deception was destined to play a major part in persuading the Turkish army that the British intended to strike east of the Jordan. However, even if the Turkish Fourth Army in the Jordan valley correctly anticipated Allenby's real plan and started to evacuate the area, the Australian and New Zealand Mounted Division would be available to deal with the problem.

In essence it was a daring strategy, even against an enemy clearly inferior in numbers and morale. It would involve a continuous ride of over 50 miles for the majority of the horsemen and over 60 miles for some, in the course of which they would have to cross a range of hills in the enemy's possession, passable only by two difficult tracks. According to Wavell, 'there was no parallel in military history to so deep an adventure by such a mass of cavalry against a yet unbroken enemy.'[24] Allenby's plan was the exact reverse of the third Gaza–Beersheba battle that had taken place nearly a year before. Then he struck the Turkish left flank, while persuading them that he meant to break through on their right on the coast. Now that he meant to break through on the Mediterranean coast he took every possible step to persuade them that he would attack their left flank.

Under the British plan, the key opening role was allocated to XXI Corps, commanded by Lieutenant-General Sir Edward Bulfin, who had served at Salonika, and was associated with notable victories at Gaza and the Nahr el Auja. His corps, which was on the extreme left of the British line, was given the task of breaking the enemy's defences in the coastal plain and clearing a path for the mounted troops. It originally consisted of four infantry divisions – the Third Indian, Seventh Indian, 54th and 75th – as well as French and Italian units, but a fifth division (the 60th) was transferred from XX Corps for this operation. Most of the available medium and heavy artillery was also allocated to XXI Corps, together with the Fifth Australian Light Horse Brigade. The Desert Mounted Corps, consisting of the Fourth and Fifth Cavalry Divisions and the Australian Division, was moved from the Jordan valley and assembled in complete secrecy immediately behind the left of XXI Corps. To the right, XX Corps, which had been reduced in strength through transfers to the XXI Corps, was required to operate on an extended front. This would give XXI Corps the opportunity to bring its entire strength to bear on a relatively small area of the enemy's right flank. In the Jordan valley, on the right of XX Corps' line, a new detachment was formed, led by the New Zealand cavalry commander Major-General Sir Edward Chaytor. It consisted of the Australian and New Zealand Mounted Division and eight infantry battalions and would operate against the Turkish Fourth Army.

As a result of these movements, the British had concentrated some 35,000 infantry, 9,000 cavalry and 383 guns on a short front of only 15 miles adjoining the sea. They heavily outnumbered the Turks who only had 10,000 men (including 1,000 mounted troops) and 130 guns deployed in the same area. The Turkish defence system on this part of the front formed a continuous line. Built on a sandy ridge, these defences went to a depth of about 3,000 yards and were protected by barbed wire. The second line of Turkish defences was constructed some three miles behind the first line and ran from the Nahr el Falik on the coast eastwards to Et Tireh. These secondary defences were significantly weaker than the first as they did not have the protection of barbed wire and were not continuous. The rest of the front line was some 45 miles in length and here the balance of opposing forces was more evenly distributed: there were 25,000 British infantry and 157 guns opposing 24,000 Turkish troops and 270 guns.

On the appointed day, the attack on the left would open with a heavy bombardment at dawn. It would be followed by an attack on the Turkish line between the Mediterranean and the main railway line by leading units of XXI Corps. Once a hole had been punched in the line and the Nahr el Falik had been crossed, the XXI Corps would then move north-eastwards, pivoting on its right. Its left flank would be protected by the Fifth Australian Light Horse Brigade, which was ordered to advance on Tul Keram. XXI Corps would force the enemy back through the Judean foothills in the direction of Messudieh and then on to Jenin. The Turkish army's retreat would be blocked by the cavalry at El Afule.

Once the XXI Corps had punched a hole in the Turkish line, the Desert Mounted Corps, under the command of Sir Harry Chauvel, was expected to race through it and advance north along the coast. It was ordered not to engage the enemy except where they attempted directly to block its progress. The cavalry would be ordered to go northwards as far as the line of the Nahr el Mefjir, where there were limited Turkish defensive positions. After these had been taken, the Desert Mounted Corps was to turn inland in a north-easterly direction. Negotiating the two hill passes, it would enter the Plain of Esdraelon and advance on El Afule, Beisan and the bridge over the Jordan at Jisr el Mejamie, cutting off the retreating enemy troops. If successful the result would be complete surprise. The enemy would have no idea that the British cavalry was behind it until it was too late. The speed of the cavalry, and its ability to avoid a premature engagement with the enemy, would be the keys to success. Liman's headquarters at Nazareth were to be taken by a detachment operating separately from the main force.

To the right of the XXI Corps, the XX Corps, which had been commanded by Sir Philip Chetwode since August 1917, was to time its advance according to the progress made on the main front adjoining the coast. Its principal task was to block the main exit routes leading from the Judean hills to the crossing point at Jisr ed Damieh on the River Jordan. The XX Corps was also instructed to advance on Nablus. The detachment commanded by General Chaytor in the Jordan valley was given several different tasks: they were to maintain the deception that another raid was planned on Amman, in the hope that Turkish troops would be redeployed accordingly. They also played a role in concealing the departure of mounted troops from the Jordan valley to the coast in preparation for the new offensive.

Beyond these acts of deception, the main role of Chaytor's force was to protect the right flank of XX Corps.

★

Allenby's plan also assumed that the Arabs would play an important but secondary role in the final offensive against the Turkish army. They were given a specific task in relation to the disruption of Turkish communications north and west of Deraa, and were asked to isolate the town days before the main British offensive. Such an action would disrupt supplies to the Seventh and Eighth Armies at the front line in Palestine and prevent Turkish reinforcements arriving from the north. It would also add to the Turks' conviction that the weight of the British attack was to fall in this area, causing the transfer of further troops from what was intended to be the main area of action.

Lawrence, Joyce and others had been preparing Arab forces for this final effort for some time. The new regular Arab army, commanded by Jafar Pasha, had now reached a strength of some 8,000 men. Former Arab prisoners of war, who had served in the Turkish army, formed the majority of the rank and file. The transfer of 2,000 riding camels from the British army in Palestine provided the basis of an Arab mobile column, which formed an important component of the new army. These troops were supported by a small British contingent, which operated in armoured cars. Supplementing these regular troops were the Bedouin tribesmen who had played such a key role in spreading the revolt northwards from its origins deep in the Hejaz. It was decided that these irregular forces should assemble early in September some 50 miles east of Amman at the oasis of Azrak, under the command of Sherif Nasir of Medina, a veteran of the earliest days of the revolt. They were described by Lawrence as follows:

> four hundred and fifty camel corps of the Arab regular army, four Arab Vickers, twenty Arab Hotchkiss, a French battery of four mountain quick-firing guns, two British aeroplanes, three British armoured cars with necessary tenders, a demolition company of Egyptian Camel Corps and a section of camel-ghurkas . . . This made our total force one thousand strong, and its prospects were so sure that we made no provision (and had no means) for getting it back again.[25]

Lawrence knew that the presence of a large force at Azrak could not be kept secret from the Turks for long. He was confident, however, that they would see it as further proof that the Arabs were about to launch an attack on Amman, which was almost due west of Azrak and much closer to them than the real target – Deraa. Steps were taken to spread rumours among local Arabs of an impending attack on Amman by Feisal's army. This deception on the Arab side would reinforce the Turkish expectation, carefully nurtured by Allenby, that the British were planning a third attack on Es Salt.

These plans were threatened by evidence of a Turkish intention to launch a new offensive from Amman. In order to delay such an offensive and allow the Arabs time to concentrate their forces, a diversionary attack was launched from Aqaba early in August 1918. The two remaining companies of the Imperial Camel Corps (which was in the process of being disbanded) were loaned to Feisal for this purpose. During a march that was to last forty-one days, the corps attacked various Turkish positions along the Hejaz railway. This included the enemy post at Mudawara, which had survived several previous attempts to capture it. Apart from its intended purpose, the attack also had the effect of adding weight to the impression that the main British attack would fall in the east.

The need for complete secrecy was at the heart of Allenby's plan to break through on the coast while persuading the enemy that he intended to attack on the other flank. The British went to considerable lengths to conceal their real intentions. This was all the more necessary because Allenby's plans required three full divisions – Fourth Cavalry, Australian Mounted and the 60th – and other units to be transferred from the Jordan valley and the Judean hills to the coast. The movement of such a large number of troops was carried out in great secrecy only during the hours of darkness. The journey to the front line was described by Charles Harvey, an officer of the Imperial Service Cavalry Brigade:

> Still trekking! We have been at it a month all but two days now. We left Deiran, the place near Ramleh where we spent our spells out of the Jordan valley, on September 17th at night: hid . . . in orange groves north of Jaffa all the 18th so that not even our own aeroplanes could find us, and marched that night to just behind the coastal section of the front line [in readiness for the offensive which began the next day].[26]

When they arrived in the area north of Jaffa they were concealed in orange groves and olive woods and shared the tents of British units that were already camping in the area. These tents were intended to have excess capacity so that all the new arrivals could be accommodated within them. No increase in the number of tents would be made and aerial reconnaissance would thus find no evidence of a growth in the number of troops concentrated there. All movement in the camps was prohibited between the hours of 4.30 a.m. and 6.30 p.m. and no fires were permitted. The watering of horses took place, if necessary, between 12 noon and 2 p.m., when the Royal Air Force kept enemy aircraft at bay in order to conceal British movements. This was of less concern, however, by the summer of 1918, since by now the Royal Air Force dominated the skies of northern Palestine and it was virtually impossible for an enemy aircraft to fly freely over British lines. In Allenby's view:

> the chief factor in the secrecy maintained must be attributed . . . to the supremacy in the air which had been obtained by the Royal Air Force. The process of wearing down the enemy's aircraft had been going on all the summer. During one week in June [1918] 100 hostile aeroplanes had crossed our lines. During the last week in August this number had decreased to eighteen. In the next few days a number were shot down, with the result that only four ventured to cross our lines during the period of concentration.[27]

Although large numbers of British troops were moved from the Jordan valley, the Allies spent much time in creating the impression that a major attack would soon be launched against the enemy right. Several measures were taken to convince the enemy that British forces were being massed in the Jordan valley rather than being withdrawn, as was actually the case. When the Desert Mounted Corps departed for the coast, their tents were left behind and their horses were replaced with 15,000 dummies made with canvas.

Action was also taken to give the appearance of continuing activity on the extreme east of the British line. New bridges were built across the Jordan. Radio signals continued to be transmitted from the Desert Mounted Corps' headquarters at Talaat ed Dumm long after these troops had left for the Mediterranean shore. Large quantities of supplies were sought in local markets. Rumours were spread that GHQ was about to commandeer the main hotel in Jerusalem as its new base. To reinforce the impression of normality, it was announced that a race meeting was to be held near Jaffa on 19 September. At the same time the actual objectives of the attack were not explained to brigade or regimental commanders until two or three days before the attack was due to begin.

There is no doubt that this elaborate deception for concentrating forces on the left of the British line was successful. It convinced the Turks that the main enemy attack would be launched on the British right and the Turks responded accordingly. Captured Turkish maps dated 17 September bore no record of the substantial movement of troops from the Jordan valley to the coast. In the view of the British official history, the 'enemy was thoroughly deceived, wholly unaware of the devastating blow that was about to be dealt him'.[28]

If the Turks had any remaining doubts about British intentions, the preliminary operations, which Allenby launched on 16 September, were designed to concentrate his attention on Deraa and his left flank, as well as disrupting his communications. The Royal Air Force launched a series of raids on Deraa, the first time it had been subject to aerial attack during the war. The bombing was not sufficiently intensive, however, to enable Lawrence and the Arabs to launch a direct assault on the town as originally planned. Instead, as Lawrence described it, the Arabs would 'carry out a flying attack on the northern, western and southern railways at Deraa'.[29] The line south of Deraa was given priority in this operation as it would have the double benefit of preventing the movement to Deraa of troops based in the south and also adding to Turkish fears of an Arab military threat to Amman.

The first attack, on 14 September, directed at a point on the railway south of Deraa, had to be abandoned when it was found that the area was heavily guarded by local Bedouin who were in Turkish pay. As the Arab troops involved in this abortive attack were needed for the assault north of Deraa, the second attempt to the south was made by a detachment of armoured cars alone. Led by Lawrence, this unit, on 16 September, destroyed a bridge on the line south of Deraa. Meanwhile, on the following day, the main force had moved north of Deraa and, as Lawrence wrote, was soon in control of a section of the Hejaz railway: 'the southern ten miles of the Damascus line was freely ours . . . It was the only railway to Palestine and the Hejaz and I could hardly believe our fortune; hardly believe that our word to Allenby was fulfilled so simply and so soon.'[30]

Before completing their work with an attack on the branch line to

Palestine, the force spent a day demolishing the track north of Deraa. They soon attracted the attention of the Turkish air force but, according to Lawrence, it made little impact on their progress:

> with some energetic encouragement, the process of demolition got under way, only to be threatened with interruption by the appearance of eight Turkish aeroplanes, hastily sent up from Deraa. Although untrained in air precautions the Arabs' instinct taught them the right action, and they scattered so effectively that after an hour's rain of bombs and bullets there were only two casualties. Then, providentially, the Arab army's one surviving aeroplane, an obsolete B.E.12 . . . appeared on the scene and drew off the attention of the Turkish machines, although at the sacrifice of itself.[31]

As a result of these attacks, all through railway traffic to Palestine from the north was brought to a halt. Valuable resources were diverted to help repair the damage to the Hejaz railway. Expecting an offensive to be launched during this period, Liman responded to these preliminary attacks by moving some reserves in the wrong direction – from Haifa to Deraa. The real focal point of the British offensive was still unclear to the Turks, even though they learned from a havildar who had deserted from an Indian unit and was captured on 17 September that a great assault was to be launched by the Allies in the coastal area of Palestine. Liman dismissed him as an agent planted by the British and refused to abandon any ground on his account, despite the pleas of his subordinates General Djevad Pasha, Eighth Army commander, and Colonel Refet Bey, XXII Corps commander. According to Refet, he 'begged to be allowed to withdraw his front on the coast so that the bombardment predicted by the deserter "might uselessly exhaust itself in battering empty trenches" '.[32] Although a tactical withdrawal by the Turks would not have undermined Allenby's plan, it would have made the operation much more difficult and risky. When it became clear at the beginning of the offensive that the Turks were still in position, British staff officers, as reported in the official history, 'declared that, though all was yet before them, they then felt that all was won. The enemy was there indeed, and so doomed.'[33]

Within two days of these preliminary moves, the Allied forces were positioned correctly to carry out their allotted roles. On 18 September 1918, the first stages of the great offensive were initiated by units of General Chetwode's XX Corps, which were based in the Judean hills. The corps, reduced to two divisions (10th and 53rd), occupied a front of some 20 miles and was charged with capturing the town of Nablus. A direct attack was ruled out because the main road from Bireh to Nablus was heavily defended and the Allies would have no advantage of surprise. As an alternative, a converging movement from both flanks was decided on. The strength of the corps was concentrated in the flanks, leaving the centre relatively exposed. This central area was monitored by a detachment of XX Corps, including units of the Worcestershire Yeomanry.

A preliminary action began during the night of 18/19 September when the 53rd Division on the right flank moved forward with the aim of negotiating the Wadi es Samieh, an obstacle to rapid movement in the Judean hills. Once this deep wadi was crossed, there were no serious barriers to the division's further progress as it was to advance along a watershed. The division would need to move quickly as soon as XXI Corps launched its attack because it was expected to block possible escape routes from the Nablus area into the Jordan valley. The operation to cross the Wadi es Samieh, which was led by the 160th Brigade, took the Turks by surprise and was a complete success. Later the same night, it was followed by an assault by the 10th Division further to the west, which was also largely successful.

This operation had barely come to an end when the main offensive was launched. Heavy artillery opened up and the Royal Air Force took to the skies. There was a gun every 50 yards – 385 in total, of which 315 were field guns or howitzers. Air attacks were primarily aimed at Turkish army command structures and communications. These included the headquarters of the Seventh Army at Nablus and of the Eighth Army at Tul Keram, together with the telephone exchange at El Afule. At the same time, Allied troops were largely immune from sustained air attacks as there were few enemy aircraft still capable of flying. Lawrence went as far as to say that air power played an 'indispensable part in Allenby's scheme . . . it was the RAF which had converted the Turkish retreat into rout, which had abolished their telephone and telegraph connections, had blocked their lorry columns, scattered their infantry units.'[34]

The front of the XXI Corps was even shorter than that of the XX Corps – a distance of some 15 miles, although the actual fighting was contained within about 10 miles as parts of the front were not suitable for launching an offensive. The whole front extended from the Mediterranean just to the north of Arsuf to Rafat in the Judean foothills. The right flank, based in the foothills, was held by the French contingent and the 54th Division. The French were instructed to seize a Turkish-held ridge opposite Rafat and act as the pivot for the XXI Corps as it wheeled to the right. To the right of the French was the 54th Division, which covered the front from Rafat to Mejdl Yaba. The 54th Division was ordered to advance on Kefr Kasim and then proceed in a north-easterly direction.

The main British line, which ran immediately to the west of these positions, crossed an exposed plain that did not feature in the first stage of the planned offensive. Any attacking force that advanced directly across the plain would be highly vulnerable to defensive fire from well-entrenched Turkish forces. It was decided to tackle these positions in the second phase of the offensive by an attack on their western flank. Beyond the open plain, the line was held by three divisions: the Third (Indian), the 75th and the Seventh (Indian). Their immediate task was to take the Turkish positions – known as the Tabsor defences – directly in front of them; they were then to capture the line that extended from Jiljulieh to Et Tireh.

Beyond these defences to the west was a second gap in the line before the coastal entrenchments – held on the Allied side by the 60th Division – were reached. This division was to break the enemy line and advance to the Nahr el Falik. Through this half-open door would pass the Fifth Cavalry Division on its way north. Once the cavalry was safely on its way, the 60th Division, protected by the Fifth Australian Light Horse Brigade on its left, would advance in a north-easterly direction to Tul Keram. It was here, by the Mediterranean shore, that the success or failure of the whole venture would be determined.

# 9

# *The Battle of Megiddo*

THE BATTLE OF Sharon – as the engagement on the British left south of Haifa was often known – finally began at 4.30 a.m. on 19 September 1918. According to Charles Harvey, who was serving as brigade major of the Imperial Service Cavalry Brigade, 'all was absolutely still and peaceful that night . . . [until] 4.30 [when] the artillery belched forth their fire'.[1] The British gunners 'fired like fury until five'. A short, intensive artillery bombardment preceded the infantry assault by some thirty minutes. More than 1,000 shells a minute poured into the enemy lines. The attack was supported by two torpedo-boat destroyers, which fired on the coastal road to the north. The Turks could not match the impact of the British artillery; according to the official history, the 'intensity and accuracy of [its] counter-battery fire caused the Turkish [shelling] to be ragged and intermittent'. Within minutes of the pre-dawn attack, the 'assaulting infantry swarmed into the [Turkish] trenches'.[2] The British artillery then lengthened its range on to the second line of enemy trenches.

Within a few hours the action had been successful along the whole extent of the line. As soon as the infantry had gained the first line of Turkish trenches, the British field artillery moved forward and the horse artillery was prepared to join the cavalry. The heavy artillery continued to fire at a lengthened range. When the bombardment began, they fired at 4,000 yards; by 8 a.m. it had been extended to 15,000 yards and soon came to an end because the Turkish army was out of range.

The intensity of fighting varied considerably along the front line. On the British right flank, the French detachment and the 54th

Division both experienced strong resistance, but were able to achieve their objectives without undue delay. This was of considerable importance since the French position served as the pivot for the rest of the British line. Further west, the Third (Lahore) Division advanced rapidly and seized the enemy's first line of defence between Bir Adas and the Hadrah road. On its left the 75th Division attacked the Tabsor defences, while the Seventh (Meerut) Division assaulted the enemy works west of Tabsor. The defending enemy forces, which had not been expecting an attack, returned the British artillery fire, but in most cases it fell behind the advancing infantry. The Turkish forces in the front line were soon forced to capitulate. The Third (Lahore) Division turned right following this initial success and made a flank attack on the Turkish defences at Jiljulieh and Kalkilieh, while the 75th Division advanced to Et Tireh, 'a strongly fortified village standing on a sandy ridge', which fell at about 11 a.m.[3] The Seventh (Meerut) Division advanced northwards along the coastal plain before turning to the right to the north of Et Tireh.

On the coast, the Turkish defences did little to impede the advance of the 60th Division which, despite increased efforts by the Turks, made rapid progress. According to Charles Harvey, resistance at the second line of defences was a 'bit stiffer, and the third line they had to fight for'.[4] Nevertheless, the British had advanced some 7,000 yards in two and a half hours and, by 7.30 a.m., they had established a bridgehead at the mouth of the Nahr el Falik. In accordance with Allenby's plan, the Fifth Cavalry Division galloped through the captured positions and advanced rapidly northwards, over the Plain of Sharon – described by Private Wilson, 179th Machine Gun Corps, as 'a desolate moorland which yet here and there will be springing into green despite Turk and torpitude'.[5] The 60th Division followed in its wake, turning north-eastwards in the direction of Tul Keram, its left flank protected by the Fifth Australian Light Horse Brigade. Rapid progress was also made further to the east of the first breakthrough, as Charles Harvey recorded:

> The other Indian cavalry division went through another gap a little further inland shortly after, and moved up parallel to us. Our leading brigade galloped or trotted the 18 miles to Hudeira, which they reached at 10.30, and caught 500 unsuspecting prisoners of whom about 60 were Germans.[6]

The scale and intensity of the Allied offensive had taken the Turks completely by surprise. They had no knowledge of the shift of British troops to the left until they received, at the last moment, accurate details of the attack from the deserting havildar whom they had captured. However, as we have seen, the Turkish authorities questioned the reliability of this information and decided not to act on it. The role of the Royal Air Force continued to be critical and there is no doubt, in the view of the British official history, that it

> contributed vastly to the day's great victory. Its reports of the advance had almost always been the first to reach the eyes of the commander-in-chief, but its most valuable service had been the spreading of destruction, death and terror behind enemy lines. All the nerve centres had been paralysed by constant bombing.[7]

With command in the air, the RAF succeeded at an early stage in the battle in disrupting the Turkish army's main communications links, including those between Liman and his forces. As a result, Liman lacked access to up-to-date information about the progress of the Allied offensive or the condition of his own troops. In the absence of this information he was unable to develop new plans or to communicate new orders to his men. In the event those forces rapidly ceased to exist, an outcome that Liman had entirely failed to foresee: 'I made only one mistake in my calculations. I hoped that individual units would only be pressed back step by step: I did not expect the complete failure of whole divisions.'[8]

The offensive caused the rapid collapse of the Turkish Eighth Army, with survivors – described by the British official history as no more than 'mere bands of terrified fugitives'[9] – escaping northwards across the coastal plain in the direction of Tul Keram. From there they made for Messudieh junction as a staging post in their escape route across the Jordan. The progress of the retreating army was hindered by continuous aerial attacks by the RAF. During the afternoon of 19 September the road between Tul Keram and Messudieh became blocked and the Fifth Australian Light Horse Brigade moved in to take prisoners. As Allenby reported, in his official record of the campaign:

> Great confusion reigned at Tul Keram. Bodies of troops, guns, motor lorries, and transport of every description were endeavouring to

escape along the road leading to Messudie and Nablus. This road, which follows the railway up a narrow valley, was already crowded with troops and transport. The confusion was added to by the persistent attacks of the Royal Air Force and Australian Flying Corps, from which there was no escape. Great havoc was caused, and, in several places, the road was blocked by overturned lorries . . . Later in the evening an Australian regiment, having made a detour, succeeded in reaching a hill four miles east of Tul Keram, overlooking the road. As a result, a large amount of transport, and many guns, fell into our hands.[10]

The 60th Division had achieved its objective of capturing Tul Keram before the end of the first day, after a hard march of 17 miles from the starting line. Beyond Tul Keram the line achieved by the XXI Corps by nightfall extended eastwards to Et Taiyibeh (Seventh Division), Felamieh (Third Division), Bidieh (54th Division) and Rafat (French detachment), with the 75th Division in corps reserve at Et Tireh.

There is no doubt that the XXI Corps had fully achieved the objectives that Allenby had set for it during the opening stages of the campaign. The Turkish Eighth Army had been routed and the coastal route to the north had been opened up for the cavalry. Under Allenby's plans, the cavalry was to press its advance northwards with the aim of capturing Beisan and El Afule at the earliest opportunity. The enemy was only to be engaged en route if it posed a direct obstacle to achieving these objectives. Before the main attack began, the Fourth and Fifth Cavalry Divisions had been based at Sarona and Selmeh but they moved up behind the infantry during the early hours of 19 September. On the British left, the Fifth Cavalry Division was positioned behind the 60th Division, with the Fourth Cavalry Division to its right behind the Seventh (Indian) Division.

Some two hours after the main attack began, at 6.30 a.m., the Fifth Cavalry Division advanced along the beach, using the adjoining cliffs to provide it with cover. Within two hours the division had crossed the Nahr el Falik and was moving northwards along the coast, as Allenby had planned. On the right of the Fifth Cavalry Division, the Fourth Division moved northwards in parallel, although it started later and made slower progress. It was delayed because of difficulties in passing through the barbed-wire defences of the Turkish front line but, even so, it had cleared the Nahr el Falik by 10 a.m. Despite this slow start the Fourth Cavalry Division was to cover 85 miles in thirty-six hours, reaching Beisan during the late afternoon of 20 September.

Both divisions made good progress along the coastal route and the Fifth Division reached Liktera on the Nahr el Mefjir just before noon. The Fourth Division also reached the Nahr el Mefjir a few miles upstream not long afterwards. Having made such good progress the two divisions needed to rest and resupply before the general advance could be restarted. They were now responsible for feeding several hundred Turkish prisoners of war who had been taken captive on the way north. During this short break in the advance, a squadron of the Fifth Cavalry Division was sent ahead to reconnoitre the passage across the Samarian hills to Abu Shusheh, en route for Nazareth and El Afule. The Fourth Division dispatched a brigade supported by armoured cars to capture the Musmus defile which gave access to El Lejjun (Megiddo) at the mouth of the pass. Beyond this point could be seen the Plain of Esdraelon with the town of El Afule in the centre.

The Fifth Cavalry Division left Liktera and advanced in a north-easterly direction, moving through the pass and out on to the plain during the early hours of 20 September. At this point it was reduced to two brigades – the 13th and 14th – as the 15th Brigade and the artillery had been delayed until daylight when they could negotiate the pass more easily. As soon as they were free to do so, the 14th Brigade moved towards El Afule, while the 13th Brigade advanced straight towards Nazareth, where Liman's headquarters was based.

The 13th Brigade reached the outskirts of the town at 5.30 a.m. on 20 September. Nazareth, Charles Harvey recorded, was

> picturesquely situated on the inward slopes of a cup with the rim of hills surrounding it entirely on the north, north-east, and north-west, but with the rim a little lower to the south, so that you can look right over the Esdraelon Plain to the Judean Hills to the south.[11]

As a result of the destruction of Turkish communications, Liman had no warning of the arrival of British forces, nor was he aware of how much ground had been lost by the Turkish army in the first twenty-four hours. For Liman personally, however, all was not yet lost. The British did not know the exact location of his headquarters and would need to conduct a house-to-house search of the town in order to find it. It became clear that such a search would face heavy opposition from the occupying troops, who soon regained their composure. Street fighting then developed, as the British official history relates: 'machine guns opened from the buildings on the high ground, while German clerks and orderlies boldly fired down upon the troops from balconies and windows.'[12] The British had to work hard to gain the upper hand, particularly as mounted troops were not well equipped for this kind of combat.

Before long the British had occupied the Germania Hotel in the town centre, and located Liman's headquarters in a private house some 200 yards away. Although important official documents were seized, there was no sign of the commander-in-chief or his immediate staff. They had escaped, possibly minutes earlier, to the French orphanage on the outskirts of the town. From here Liman directed three attacks on the British troops advancing through the centre of Nazareth, eventually forcing them back in the direction of Haifa: as he later wrote, the 'bold attempt by the British brigade to capture the staff of the Group of Armies, after a hard ride during the night had failed'.[13] On their return to the plain the British took about 1,500 prisoners (including many Germans) with them. The 13th Brigade subsequently reoccupied Nazareth on 21 September. As a result of this operation, Charles Harvey reported,

> the G.H.Q. of the Turkish army was . . . destroyed and all communications were cut, and from that hour onwards the Turks who were in the firing line received no orders from their headquarters. This was largely responsible for their total defeat and capture.[14]

Meanwhile, Liman had left Nazareth at 1.15 p.m. in the direction of Tiberias, having taken one of the northern exits from the town that the British had failed to block. Such roads were rocky and inaccessible and it was impossible for the British to seal off all the potential escape routes before entering the town. Liman made his way to Deraa, leaving there for Damascus on 22 September. On his arrival he tried to organize resistance to the Allied advance but had little success. The Turkish Second Army was finally placed under his direct command but its battalions were largely devoid of staff.

★

While Liman was engaged in the thankless task of raising more troops, the Allied advance continued to make progress. It was difficult to see what force – or combination of forces – could stop it now. After crossing the Nahr el Mefjir, the Fourth Cavalry Division passed through the Musmus defile during the hours of darkness and entered the plain at El Lejjun by dawn on 20 September. It soon encountered the small advance guard of a Turkish force which Liman had dispatched from Nazareth and El Afule with the aim of blocking the defile in case a British cavalry raid had been planned. As soon as these troops had been captured, the British saw the main enemy force, which consisted of six companies equipped with 12 machine guns. The Second Lancers, the leading regiment of the Fourth Cavalry Division, supported by several armoured cars, launched an attack on the Turks, who were once more taken by surprise. Within a few minutes, 46 Turks had been killed and 500 taken prisoner.

The route ahead was now clear and the Fourth Cavalry Division reached El Afule at about 8 a.m. The 14th Brigade of the Fifth Cavalry Division arrived there at about the same time. There was clear evidence that the Turks had not expected the enemy's early arrival and that they had evacuated the town in a hurry. There were large quantities of military supplies in good condition, the railway was intact and there were eight aircraft ready to fly from El Afule airstrip. In fact the unexpected appearance of the British army did nothing to prevent the arrival of a regular German mail delivery, as Charles Harvey explained:

> On the afternoon of the 20th [September], one aeroplane landed there with all the official mail which had been brought in a submarine from Germany to Beirut and thence by air again. He landed and walked towards the aerodrome when he suddenly saw Indian soldiers guarding it instead of Turks. He rushed back to his machine and started the engine, but before he could get off the ground one of our armoured cars had overtaken him and caught him and his mails.[15]

The Fifth Division was ordered to occupy El Afule while the Fourth Division pressed on to Beisan. It advanced down the Valley of Jezreel and arrived at Beisan at about 4.30 p.m., where the Turkish garrison surrendered without much of a fight. Although the division had now covered 85 miles since the offensive began, one of its regiments, the 19th Lancers, was dispatched to the River Jordan, a ride of a further 12 miles, during the night. They succeeded in taking control of a railway bridge over the Jordan at Jisr el Mejamie and thus blocking a Turkish escape route to the east.

With the main cavalry force in control of El Afule and Beisan, the remainder of the mounted troops had reached the Plain of Esdraelon during 20 September. The 15th Brigade of the Fifth Cavalry Division, which had delayed its departure from Liktera, joined the rest of the division at El Afule later in the day. The Australian Mounted Division, which had been following in the path of the Fourth and Fifth Cavalry Divisions, arrived at Lejjun at 11 a.m. the same day. The Third Australian Light Horse Brigade moved on to Jenin, where it arrived in the afternoon. The Turkish garrison, which had no idea it was about to be attacked, rapidly abandoned any resistance in the face of a superior force. The brigade remained at Jenin to await the arrival of Turkish units retreating from Nablus and Tul Keram as the British infantry maintained its offensive pressure further south.

It had thus taken no more than thirty-six hours for the British cavalry to encircle the retreating Turkish armies. Now that the key towns were under British control, the Turkish Seventh and Eighth Armies would find their natural escape routes barred. With their command and communications systems in ruins – and in the absence of good quality intelligence – they were unable to develop a coordinated response to this difficult situation. The Turks had little idea of how bad their predicament was and were not yet aware that the only way out of the battlefield still available was to the east across the River Jordan. All the direct routes to the north had already been closed.

The task of closing the remaining escape routes into the Jordan valley had been given to XX Corps on the right of the main British line. Allenby's plan was based on the assumption that XX Corps would only begin its advance when XXI Corps had succeeded in breaking through the Turkish lines and was moving north to its next objectives further along the coast. At about noon on 19 September, the high command decided that these conditions had been met and the XX Corps was ordered to begin its attack later that night. Apart from blocking the enemy's remaining escape routes, XX Corps, which consisted of the 10th and 53rd Divisions, was ordered to advance on Nablus. On the right of the 10th Division, the 53rd Division was to move along the route of a watershed, which provided a clearly defined route for it to take. This ridge proved difficult to negotiate and progress was relatively slow. To the east of the ridge the hills ran steeply down to the River Jordan; to the west there was a more gradual descent to the road from Jerusalem to Nablus.

The 10th Division was concentrated on the far left of this line and operated to the west of the Nablus road. The hills in this area were marked by a series of ridges and the main ridge was identified by the three villages located on it – Iskaka, Selfit and Furkhah. The Turkish front line centred on Furkhah and was directly opposite the British positions manned by the 10th Division. The Turkish line was well defined and was specifically designed to withstand a direct attack from the south. The British were well aware of this feature and sought to give the Turks the impression that they intended to attack from this direction. However, their real intention was to mount a flanking attack on the western end of the ridge. The 10th Division's assault on Furkhah began at 7.45 p.m. on 19 September. The enemy was taken by surprise and although they fought strongly the British prevailed in the end. The attack was also well timed as any delay would have given the Turks the opportunity to withdraw from their positions.

The Turks were indeed planning to leave the area, having heard of the success of the massive British attack in the coastal area of Palestine. The 10th Division moved forwards and by 4.30 a.m. on 20 September the left column was near Kefr Haris, while the right column was at Selfit. However, further progress was slow owing to effective action by enemy rearguards. On the rest of XX Corps' front, progress was also slow, with the 53rd Division encountering heavy resistance throughout 20 September. To the left of the 10th Division, the infantry of the XXI Corps made steady but unspectacular progress. The Third and Seventh (Indian) Divisions proceeded north-east through the hills towards ancient Samaria. The 60th Division moved east along the Tul Keram–Nablus road. By the end of 20 September, more than forty hours after the offensive had begun, the main British achievements were the expulsion of the enemy from the coastal plain and the success of the cavalry in blocking his main lines of retreat.

Elsewhere the situation was more mixed. The infantry's progress in the Judean hills had been much less spectacular, largely because the enemy had far greater opportunities to delay the British advance. The infantry was instructed to maintain the pressure on 21 September; in particular, priority was to be given to sealing off the enemy's escape route to the bridge over the River Jordan at Jisr ed

Damieh, a task which would entail capturing the high ground to the north and north-east of Nablus.

The British infantry advanced more rapidly on 21 September. Enemy resistance faltered during the early morning and the 10th Division was able to reach Nablus by noon. They were met by the Fifth Australian Light Horse Brigade which arrived there from the west at about the same time. There is no doubt, in the words of the British official history, that the 10th Division's

> final effort had been magnificent, and in particular the march on Nablus deserves an honourable place in our military records . . . in forty-eight hours individual men cannot have had more than five or six of uneasy sleep, snatched at intervals. In the last few miles it was only the driving force from above, through divisional commander, brigadier, battalion commanders, and their own resolution, aided by the inspiration of victory, which had kept them on their feet.[16]

By this point the Turkish Seventh and Eighth Armies had effectively ceased to exist. Most of the Eighth Army had already been captured. Large numbers had been taken in the opening stages of the offensive or in the pursuit up the coastal plain. Many of the survivors were subsequently captured when they marched towards Jenin and were rounded up by the Australians. Surviving members of the Seventh Army (together with the remnants of the Eighth) had left Nablus during the night of 20/21 September, planning to pass through Beisan on their way to the River Jordan. They never made it. During the early hours of 21 September, as they moved along a road cut in the side of the Wadi Fara, these troops came under heavy and sustained air attack. The bombardment continued for four hours, blocking the road and forcing the Turks to abandon their vehicles. In the chaos that followed there was a race to find cover in the hills. A few managed to escape across the Jordan, but most of the survivors were rounded up in the hills over the following few days. Over a thousand Turkish vehicles and 90 guns were later recovered from this 'valley of death'.

This phase of the offensive – the most significant part of the Battle of Megiddo – was now complete, with one exception: the capture of the port of Haifa, which remained in Turkish hands. Described by Charles Harvey as a place of 'extraordinary beauty . . . The view from the top of Mount Carmel across the bay to Acre is perfectly lovely',[17] the port was a crucial staging post in the British assault, as they were reminded during the early hours of 22 September when, on the Acre road west of the town, the 18th Lancers were attacked by a Turkish battalion based at Haifa. The Turks were soon defeated with 30 killed and 300 taken prisoner. At about the same time Allenby met Chauvel at Megiddo and warned him to be prepared for further action, which would include, as a first step, the seizure of Haifa and Acre. With these towns in British hands, the conquest of Palestine would be complete.

Orders were then issued to the Fifth Cavalry Division, which was now based at Nazareth, to take both Haifa and Acre, although by this time intelligence reports had been received that the Turkish army had already evacuated Haifa. In the light of this information a small detachment of armoured cars was sent to occupy the town but it soon became clear that these reports were inaccurate. As the armoured cars reached the outskirts of Haifa they were greeted with a heavy barrage of artillery fire, indicating that the Turkish garrison was still in position. It was clear that a much more substantial force would be needed to free the port. The entire Fifth Cavalry Division was therefore dispatched with orders to take Acre as well as Haifa. The 13th Brigade was allocated the task of capturing Acre, which it did without serious difficulty, and some 200 members of the garrison were taken prisoner.

Events did not proceed so smoothly at Haifa where, according to Harvey, 'it soon became apparent that the enemy meant to resist, and they were slinging about some heavy shells pretty freely'.[18] Harvey, serving in the Fifth Cavalry Division, summarized what happened:

> we had a pretty fight . . . to take this place. It was the only real opposition the Turks put up in the whole show. However, we eventually galloped in at a place which anyone who saw the ground would have called impregnable. So it would have been if there had been Britishers behind the guns and machine guns instead of Turks.[19]

The strength of the Turkish defensive position was attributable in part to the fact that their guns had been effectively positioned on the dominating heights of Mount Carmel. The approach road from the east ran between the mount and the Nahr el Muqatta. This river could not be crossed because it was surrounded by marshland and the road was protected by a detachment of Turkish machine-gunners.

On 23 September, the Fifth Cavalry Division approached Haifa. Its first priority was to silence the Turkish guns on top of Mount Carmel: a squadron of the Mysore Lancers (reinforced by a squadron of the Sherwood Rangers) was dispatched for this purpose. At 2 p.m., after a delay to give the Mysores a chance to move into position, the Jodhpur Lancers (supported by the remaining Mysore squadrons) launched the main attack, advancing on the Turks blocking the road ahead. Harvey continues:

> The leading regiment and machine-guns acted as a fire pivot, the battery fired on to the enemy positions, and one regiment was sent from about three miles behind to gallop the place. It was a ticklish situation as an impassable stream . . . forced them to wheel to the left and go through the narrow defile along the main road. However, a stout-hearted body of men on galloping horses takes a lot of stopping and, within half an hour from the word 'go', Haifa was ours.[20]

There was now nothing to prevent a British advance on the town. As the attack was being made, the squadrons climbing Mount Carmel reached their destination. They charged the Turkish positions and took 17 guns and 1,350 prisoners of war. There is little doubt that the relative ease with which the British captured Haifa is explained by the collapse in Turkish morale following the defeat of the Seventh and Eighth Armies; more highly motivated troops could almost certainly have held on to the Turks' well-protected positions for much longer. The capture of Haifa eased the British army's supply problems considerably since it meant that stores could be unloaded at the port and transferred thence to the Palestine railway network.

★

With the capture of Haifa the first phase of the Megiddo offensive was virtually complete, apart from some minor mopping-up operations in which the Fourth Cavalry Division played an important role. The overwhelming majority of the Turkish Seventh and Eighth Armies had been captured and no more than a few hundred managed to escape the trap. Only the Turkish Fourth Army to the east of the Jordan remained intact and it was to the destruction of this force that Allenby now gave priority. At this point, he summarized the position in a letter to his wife dated 23 September 1918:

I've been going round hospitals today . . . I've told them that they've done the biggest thing in the war – having totally destroyed two armies in thirty-six hours. The VII and VIII Armies, now non-existent, were the best troops in the Turkish Empire, and were strongly backed by Germans and Austrians . . .[21]

Unlike the coastal area, the Jordan valley was notable for its inactivity during the first three days of the British offensive. The Turkish Fourth Army, which was based in the Jordan valley and on the hills of Moab, remained at its stations on the defensive. Commanded by Djemal the Lesser from headquarters in Amman, it consisted of II Corps (24th Division and Third Cavalry Division) and VII Corps (48th and Composite Divisions, including the 146th German Regiment).

The Turkish Fourth Army remained in position partly because it lacked reliable information about what was happening west of the Jordan. It was not until 22 September, after the extent of the Turkish defeat had become clear, that Djemal the Lesser decided to order a retreat. Although advised by Liman two days earlier to pull his forces back – advice reinforced a day later by an order to that effect – Djemal had decided to await the arrival in Amman of II Corps, following its withdrawal from Maan and other southerly points on the Hejaz railway. Such delays however were potentially costly since, hour by hour, events were turning against the Turkish army. Apart from the progress of the British offensive, the Arab revolt was gaining momentum and Arab forces were active in the area separating the Fourth Army from Deraa and the north. It was not long before the Arabs were to cut the Hejaz railway, breaking Djemal's supply lines with the north.

A more significant factor in determining the fate of the Turkish army in the east was the force assembled under the command of Major-General Chaytor. Consisting of the Anzac Mounted Division, the 20th Indian Infantry Brigade and other units, it was charged with occupying the attention of the Fourth Army while the coastal offensive was launched and preventing the transfer of Turkish units to the main battlefield west of the Jordan. Chaytor was also instructed to protect the right flank of XX Corps on his left as it advanced. As he moved forward Chaytor was ordered to capture the river crossing at Jisr ed Damieh and then advance on Es Salt and Amman, both of which had eluded two previous British attempts to capture them earlier in the year.

While the Fourth Army remained stationary, Chaytor's force was on the move. On 21 September, the New Zealand Mounted Brigade advanced northwards along the west bank of the Jordan towards the Nablus–Jisr ed Damieh road. Despite some opposition on the way, it reached the road during the early hours of 22 September and, within a few hours, had captured the vital river crossing at Jisr ed Damieh: an important step in sealing the ring that prevented the escape of survivors of the Turkish Seventh and Eighth Armies. By this time Chaytor was in receipt of intelligence reports confirming that, during 22 September, the Fourth Army had finally started its long-delayed retreat. Within a day the Anzacs had taken Es Salt for the third time; this time they held on to it. Amman was taken during the late afternoon of 25 September after overcoming heavy resistance from Turkish rearguards. Chaytor then received instructions from headquarters to give priority to intercepting and defeating the Turkish II Corps as it retreated northwards.

Intelligence reports indicated that by the evening of 25 September this enemy force was about 30 miles south of Amman. Chaytor sent a brigade south to intercept the Turks, but sent another north of Amman to the Wadi el Hammam. This wadi provided the only water supply to the north of Amman and the enemy would need to stop there if it succeeded in evading the main body of Chaytor's force. A third brigade, together with the Indian infantry brigade, was positioned just east of Amman. On 28 September, as the Turks drew closer to Amman, the commander of the Second Australian Light Horse Brigade initiated talks with his Turkish counterpart. The Turks recognized the reality of their position but, being surrounded by hostile Bedouin of the Beni Sakhr tribe, they were unwilling to lay down their arms. The British were unable to muster sufficient manpower to guarantee the safety of the Turkish corps overnight and the two forces mounted a joint defence of the area, which was sufficient to deter an Arab attack. These 4,000 Turkish troops surrendered their weapons the following morning and were then taken to Amman and into captivity. The surrender of II Corps marked the successful completion of Chaytor's operations east of the River Jordan. All of his main objectives had been achieved and some 11,000 prisoners and 57 guns had been taken.

★

The Arabs, who were to play a useful role in hindering the withdrawal of the remnants of the Turkish Fourth Army, had first been

given news of Allenby's successful offensive and the destruction of the
Turkish Seventh and Eighth Armies on 21 September. The information was delivered by an RAF aircraft which landed at Azrak, the
forward base of the Arab army. It also brought a message from the
commander-in-chief expressing the hope that the Arabs would help
close the remaining gap across the Jordan to prevent the escape of
defeated Turkish troops. The aircraft also carried instructions from
Lieutenant-Colonel Alan Dawnay, who was responsible for liaison
between the EEF and the Arabs. The orders stressed the fact that
every escape route had been 'closed except, possibly, that east of the
Jordan by way of the Yarmuk Valley. If the Arabs can close this, too –
and close it in time – then, not a man, or gun, or wagon ought to
escape – *some* victory!'[22] The same aircraft brought a formal
command from Allenby expressing his wish that Feisal should not
'embark on any enterprise to the north, such as an advance on
Damascus, without first obtaining the consent of the commander-in-
chief'.[23]

The victory in Palestine was so complete that Allenby decided to
push forward immediately, before the Turks could establish a new
line of defence. His next objectives were to be Deraa and Damascus,
which were defended by no more than their regular Turkish garrisons, together with such survivors as had reached these towns from
the defeated armies in Palestine. Under these plans, the Fourth
Cavalry Division led by General Barrow would advance to Irbid en
route for Deraa. Australian troops under Chauvel would make for
Damascus by the direct route – part of the old caravan road from
Egypt to Syria – which would take them round the north end of
Lake Tiberias and on to Kuneitra, further north.[24] When Deraa and
Kuneitra had been taken, the forces under Barrow and Chauvel
would close on Damascus, while Chaytor would continue to hold
Amman. Arab forces were expected to cooperate with these plans
and in particular to join in actions against the Turkish Fourth Army.
When Lawrence was briefed on Allenby's intentions it was again
emphasized that there was to be no independent Arab offensive.
Assured, however, that Feisal would be given the opportunity to set
up an Arab government in Damascus, Lawrence returned to Azrak
on 22 September with this news, at the same time explaining to Feisal
the need to cut the railway south of Deraa to hold up any movement
northwards by the Turkish Fourth Army.

Feisal's troops attacked the Hejaz line repeatedly on 23–24

September and succeeded in damaging it beyond repair. By the time the retreating Turkish forces had reached the break in the line, they were forced to abandon their trucks and carriages and continue their journey by road – a departure which threw their retreat into chaos. The Arab force now moved to Sheikh Saad, north-west of Deraa, where it was able to watch over the Turkish line of retreat. From this vantage point, it could attack any units of the Turkish Fourth Army trying to go north, as well as any remnants of the formations that had fought in Palestine and now sought to escape through the Yarmuk valley. At the same time they would also be able to prevent the railway north of Deraa from being returned to use, thus forcing the Deraa garrison to choose between a retreat by road (leaving most of its equipment behind) or making a stand in the town itself, which would soon be surrounded by Barrow's cavalry as it arrived from the west.

On 25 September, Lawrence reported the Turkish force retreating from Amman as being about 4,000 strong. He expected 'to knock out nearly half. I think the others will not stand at Deraa (where they will find about two thousand of the relics of the Palestine army) but will go off to Damascus at once.'[25] On the same day Allenby gave Feisal good reason to reinvigorate his military actions against the Turks. The Foreign Office in London had confirmed that there was to be an Arab administration in Damascus and there was no reason to prevent Feisal going there. Allenby informed him that he was

> sending troops to Damascus and hope that they will arrive there in four or five days from today. I trust that Your Highness' forces will be able to cooperate, but you should not relax your pressure in the Deraa district, as it is of vital importance to cut off the Turkish forces which are retreating north from Maan, Amman and Es Salt.[26]

The way was now open for Feisal to establish an Arab government in Damascus which would assume responsibility for civil administration as soon as the Turks had left. To help to ensure this, the Arabs were given a free hand: on 26 September Allenby issued an order prohibiting British troops from entering Damascus unless forced to do so for tactical reasons.

In the advance on Damascus west of the Jordan Allenby's next move was to close on Semakh and Tiberias. On 24 September, the Australian Mounted Division was ordered to strike northwards from

Jenin, with the aim of holding a new strategic line running from Tiberias through Nazareth to Acre. These orders cut across plans made by Liman following his enforced departure from Nazareth on 19 September. Intending to create a new defensive line running from Deraa to Semakh and then west of the Sea of Galilee by Tiberias to Lake Huleh, Liman sought to give his forces the opportunity to reorganize and to buy time to prepare the defence of Damascus. The Fourth, Seventh and Eighth Armies were each allocated segments of this east–west line.

Though perfectly logical, Liman's plan had little basis in reality. With the rapid disintegration of the Seventh and Eighth Armies the forces on which his plan relied had for the most part ceased to exist. Further hindered by the collapse of communications, his orders could no longer be conveyed to commanders in the field. In practice he could do little more than issue orders in person to those troops still in position as he travelled northwards from Nazareth in the direction of Damascus. At Semakh, a large village on the Sea of Galilee which both sides regarded as a key strategic point in the campaign – for the Turks it was to be a critical link in the new defensive line and the intersection between the Seventh and Eighth Armies – Liman placed the garrison under German control and left behind a number of German machine-gunners to strengthen its defence. By this means he was to ensure that there would be a determined struggle for the control of the village.

As the Australian Mounted Division moved forward, the Fourth Australian Light Horse Brigade, commanded by Brigadier-General Grant, was ordered to lead the attack on Semakh. With limited resources – only the 11th Australian Light Horse Regiment and a squadron from another regiment were immediately available – the attack was made in darkness during the early hours of 25 September. As the Australians approached the Turkish positions, the German machine-gunners opened fire. The Australians responded by forming into line and charging although, in the darkness, their destination was unclear. They succeeded in reaching the centre of the village but not without sustaining heavy losses, particularly of horses. There they dismounted and the exchange of gunfire continued. The defending forces were well protected by stone buildings and it was only after the Australians entered the buildings and engaged in heavy hand-to-hand fighting that the enemy was forced to surrender. Enemy losses amounted to 100 dead and 350 prisoners; Australian losses were small by comparison, with 14 killed and 29 wounded. However, they lost nearly 100 horses.

With Semakh secured, a squadron was dispatched later the same day along the lake road in the direction of Tiberias. Joined as it approached the town by the Third Australian Light Horse Brigade, which had been based at Nazareth, the combined force had little difficulty in taking Tiberias, where the Turkish garrison offered only token resistance. By the time Tiberias had been taken, General Allenby had issued orders instructing his forces to advance on Damascus. Further west, the Australian Mounted Division, which was now in the Tiberias area, and the Fifth Cavalry Division, based at Nazareth, were ordered to advance to Damascus by the most direct route. This meant a journey of 90 miles travelling round the northern end of the Sea of Galilee and through Kuneitra. They left a day after the Fourth Cavalry Division but arrived in Damascus within an hour of each other.

The Fourth Cavalry Division, now at Beisan, 170 miles from Damascus, was to advance to Irbid and then on to Deraa. If the division was unable to intercept the Turkish Fourth Army at Deraa it was to pursue it northwards to Damascus. Following its departure from Beisan on 26 September, the division first encountered the Turks at Irbid later the same day when it made contact with a flank guard of the Turkish Fourth Army. The Second Lancers charged the position held by the Turks but were repelled with heavy losses, reflecting the fact that part of the Fourth Army was still intact as a fighting force even though it was in rapid retreat. During the night the Turkish flank guard withdrew to Er Remte where, on 27 September, they fought a difficult battle with the 10th Brigade but were eventually forced to withdraw. The Fourth Cavalry Division spent the night of 27 September at Er Remte before arriving at Deraa the following day.

At the same time as the British cavalry had left Beisan, Arab attacks on the railway north of Deraa were renewed. The line had only just been restored to use after the original assault nine days earlier and the damage caused by this second wave of attacks was much more extensive. Soon after the Arabs reached Sheikh Saad, news arrived that Deraa was being evacuated by road. Later intelligence confirmed that two columns of Turks were approaching – one from Deraa, about 6,000 strong, and the other from Mezerib, some 2,000 strong. The Mezerib column was similar in size to the Arab force and it was decided to intercept it just north of Tafas.

The Arabs arrived too late to prevent the enemy entering the village, a delay that was to cost many lives, both civilian and military. As described by Lawrence,

> they allowed themselves to rape all the women they could catch. We attacked them with all arms as they marched out later . . . When Sherif Bey, the Turkish commander of the Lancer rearguard in the village, saw this he ordered that the inhabitants be killed . . . These included twenty small children . . . and about forty women.
>
> With Auda's help we were able to cut the enemy column in three. The third section, with German machine-gunners, resisted magnificently, and got off, not cheaply . . . The second and leading portions after a bitter struggle, we wiped out completely.[27]

The desire for revenge was so strong that an order to take no prisoners was given. This was generally obeyed, except for the reserve company which took 250 prisoners. Later, however, they found 'one of our men with a fractured thigh who had been afterwards pinned to the ground by two mortal thrusts with German bayonets. Then we turned our Hotchkiss on the prisoners and made an end of them, they saying nothing.'[28]

That night (26/27 September) Arab horsemen were sent into Deraa 'with orders to scatter any formations met with on the road, and to occupy the place'.[29] When Lawrence arrived at dawn on 28 September – shortly before the arrival of British forces under General Barrow – he found the town in chaos. It had been 'one of the nights in which mankind went crazy, when death seemed impossible, however many died to the right and left, and when others' lives became toys to break and throw away'.[30] The Arabs put in place new administrative arrangements before Barrow's cavalry arrived but, following a dispute over control between Barrow and Lawrence, a British army of occupation assumed responsibility for the town.

On 28 September, Barrow's cavalry left Deraa with Damascus, 70 miles away, as its next objective. Under arrangements agreed between British and Arab commanders, Arab regulars under the Iraqi volunteer Nuri es-Said would march up the railway and cover Barrow's right flank, while Arab irregulars would continue to harry Turkish troops as they retreated towards Damascus. As the Arabs approached the city, Lawrence recorded the impact of the final phase of the revolt on the Turkish Fourth Army: 'in all, we had killed nearly five thousand of them, captured about eight thousand . . . and counted spoils of about one hundred and fifty machine guns and from twenty-five to thirty guns.'[31]

★

West of the Jordan, the converging advance of the Australian Mounted Division, which began on 27 September, was also not without its difficulties. The division had reached Jisr Benat Yakub, a Jordan river crossing, by midday to find that the enemy had destroyed the stone bridge. An enemy rearguard, which included German machine-gunners, had been positioned on the opposite (eastern) bank. Heavy machine-gun fire prevented the Australians from approaching the river or a nearby ford. The French contingent of the Fifth Australian Light Horse Brigade was ordered to try to force a way through, while other units were sent north and south to search for alternative routes across the river.

While the remainder of the Fifth Australians went south in search of a ford, the Third Australian Light Horse Brigade went north to a point at the south end of Lake Huleh where it was thought that the river could be crossed. Although this belief turned out to be incorrect, some members of the brigade managed to cross the river between the demolished bridge and Lake Huleh. Meanwhile, the Fifth Australian Light Horse had also managed with great difficulty to cross the Jordan. The Australians were now in a position to attack the enemy rearguard at Jisr Benat Yakub on both flanks, forcing it to withdraw as soon as darkness fell. Most of the mounted troops crossed the river unopposed by means of the fords, as repairs to the bridge were not completed until the following day (28 September).

By this time, the mounted troops had reached Kuneitra and were thus still some 40 miles from Damascus. They moved on during the afternoon of 29 September. The presence of another Turkish rearguard on a ridge south of Sasa delayed a plan to march during the night of 29/30 September so that the mounted troops would be closer to Damascus the following morning. The Australians were to encounter the rearguard once more as it took up position to make a last stand between Kaukab and Kantana. This was some ten miles from Damascus and five miles west of Kiswe, which was on the main route from Deraa to Damascus where the retreating Turkish Fourth Army was still ahead of the Fourth Cavalry Division.

On the morning of 30 September, the British, who were still some

30 miles south of Damascus, were given their orders for the capture of the city and for rounding up the remaining Turkish forces. The Australian Division was instructed to overcome any final Turkish opposition in the Kuneitra area and move round Damascus to the west with the aim of blocking the northern escape routes to Beirut and Homs. The Fifth Cavalry Division was to change direction and move eastwards to the road from Deraa to Damascus at Kiswe, where they were to attack and capture the remaining elements of the Fourth Army. The Fourth Cavalry Division was to continue up the Deraa road to join forces with the Fifth Division with the aim of bringing the Turks to a final battle. During further fighting in the Kiswe area, the two divisions completed the elimination of the Fourth Army and most of the survivors were taken prisoner.

Only one organized enemy unit – a German battalion – reached Damascus intact on 30 September. On the Kuneitra road the Australians soon overcame the resistance of the Turkish rearguard at Kaukab. The Fifth Australian Light Horse Brigade then advanced towards the Beirut road, closely followed by the Third Australian Light Horse Brigade which had orders to move round the north of Damascus and block the route to Homs. It became clear however that there was no such access to the Homs road, as the Barada gorge blocked the way and the cliffs of the gorge were too steep to be negotiated. The only route lay through the centre of Damascus, but British troops had been banned from entering the city. Both brigades therefore turned their attention to the Beirut road which was packed with defeated enemy troops making their escape. From their vantage point on the cliffs over-looking the road, the Australians opened fire on the head of the column, causing large numbers of casualties. Those in the rear of the column abandoned any hope of escape and returned to Damascus.

By the night of 30 September, the escape routes from Damascus had effectively been closed. Chauvel's forces had circled the town to the north-west, while Barrow had covered routes to the south-west. The Arabs were camped at Kiswe, a few miles to the south of the city. Before them lay the oldest city in the world – the prize they had often dreamt about but until recently had not expected to win. Despite its antiquity it had never been fortified or enclosed in walls. Like Jerusalem, it was more strongly associated with trade than with war. In the words of Charles Harvey, the city was very disappointing, being nothing more than a very big native bazaar . . . on the other hand, the gardens all round the city on the north-east and south are perfectly wonderful. There is a most extensive system of irrigation, the rivers being split up into hundreds of canals; and the gardens stretch for about fifteen miles to the east and are quite eight miles wide.[32]

Within the city Turkish rule was rapidly coming to an end; on 30 September their administration finally collapsed. For a brief period before the Allied occupation the inhabitants demonstrated their opposition to the continuation of Ottoman rule by raising the Sherifal flag and denying supplies to the Turkish forces. At the same time, 'parties of armed Arabs entered the town daily, at first contenting themselves by displaying their skill in horsemanship and firing in the air'.[33] By now, with the British and Arab forces approaching, it was evident that the city could not be successfully defended against the Allied armies on its doorstep. Arab flags replaced Turkish ones and control of the city's administration passed to a committee of Arab notables. There were chaotic scenes as Turkish troops abandoned the city for the escape routes to the north. The last Turkish troop train left Damascus at 9 p.m. on 30 September. It arrived safely at Rayak, north-west of Damascus, where the retreating Turkish and German forces had been ordered to assemble as they withdrew northwards.

It soon became clear, however, that the Rayak position could not be safely held and the retreating forces were ordered back to Homs. Veterans of the Palestine campaign, most of whom were in poor physical condition, mingled with recently arrived reinforcements. Those able to escape took one of the two roads to the north, both of which soon became crowded with retreating Turks. The road to Homs ran in a north-easterly direction from Damascus and skirted the edge of the desert; the alternative route, to Rayak and Beirut, passed through the gorge of the River Barada in a north-westerly direction; it had already come under Allied attack.

The Third Australian Light Horse Brigade gained permission during the course of 30 September to enter Damascus in order to close the Homs road to retreating soldiers. The brigade entered the city at dawn the following day – the first British force to do so. It pursued the enemy down the Homs road and fought several engagements with enemy rearguards, taking 750 prisoners and capturing several machine guns. The pursuit continued on 2 October when they caught up with another Turkish column, taking some 1,500 prisoners, 3 guns and 26 machine guns. This concluded the fighting in the Damascus area and was the last engagement fought by the Australians in this campaign. Leading units of the Fifth Cavalry Division were also occupied within the city boundaries, where they spent some time taking charge of the 12,000 Turkish soldiers who were still free but had made no real attempt to escape.

The arrival of the Third Australians in Damascus early on 1 October was rapidly followed by the entry of Lawrence of Arabia and other military leaders, including Sherif Nasir and Nuri Shafaan, Emir of the Ruwalla, and their forces. Together with Lawrence and Auda they went straight to the town hall, where they learned that an Arab government had been proclaimed the previous afternoon, well before the last enemy forces had evacuated the city. The new administration had declared its loyalty to Sherif Hussein as king of the Arabs.

Within hours of the liberation of Damascus, however, the Arab victory started to turn sour as Allenby began to impose restrictions on the Arabs in accordance with the Sykes–Picot agreement. On his arrival on 2 October, Allenby's immediate tasks were to restore law and order and thereafter to ensure that the terms of the agreement were implemented. He conferred with Lawrence and then held a meeting with Feisal, as he explained in a letter to his wife:

> On arrival, I went to the Victoria Hotel. Later, the Sherif Feisal arrived, and came to see me there. He was mounted on a big Arab, with a large escort of Arabs, all mounted. He is a fine, slim, sharp-featured man of about 35 . . . I had a long and satisfactory talk with Feisal. He will take over the administration of Damascus; or, rather, will put in a military administration. His flag now flies.[34]

Under these arrangements Feisal would be responsible to Allenby, but would also have to communicate with a French liaison officer who had yet to be appointed.

Feisal claimed to know nothing about the role allotted to France in the post-war government of Syria. His understanding of the position from Lawrence was that the Arabs were to administer the whole of Syria, including the Lebanon, provided their forces had reached northern Syria by the end of the war. Under the plans agreed by British representatives with Georges Picot, however, France was to be allocated the Lebanon – although, when questioned by Allenby soon after they arrived in Damascus, Lawrence claimed that he was unaware of the plan and could not, therefore, have mentioned it to Feisal. Without access to the Mediterranean, Syria would be a land-locked country with a much less promising economic future. This issue remained unresolved, but by the conclusion of the meeting Allenby had persuaded Feisal to accept the de facto situation. The consequences of direct action by the Arabs would be serious, as Allenby indicated to the War Office: 'Feisal is being warned that if he attempts to control the blue area [the Lebanon, a proposed French sphere of interest], the settlement of which must await the Peace Conference, he will prejudice his case. He is also being told that the Lebanon's status is a peculiar one.'[35] These exchanges about the scope of the Sykes–Picot agreement undermined Lawrence's cred-ibility as an intermediary between Allenby and Feisal and it was one of the reasons behind Lawrence's early departure for London on 4 October.

As a semblance of normality returned to Damascus, the Allied forces pressed on northwards in pursuit of the remnants of the Turkish army, with Aleppo as the final objective. It was clear that while the Arabs' major goal had been achieved, more Ottoman terri-tory would have to be taken before the Turkish government would come to the negotiating table to discuss its withdrawal from the war.

# 10

# *Pursuit to Aleppo*

B Y THE TIME Damascus had fallen into Allenby's hands on 1 October 1918, some 19,000 Turkish soldiers – from a total of 100,000 serving in Palestine and Syria before the final British offensive – had escaped the Allied net around the city and were able to continue the retreat northwards. But this gave no real indication of the residual strength of the Turkish forces still operating in northern Syria. Successive defeats in adverse conditions meant that their morale and physical condition were generally poor, they had no artillery support and transport was virtually non-existent. With no more than 4,000 of these troops equipped and able to fight, they were unlikely to be able to offer much solid resistance to a determined British cavalry force operating north of Damascus.

In these promising circumstances, Allenby came under early pressure from the War Cabinet which, reviewing British strategy immediately following the initial success of the offensive of 19 September, had come to the conclusion that a quick cavalry raid on Aleppo, some 200 miles north of Damascus, would be desirable. It was believed in London that the capture of this ancient city in northern Syria, on top of the dramatic losses that the Turks were already facing, could be sufficient to persuade Turkish leaders that it was time to negotiate an end to their involvement in the war.

Allenby took a much more cautious view of the situation both during the Megiddo offensive and afterwards. Not even the fall of Damascus and the chaotic withdrawal of the Turkish army persuaded him to change his basic approach. Unless the government were willing to reconsider the idea of a major amphibious landing at

Alexandretta (first mooted at the beginning of the war), he was only prepared to advance in stages, as circumstances permitted. The first step was the advance to Damascus and Beirut. If it succeeded, further progress northwards would have to be made on the same conditional basis. Operating at such an extreme distance from his main bases, which lay 150 miles south of Damascus, would place his supply arrangements under considerable strain, even though there were no significant physical barriers along the route. Keeping even a small force in the field at that distance would be difficult, although the capture of the main Syrian ports would provide easier access by sea and would eventually make the supply problem more manageable.

More important, Allenby's forces in Damascus were being severely incapacitated by disease. Malaria had afflicted the Allied armies throughout the Palestine campaign, but it was particularly prevalent in the Jordan valley where no effective action had been taken to control the disease. All Allied units were affected to some extent but the Fourth Cavalry Division and the Australian Mounted Division, which had served in that area before moving on to Damascus, suffered particularly badly. While cases of malaria were increasing rapidly, a new danger – influenza (or Spanish flu) – was beginning to emerge by early October. It represented the first stirrings of an epidemic that was to kill millions of people throughout the world in the immediate post-war period. Soldiers who had survived the hardships of the Palestine campaign without injury were being struck down in hours. According to the official account, 'the death rate was not high, yet nearly four times as many men of the [Desert Mounted] Corps died in Damascus as had been killed between the opening of the [September] offensive and the capture of the city'.[1] The British were also faced with the even greater problem of managing illness among Turkish prisoners of war in Damascus and the surrounding areas. These troops, the official history continues, 'were suffering from almost all the diseases which warfare brings in its train'.[2] Not all of these prisoners could be accommodated in hospital; many were confined in compounds with only the most primitive medical facilities. At one such compound, which held some 10,000 prisoners, as many as 70 men were dying of disease every day.

Allenby's plan to advance northwards from Damascus by stages, in order to avoid exposing his weakened forces to further strain, was soon conveyed to his subordinates. On 3 October, he met with General Chauvel in his new headquarters – a former Yilderim building in the south-western suburbs of Damascus – to brief him on his plans for the Aleppo campaign. Leaving the Australian Mounted Division to maintain public order in Damascus, Chauvel instructed the Fifth Cavalry Division, under the command of Major-General H.J.M. MacAndrew, an experienced cavalry leader who had served in France, to advance to Rayak, some 30 miles north-west of Damascus. This important railway junction was the terminus of the standard-gauge railway from Constantinople; the Hejaz railway ran from Rayak to Damascus, Deraa and the south, while a branch line connected it to Beirut. Situated in a valley that divided the mountains of Lebanon and Anti-Lebanon, Rayak was an obvious first target for the Allies as the place where Turkish and German troops retreating from the south and from Haifa had been ordered to assemble as they struggled to regroup.

The Fifth Cavalry Division, which left Damascus on 5 October, arrived in Rayak during the afternoon of the following day. An RAF raid four days earlier had caused much death and destruction in the town but the occupying forces still found some surviving Turkish soldiers as well as serviceable military equipment and rolling stock, all of which fell into Allied hands. Most of the retreating enemy forces had left Rayak in good time and were continuing their withdrawal northwards in the direction of Baalbek and Homs. The Fifth Cavalry Division was followed, a day later, by the Fourth Cavalry Division, which had left Damascus on 6 October. However, its progress was soon brought to a halt when virtually the whole division was taken ill with influenza or malaria. Robert Wilson, of the Royal Berkshire Yeomanry, who participated in the march along the road to Aleppo, described the impact of the disease:

> We had chased and chivied the retreating Turk from Damascus to Baalbek with only slight resistance, which was fortunate as we were now suffering very seriously from malaria – a frequently fatal type – which we had, no doubt, contracted in the Jordan Valley. There was no quinine and no medical aid. Several of my friends died and I, myself, was in a very bad way for about two days before reaching Baalbek but I badly wanted to keep going until the Turk threw in the sponge – an event expected at any moment.[3]

As the Fifth Division advanced northwards unopposed there was time for the battle-weary officers to appreciate their new surroundings and gauge the reactions of the local population. On 8 October, Charles Harvey reported to his parents that he had been

> resting for a few days in one of the most delightful spots I have ever been in. The trek along the pass over the Anti-Lebanon mountains from Damascus was dull and monotonous, but this valley which separates Lebanon from Anti-Lebanon is perfectly lovely. The eastern slopes of Lebanon, on the western side of the valley – which is only about eight miles broad – is thickly populated and most fertile. The people are Syrians, mostly Christians, and are perfectly delighted to see us.[4]

In parallel with this movement, the Seventh Indian (Meerut) Division (a component of Bulfin's 21st Corps) left Haifa on 3 October and was ordered to march up the coast as far as Beirut (to establish a new forward line eastwards to Rayak). It advanced northwards in three columns, with Tyre as its first target. The poor state of the coastal route, which was in places no more than a narrow track cut from the cliff face, did not delay the arrival of the Corps Cavalry Regiment in Tyre on 4 October, but the units that followed, including the artillery, took longer to complete the journey. It advanced to the rival port of Sidon on 6 October.

In the absence of any Turkish opposition, the much bigger prize of Beirut was in British hands only two days later. Armoured cars operating from Rayak had established the previous day that the city was unoccupied (although 600 Turks who had not left in time were rounded up by the local population and handed over to the British). Although Beirut was no longer occupied by the Turks, the Allies found that the French navy and Arab irregular forces had already arrived to stake their respective claims. In the end the French prevailed and the Arabs were forced to withdraw. Beirut was Syria's second city and had a population of 190,000 in 1918. Its port facilities were to prove invaluable for unloading the supplies that would help sustain Britain's military efforts further to the north.

Bulfin established himself in the city's main hotel, the Deutscherhof, although prime responsibility for local administration was rapidly devolved to the French in conformity with the terms of the Sykes–Picot agreement. French military governors for Beirut, Sidon and Tyre were appointed and French troops were soon landed to maintain civil order. A brigade of the Seventh Indian Division continued the coastal advance northwards until the next stage – a line running from Tripoli to Homs – was reached. On 13 October, Tripoli – together with its port of El Mina – was occupied by the XXI Corps Cavalry Regiment and a few armoured cars. Access to the port helped to ease the supply problems of the British force as it advanced further and further away from Damascus.

Inland, Allenby was sufficiently encouraged by the cavalry's steady progress and the hasty withdrawal of the enemy to give the Fifth Cavalry Division the task of taking Baalbek and then Homs (the latter target being the subject of a separate order issued by Allenby on 9 October). The division was to proceed along the route of the railway and through country which, according to the British official history, 'far exceeds in beauty and grandeur that which [the troops] had known for the past year'.[5] This was the same route used by the Turks a few days earlier following their enforced evacuation of Rayak; they were still in a disorganized state and Liman feared that it would not be possible for them to regroup before they reached Aleppo. In order to gain time for preparations for a final stand at Aleppo, the remnants of the Turkish Fourth Army, commanded by Djemal Kuchuk, were ordered to remain at Homs for as long as they could. In the meantime, one of the main surviving units, Colonel Gustav von Oppen's Asia Corps, was dispatched direct to Aleppo, where Mustapha Kemal had been instructed to prepare the defences against a likely British cavalry attack.

The British armoured cars spearheading the advance reached Baalbek on 10 October and found it completely deserted. The temporary location of Liman's headquarters on his way north, he had soon been forced to abandon it. General MacAndrew was now ordered to reach Homs by 16 October. He organized his division into two columns, which were separated by a day's march; the leading units included the armoured cars and the 13th Cavalry Brigade. Feisal was asked to cover the right flank of the advance from Baalbek and regular troops, under the command of Nuri Bey, advanced from Damascus, travelling through the desert to the east of the railway. Progress as far as Homs had been maintained without a single shot being fired in anger but this situation was unlikely to continue for much longer.

At Homs, a town of 70,000 inhabitants and the site of a commanding crusader castle, General MacAndrew was joined, on 16 October, by 1,500 Arab regulars, under the command of Sherif Nasir.

Requested by Allenby, they had arrived direct from Damascus in order to strengthen his offensive troops as they faced their final challenge of the war. The two forces were very similar in strength, although the British had additional support from two Royal Horse Artillery batteries and an RAF squadron. Allenby also ordered a strengthening of MacAndrew's armoured car capability so that he 'had the strongest column of light armoured motor batteries and light car patrols yet employed in the theatre'.[6] Several more armoured cars were added to the division, thus enhancing its mobility and reconnaissance capability.

At the same time, new intelligence information encouraged Allenby to abandon his cautiously staged advance: he had received news that the Turkish army seemed to be evacuating Aleppo by train post-haste, while the RAF was able to confirm that Hama, a town 27 miles to the north of Homs, was no longer occupied by enemy forces. Allenby ordered General Chauvel to make preparations to continue his offensive on 20 October, with the aim of reaching Aleppo, some 120 miles from Homs, within six days. According to one of Allenby's biographers, it was to be 'the last great cavalry action in history'.[7] The Fourth Cavalry Division would move up to Homs should reinforcements be needed.

However, as MacAndrew was leaving Homs on 20 October, Allenby received further reports that caused him to reconsider his decision to authorize a further advance. The main problem was the rapidly declining strength of the Fourth Cavalry Division which was being decimated by disease. With only 1,200 men fit for service there were real doubts about its ability to reach Homs, let alone Aleppo; the chances of it being able to act in support of the Fifth Cavalry Division in a final battle with the Turks seemed remote. His concern about the vulnerability of the division increased as it became clear that the retreating forces would have sufficient time to organize their defences in the Aleppo area before the British arrived. In addition to the 4,000 effective Turkish troops on the road to the north, there were about 20,000 men in the city and nearby. These forces were being organized by Mustapha Kemal, former commander of the Turkish Seventh Army, who was working in cooperation with Nehed Pasha, Second Army commander, to form a new defensive line against the British.

The normally bold and determined commander-in-chief concluded that on this occasion caution was the best approach and he

decided to postpone the final stage of the offensive. He ordered the
Fifth Cavalry Division not to advance beyond Hama, while Chauvel
instructed other units under his command to postpone planned
moves until they received new orders. These instructions reached the
Fifth Cavalry Division during the evening of 20 October after it had
completed a day's march. General MacAndrew, a notably 'vigorous
and headstrong commander',[8] objected strongly to the order on the
grounds that he believed he would not face any serious opposition at
Aleppo, since the main town en route – Hama – was already in local
hands. A flurry of telegrams, initiated at once by MacAndrew, followed in response to the arrival of the unwelcome order:

> Not understood. Troops far in advance, and I propose advancing with
> armoured cars to Aleppo. Believe the railway road avoids all blown
> bridges. Shall be in Hama by midday tomorrow, which is already
> occupied [by the Arabs]. No opposition worth thinking of expected
> at Aleppo. Hoped advance may secure engines and rolling stock.[9]

This forthright response led to further consultations between Allenby
and Chauvel, as a result of which they modified their original stance.
It was agreed that MacAndrew's thrust to the north could continue
without waiting for the arrival of reinforcements. Allenby was prepared to abandon his caution when he received sound advice from an
able subordinate whose judgement he trusted.

During 21 October, MacAndrew's car column advanced at speed
with the aim of making contact with the enemy, which was reported
to have reached as far as Khan es Sebil, a village some 44 miles north
of Hama. By the time the British approached this point, at 2.30 p.m.
on 22 October, all that remained of the Turkish army was a well-
equipped rearguard. It had, however, made a rapid escape in six
lorries with an armoured car in the rear in support. A chase followed
and, within a mile, the British column caught up with the armoured
car and captured it. The chase continued for a further 15 miles until
the last lorry in the convoy eventually broke down. The Turkish
troops in this vehicle escaped into the surrounding hills under heavy
British machine-gun fire; some 24 Turks were killed and five were
captured during the course of this action.

The incident did not delay British progress for long and by the
evening of 22 October the spearhead of armoured cars had reached
Seraqab, which was no more than 30 miles from Aleppo. As the rest

of the 15th Cavalry Brigade was still a considerable distance behind, the following morning the cars pressed on in the hope of learning more about the strength of Turkish defences in the Aleppo area. They soon discovered that some 3,000 Turkish soldiers were holding defensive positions in short lengths of trench by the Hama road some three miles south of Aleppo, although much larger concentrations of enemy forces remained in the area. In order to test Turkish intentions, a British officer was sent in under a flag of truce to demand the immediate surrender of Aleppo. The reply from Mustapha Kemal's staff officer was short and dismissive: 'the commander of the Turkish garrison of Aleppo does not find it necessary to reply to your note.'[10]

By 25 October, the 15th Cavalry Brigade had joined the armoured car column at a point some 13 miles south-west of Aleppo. Under plans developed by General MacAndrew and his staff, the city would be attacked from three sides. Arab forces under Colonel Nuri es-Said had agreed to move to the east of Aleppo and launch an attack on Turkish positions from that direction. British armoured cars would attack from the south, while the 15th Cavalry Brigade would advance from the west. During the afternoon, well in advance of the major planned assault, the Arabs launched their first probing attack on Turkish defences but were quickly repulsed. Despite this apparent setback, the Turkish administration of Aleppo was already in a state of near collapse. Arab agents were active in spreading reports of the success of the Arab revolt and of the British advance from Damascus. British plans to attack Aleppo on the following day were pre-empted when 1,500 Bedouin forced their way into the city during the evening of 25 October and the authorities declared a state of siege. During the street fighting that followed, the Bedouin seized the citadel – one of the 'most splendid monuments of Arabic military architecture'[11] – and took control of key government buildings. The Turks responded by withdrawing their troops from the city as well as the two divisions holding the defensive positions to the south.

Early the following morning the 15th Cavalry Brigade moved to take a commanding ridge to the west of Aleppo and found it unoccupied. After assuming control of the Alexandretta road they learned that 1,000 enemy troops had left Aleppo earlier the same morning and were moving northwards. At about the same time air reconnaissance had apparently identified a group of no more than 300 Turkish cavalrymen on the Alexandretta road at Haritan, some eight miles north-east of the city. A British advanced guard pushed forward until it reached a ridge overlooking the Turkish position. Heavy enemy machine-gun fire forced it to retire, but it was decided to launch an immediate attack. The Mysore Lancers were to move round the eastern end of the ridge and charge the enemy; two squadrons of the Jodhpur Lancers were to follow them while the few available machine guns gave supporting fire.

As the cavalry moved forward it became clear that the Turkish flank was on a rocky knoll further to the east than had been expected and beyond the range of covering machine-gun fire. Even so, the order for the attack was given and the Mysore Lancers took the position without great difficulty. However, it was soon evident that the Turks were present in much greater strength than had at first appeared; later estimates suggested that as many as 3,000 enemy troops may have been operating in the immediate area. As Turkish reinforcements arrived, both Indian regiments in turn came under heavy and well-directed fire from enemy troops who seemed to have been reinvigorated; they were also, it was reported, being directed in person by Mustapha Kemal and perhaps giving a better account of themselves as a result. Though a counter-attack failed to materialize, the Turks started to dig in and for several hours the British position remained uncertain. However, at about 11 p.m. on 26 October the 14th Cavalry Brigade arrived and, within an hour, the enemy had gone. Thus ended the last engagement of the war in the Middle East.

★

Meanwhile, the British army had arrived at the gates of Aleppo, which was now unoccupied. General MacAndrew, accompanied by his armoured cars, entered the city at 10 a.m. on 26 October, an hour before the Battle of Haritan began. The liberators, in the words of the official history, were given 'a reception as enthusiastic as had greeted the British at any point hitherto'.[12] The last city to be captured during the Palestine campaign, it had a pre-war population of 150,000 and had been in Ottoman hands for more than four hundred years. The success of the final drive against the Turks owed much to General MacAndrew's successful leadership. In the view of Charles Harvey, 'he deserves the fullest personal credit for the taking of Aleppo. It was a much bolder deed than you probably realize . . . he is a fine clever leader with the cavalry instinct developed in him to an unusual degree.'[13] MacAndrew, who died in Aleppo in July 1919 as a result of an accident, 'left behind him a record of achievement hardly equalled by any cavalryman of modern times'.[14]

While the inhabitants of Aleppo celebrated the British army's arrival, the movements of enemy forces to the north of the city were being carefully monitored. During the course of the following morning (27 October), Turkish troops were discovered to be holding a ridge some three and a half miles north-north-west of Haritan, but within a day they had fallen back another five miles to Deir el Jemal. By 30 October, the Turkish army's outposts remained at Deir el Jemal, while the retreating forces had withdrawn a further four miles. Here they held a strong defensive line extending for some 25 miles. At this point the British were heavily outnumbered (by a factor of six to one) and there was no prospect of launching a successful attack without the arrival of substantial reinforcements. General MacAndrew, who had displayed great boldness and courage, recognized the reality of his position and prepared to wait until he had a better chance of inflicting further defeats on the Turks.

The Australian Mounted Division was sent to Aleppo from Damascus on 27 October but had not progressed as far as Homs before Turkish involvement in the war ended on 31 October 1918. One of the last acts of the war was the occupation of Muslimiya station by Arab forces loyal to Feisal. The station was located at the junction of the Syrian and Mesopotamian railways and their connection to Constantinople; its capture underlined the fact that Turks had effectively lost control of a large part of their once powerful empire. Since the beginning of Allenby's offensive six weeks earlier they had been pushed back some 350 miles. The conclusion of the campaign saved the Turks from a final engagement with the British to the north of Aleppo that could only have resulted in further heavy losses to add to the widespread destruction experienced by their armies over the previous few months. These local losses were matched by a substantial decline in fighting strength across the entire Ottoman empire. In total during the war, Turkey lost over a million and a half men from desertion, 325,000 were killed in action and 240,000 were lost from disease. She had no more than 100,000 front-line troops left when hostilities ceased.

★

Rapid British progress in Syria was reflected by major developments in other theatres of the First World War after years of wasteful

stalemate. On the Western Front, the Allied advance had broken
through the Hindenburg line in the latter part of September 1918
and within days Germany had sent proposals for an armistice to the
American president, Woodrow Wilson. On the Italian front, the
Battle of Vittorio Veneto, which began on 24 October, sent
the Austrians reeling. Within days they were suing for peace with the
Italian government. Elsewhere, the British were advancing on Mosul
in Mesopotamia, but the critical events affecting Turkey's continued
involvement in the war occurred in the Balkans. The decisive Battle
of Monastir-Doiran, which began on 18 September, resulted in the
'complete rupture of the Bulgarian front'.[15] Within days – on 30
September – the Bulgarians had signed an armistice with the Allies,
agreeing to demobilize their forces and open their transport facilities
to their former enemies.

The Bulgarian defeat had a substantial impact on Turkey, which
now had her transport links with Germany severed and was therefore
cut off from the aid that had sustained her through four years of war.
The setback also had the effect of reducing German political pressure
on Turkey, which had been directed to keep her fighting. Turkey
lacked the political will to continue and without external pressure
from her Germany ally, the inclination of her leaders was to seek an
accommodation with the Allies. The Germans were in any case
facing the prospect of imminent defeat in Europe and their main
priority was to bring their own troops home. Other factors, including defeat in Palestine, also pointed toward a Turkish surrender, but
developments in the Balkans brought the issue to a head.

Political changes within Turkey created the climate within which
armistice discussions could be initiated. Turkey's wartime leaders
were 'universally execrated'. Associated with military defeat and the
loss of imperial territory, the Talaat–Enver ministry had lost all
popular endorsement and early in October, following the loss of
Damascus and Beirut, the government collapsed. The Sultan
appointed Marshal Izzet Pasha, a distinguished soldier who commanded wide support, to the office of Grand Vizier. By this time
both Britain and Turkey realized that the war in the Near East was
effectively over and that a formal agreement on peace terms was
needed. When news of the Bulgarian surrender reached London, the
British War Cabinet instructed the Admiralty to prepare the naval
terms of an armistice with Turkey. The British commander-in-chief
in the Mediterranean, Vice-Admiral Sir Somerset Gough Calthorpe,

was ordered to go to the Aegean island of Mudros, which had been selected as the venue for armistice discussions between the two countries. On 22 October, an envoy of the new Turkish Minister of Marine, accompanied by Major-General Charles Townshend, who had been a prisoner of war since the fall of Kut, arrived on the island. Izzet Pasha had sent Townshend to Mudros so that he could confirm personally that the Turkish government was acting in good faith in stating that it wished to conclude a separate peace with the British.

Following these initial talks, armistice terms were prepared and formally presented to a Turkish delegation, led by Rauf Bey, the Minister of Marine, which arrived on Mudros on 26 October. After four days of 'difficult discussions' the armistice was signed on board the British battleship *Agamemnon* on 30 October.[16] The most important clause stipulated that all hostilities should cease from noon (local time) on Thursday 31 October 1918. The agreement also provided for the opening of the Dardanelles and the Bosphorus to the Royal Navy, the demobilization of the Turkish army, an Allied right to occupy key points in the empire should it wish to do so, and the immediate withdrawal of all German and Austrian troops. By the time this agreement came into effect the defeated commander, Liman von Sanders, had anticipated the outcome. He was already on a train bound for Constantinople whence he would travel on to Germany. He had handed over the supreme command to General Mustapha Kemal, whose last stand north of Aleppo had prevented a British invasion of Turkey and the further destruction of the Turkish army. Some 10,000 German troops were also on the move in various parts of the Ottoman empire, all seeking to return home by the quickest available route.

News of the armistice was circulated by radio but only reached the Fifth Cavalry Division at Aleppo two hours before the ceasefire was due to come into effect. It seems unlikely that the British advance northwards could have continued without further reinforcements but, equally clearly, a stronger British force could have disrupted Mustapha Kemal's new line with ease. The Fifth Cavalry Division's achievement had been remarkable. It had progressed nearly 600 miles in the thirty-eight days since the start of Allenby's final offensive on 19 September. The general British advance on Damascus had run for 350 miles and taken only eleven days. Rapid movement on this scale could only mean the effective collapse of the enemy and the irrevocable loss of large swathes of imperial territory. In the course of Allenby's manoeuvres three Turkish armies were destroyed and 75,000 prisoners (including 3,700 Germans and Austrians) taken from a total ration strength of 104,000 men. The Turks also lost 360 artillery pieces, 800 machine guns and many other pieces of equipment. The railway system on which the Turks had been so reliant also suffered heavily: 89 railway engines and 468 railway carriages and trucks were lost to the Allies. Allied losses in the final September offensive were relatively modest with 853 killed and 4,428 injured. (Their total battle casualties for the whole campaign, from 1915, were 51,451.)

Early in November, Allenby – in a new role as commander of the peacetime army of occupation – started to deal with the first tasks of repair and reconstruction in a country that was virtually reduced to ruins. Created a life peer and field marshal in 1919, Allenby was to have a continuing role in the rebuilding of the region as High Commissioner of Egypt, 1919–25. On 9 November, British and French warships entered the Gulf of Iskanderun. A few days later the first French troops were landed and occupied the port of Alexandretta, potentially adding to the commander-in-chief's difficulties. A British army of occupation was established with garrisons stationed across Palestine and Syria until the fate of these territories was decided at the Paris Peace Conference in 1919. More problematic was the delay in demobilizing the defeated Turkish forces caused by obstruction on the part of some Turkish generals, who ignored or feigned ignorance of the terms of the armistice. It was not until Allenby complained to the Turkish government in February 1919 about such obstruction by the Sixth Army – still based just north of Aleppo, and one of the worst offenders – that the process of demobilization began.

By this time the only centre of organized resistance that still existed was at Medina in the Hejaz where the Turkish occupation continued. The siege went on beyond the armistice and into the New Year, with neither side apparently anxious to bring it to an issue, despite the diplomatic efforts of Sir Reginald Wingate, the Egyptian High Commissioner, who offered the entire garrison a safe passage to Egypt. Abdullah, Sherif Hussein's second son and head of Arab forces in the area, wished to avoid further bloodshed, while Fakhri Pasha, the Turkish commander, was apparently determined never to surrender. In the end, however, Fakhri's own officers settled the matter. Early in January 1919, according to the British official history, they seized 'the fierce veteran on a bed of sickness and [handed] him over to the Arabs'. The garrison was, by this time, 'in a state of destitution, and over a thousand men had died in the past few months of influenza'.[17]

The belated surrender of Medina marked the final symbolic extinction of Ottoman power in the Middle East, five years after the first tentative contacts had been made between Britain and the Arabs about possible collaboration against their common enemy. In the early days of the war, the Turkish government had the political determination and military strength to contemplate an invasion of Egypt. However, it never deployed sufficient resources to match its imperial ambitions and the Turkish army barely succeeded in crossing the Suez Canal with no more than a handful of men. It had no realistic prospect of progressing further west into the heart of Egypt without considerable local support. This unwillingness to deploy sufficient resources to produce a decisive result helps to explain why the Palestine campaign extended over almost the entire course of the war, even though Allenby's final offensive in September 1918 was compressed into a matter of days. The fact that neither side was able or willing to bring the fighting to a head at an earlier point reflects the attitude of the two governments to the place of the Middle Eastern theatre in the First World War as a whole. Both Britain and Turkey regarded the theatre as a sideshow, and the degree of importance they attached to it – or were able to attach to it – varied significantly as the war progressed.

For most Turkish ministers the war against Russia and the preservation of their territorial interests in the Caucasus invariably had much greater priority than the retention of Ottoman Palestine. After the withdrawal of Russia from the war following the October Revolution 1917, territorial expansion in the Caucasus became the government's chief concern. As Russia disintegrated into warring factions the dream of recapturing long-lost Ottoman possessions suddenly seemed to be a real possibility. Despite the build-up on the British front line, Turkish troops were diverted from the Palestine front for this purpose and the forces opposing Allenby were consequently weakened. Turkey could justify maintaining its forces at this reduced level by reference to its belief – echoing that of British 'Westerners' – that the outcome of the war would ultimately be determined by events in France. For much of the period during which Allenby was preparing his final offensive, they were confident that the Germans would prevail in the west.

The British were also forced to withdraw units from Egypt and Palestine to meet the continuing demands for manpower on the Western Front. The requirements of British forces in France always took priority. This policy was applied from the beginning of the war when the British government had no greater ambition in the area than that of ensuring that the Suez Canal was secure and that traffic could pass through it without disruption. Experienced units were often dispatched to France well before their typically inexperienced replacements had arrived.

The pace of British operations in the Middle East was also affected by the wider policy debate between 'Westerners' and 'Easterners' about the military resources that should be devoted to a sideshow such as Palestine compared with the Western Front. Without the crucial intervention of Lloyd George, who took a broader view of the possible benefits of success in the Middle East, it seems unlikely that British forces would have reached Aleppo by the end of the war. The issue of whether Britain should be more actively involved in the defence of Egypt was eventually decided by the War Cabinet; but not until relatively late in the conflict – after the first Battle of Gaza in March 1917 – did the British government take the idea of invading Palestine seriously. In the period before the first failure at Gaza, policy had focused almost exclusively on the defence of the canal, with the aim of ensuring that the 'jugular vein' of the British empire remained unobstructed. However, the method of ensuring that the canal was secure changed quite radically during the course of the war. At first its defence was centred on the canal itself, but once the risks inherent in this strategy were appreciated a new policy was adopted. This was based on the principle of ensuring that sufficient physical distance was maintained between the Turkish army and the canal by the construction of new forward defences. Unless they could penetrate the forward lines they would be too far from the canal to attack it effectively with long-range artillery.

In pursuing this policy, British forces advanced steadily eastwards across the desert in several clearly defined stages. The policy was eventually extended to justify the use of resources necessary to recapture all the Egyptian territory east of the canal that was abandoned to the Turks in 1914. It meant assembling and equipping the largest desert column in the history of war. Several factors forced the British government to review policy in the Middle East in the spring of 1917 when General Murray's forces had reached the borders of Ottoman Palestine. Prominent among them was Lloyd George's need for a striking Allied victory – such as the fall of Jerusalem – at a time when the costly slaughter on the Western Front was reaching unparalleled proportions with no apparent benefit to the Allies. But there was more to an active policy in Palestine than the possible boost to British domestic morale provided by the capture of Jerusalem. To the 'Easterner', it offered the opportunity of taking positive action that might be decisive to the progress of the war as a whole. There was a real chance of achieving, over a relatively weak enemy, a military victory such as had so far proved impossible to achieve against the Germans in France.

It was hoped in London that military success in Palestine could trigger the collapse of the enemy alliance and accelerate the end of the war on other fronts. It now became declared policy to defeat the Turks in Palestine and Syria. This commitment to achieving a military victory was agreed in principle but could only become a reality when the demands of the Western Front for men and *matériel* began to ease. Delays in starting the final offensive in Palestine as a result of troop shortages meant that Turkey's elimination from the war did not take place until all Britain's other enemies were on the way to being defeated as well. For this reason the wider benefits of Allenby's achievements were less important than they would have been had he been able to launch a final attack earlier in the year, as he had originally intended.

There is little doubt that other events were more influential than the outcome of the war in Syria in forcing Turkey to seek an armistice. The immediate trigger was the collapse of Bulgaria, but unfavourable developments on the Western Front also had an impact on the Constantinople government. Even so Britain's military policy in the Middle East clearly had a number of tangible outcomes. It succeeded in securing the defence of the Suez Canal and keeping it open to shipping throughout the war. The few isolated interruptions to traffic as a result of enemy action could be measured in hours rather than days or weeks. Equally important, British prestige was substantially enhanced by its wartime policy in the Middle East, and its influence on the course of post-war events in the region was the greater for it. In ensuring the security of communications with its overseas possessions, it contributed to the stability of the empire in the inter-war period.

Egypt was used throughout the war as a base for training and recuperation for troops ultimately destined for the Western Front. There is little evidence that British forces in France were seriously disadvantaged by the continuing military requirements in Palestine. In 1918, when thousands of British troops were transferred to France, Allenby's final offensive used forces that were largely colonial in origin and were not required for service in Europe. Despite these external constraints, Allenby enjoyed a marked numerical superiority over the Turks, an advantage he exploited to great effect in the third Battle of Gaza and in the final Megiddo offensive. The other advantages he enjoyed included an experienced mounted arm, which he used to great effect, extensive naval and air support, and troops whose morale was high. At the same time, by maintaining regular and flexible relations with the leaders of the Arab revolt, Allenby ensured that the British and Arab armies worked in close coordination as the Turks retreated northwards. The British army also gave high priority to developing effective transport links from Egypt to Palestine and Syria. By late 1917, the waters of the Nile had been brought to Palestine, but supply shortages remained a major constraint on British action in the third Battle of Gaza and the subsequent thrust into Palestine.

Despite his many advantages, Allenby recognized that Turkey remained in many ways a formidable opponent for most of the war. Her army gave a particularly good account of itself in defensive fighting at Gaza and Jerusalem. The endurance and reliability of the Turkish foot soldier to some extent compensated for inadequate numbers and poor leadership. There are 'few nations which excel [the Turk] in martial qualities . . . the flower of his strength had been destroyed in the Balkan Wars and on the Gallipoli peninsula; but . . . he was still a fine soldier.'[18] Turkish commanders were much more mixed in quality but they were well supported by several able German military leaders, including Kress von Kressenstein, Marshal von Falkenhayn and Liman von Sanders. Falkenhayn in particular was an outstanding officer even though his period in command of the Turkish forces in Palestine was short. His two counter-offensives in the latter part of 1917, including the attempt to recapture Jerusalem, were evidence of his skills, even though both failed.

The British were far more fortunate in their leaders than were their opponents. The successive British offensives to recover lost Egyptian and Palestine territory were led by British commanders who seemed appropriate for their respective roles but would not have been interchangeable. The primary concern of the first two commanders – General Maxwell and General Murray – was the defence of the Suez Canal. Murray reorganized and retrained the Allied forces returning from Gallipoli and developed the transport infra-structure across Sinai. He pushed the Allied forces across the desert but was unable to negotiate the enemy barrier at Gaza or inspire his troops once their morale had begun to fail. For these reasons Murray was clearly not the man to sweep through Palestine and capture Jerusalem before Christmas 1917, as British policy required. The War Office recognized his limitations and the need to remove him.

The strengths of his successor – General Sir Edmund Allenby – were far more relevant to the next stage of operations: breaking into Palestine and advancing northwards. Unlike many of his fellow gen-erals of the First World War, his reputation has largely stood the test of time, despite the apparently more favourable conditions in which he operated. The contrast between the static and hugely wasteful warfare on the Western Front and a successful war of movement in Palestine may have caused Allenby's role to have been over-generously assessed. Nevertheless, there is no reason to doubt his qualities as a general. His predecessor, Archibald Murray, laid the logistical foundations of Allenby's successes but lacked the drive and imagination to achieve victory when the enemy was strongly entrenched. Allenby's other strengths included his ability to concen-trate his forces, his boldness in deception, his fortunate choice of staff officers and his skill in inspiring the rank and file, including his independent-minded Australian troops. Criticisms of Allenby have focused on his apparently risky strategy for breaking the deadlock at Gaza in late 1917 and the partial failure of the subsequent cavalry drive northwards. It is claimed – but hard to establish – that a direct assault on the town would have succeeded without difficulty at this third attempt and that the pursuit of the enemy would have been more easily achieved. This view overlooks the fact that Allenby's indirect assault was largely successful and also that there were major psychological barriers to another direct attack, given Britain's three years' experience of deadlock on the Western Front and elsewhere.

The defeat of Turkey resulted in the total loss of its empire in the Middle East and its replacement by new governments whose boun-daries bore little resemblance to the administrative units of the Ottoman empire before the war. Although it had previously recog-nized the territorial integrity of the Ottoman empire, after 1914 Britain had actively supported the process of dividing the area, reach-ing formal agreements with France and other countries to this effect. In the immediate post-war period responsibility for occupying the former Ottoman territories and maintaining peace rested largely with Britain. However, under the terms of the armistice, France was responsible for Syria and the Lebanon and she established a significant military presence in the region towards the end of the year. In November 1919, General Barrow, commander of 'Northforce', a British army of occupation, handed over Syria to the French. By this time the writ of the British and French governments ran over most of the Middle East, the former having withdrawn its support for Feisal's Arab regime in Damascus. These developments were formalized in a peace-making process that was to take longer than the war itself. Peace was not formally concluded with Turkey until the Treaty of Lausanne was signed in 1923, although the mandate system, which reflected the pattern of administration already established by Britain and France, was established by the San Remo Conference in 1920. Much to the anger of the Arabs, France was allocated the whole of Syria while Britain received Palestine and Mesopotamia.

There is little doubt that the course of wartime political events did not run as smoothly as operations on the ground. Although the British had been forced to make concessions to Sherif Hussein in order to secure the military support of the Arabs, their real intentions had been exposed even before the Palestine campaign had begun. Secret discussions held in 1916 between Britain and France on the shape of the post-war Middle East had been embodied in the Sykes–Picot agreement, which carved out spheres of influence for the two powers at the end of the war, recognizing the French interest in Syria and the Lebanon and also Britain's influential position in Mesopotamia. There was greater international interest in the fate of Palestine than in any other part of the region because of the unique standing of the holy city of Jerusalem, the claims of the Arabs and the emerging Jewish question. In order to recognize the existence of different Arab and Jewish interests, and the need to mediate between them, a trusteeship – to be exercised by Britain – was proposed. In practice it represented an extension of British colonial power (and a denial of Arab interests) in a new and more acceptable guise.

Arab demands were only partially recognized by the proposed creation of a new kingdom of Transjordan, but in other respects their legitimate nationalist aspirations were disregarded in this secret agreement. Shortly afterwards the British took another decisive step that was to erect a more permanent barrier to Arab objectives and give rise to the political and military instability that has plagued the area in the post-1945 period and is likely to continue to do so. The Balfour Declaration of 1917, which gave British support to the creation of a Jewish national home in Palestine, was viewed as a necessary response to the growing political importance of the Zionist movement in Europe and America as well as in Britain. It was also seen as another useful vehicle for extending British influence in the area. The declaration was to stimulate the mass migration of Jewish people to Palestine in the inter-war period and led directly to the creation of the state of Israel in 1948.

However, Britain's immediate post-war concern – which was shared by France – was to consolidate its position in the Middle East and fill the vacuum left by the collapse of the Ottoman empire after four hundred years of continuous rule. Cairo became the centre of Britain's new Middle East empire, although Egyptian nationalists secured a degree of independence within an agreed framework which recognized vital British imperial interests. A British military administration was established in Palestine during the final months of the war, while the French landed troops at Beirut late in 1918, occupying the surrounding coastal area. From 1920, Mesopotamia was ruled by an Anglo-Indian administration under a League of Nations mandate. As the supreme power in the region, Britain could pay lip-service to the principle of self-rule while doing everything in its power to obstruct it. Instability persisted for much of the inter-war period, but the Arabs were powerless, either at the Paris Peace Conference of 1919–20 or locally on the ground, to reverse the tide of events.

The League of Nations formally acknowledged the new Anglo-French ascendancy in the Middle East when it agreed in 1920 to the creation of five new states – Syria, Lebanon, Transjordan, Iraq and Palestine – which were to be administered under a British or French mandate in cooperation with the Arabs. The Hejaz province was recognized as a separate kingdom – all that was left of Sherif Hussein's dream of independent Arab rule in the Middle East – but even this autonomous entity soon disappeared. Occupied by Hussein's old rival Ibn Saud of the Nejd, after a protracted war (1919–25), the new kingdom of the Hejaz and Nejd was renamed Saudi Arabia in 1932.

Britain's imperial presence was almost as transient and did not survive the Second World War and its aftermath, although it had secured some key strategic interests for a generation or so. However, these gains had been achieved at a price, for Britain was to suffer the continuing enmity of the Arabs, who felt that their legitimate aspirations had been cynically betrayed when imperial ambition took precedence over the moral commitments embodied in a successful wartime alliance.

In Palestine it became clear that the price of a permanent imperial presence was likely to be high, as violence flared soon after the end of the war. The conflicting claims of Jews and Arabs eventually led to the development of open warfare between them in 1937 and was to lead to the ending of the British mandate in 1948. The territorial claims of the two groups still remain unreconciled and their relationship continues to be characterized by sporadic violence and discord. The success of the Allied campaign in the Middle East between 1914 and 1918, which helped to bring down an empire, was never matched by its political outcomes. The new state structures that were created left too many difficult issues unresolved and the result has been permanent instability in a region that continues to be a major source of international tension and conflict.

# *Notes*

## CHAPTER 1    IMPERIAL WAR AIMS

1. Two good, recent general histories are: Martin Gilbert, *First World War* (London, 1994); John Keegan, *The First World War* (new edition, London, 1999).
2. Jonathan Newell, 'Allenby and the Palestine Campaign', in Brian J. Bond, *The First World War and British Military History* (Oxford, 1991), pp. 189–226.
3. Douglas A. Farnie, *East and West of Suez: The Suez Canal in History, 1854–1956* (Oxford, 1969).
4. P.J. Vatikiotis, *The History of Modern Egypt* (London, 1991).
5. Yigal Sheffy, *British Military Intelligence in the Palestine Campaign, 1914–1918* (London, 1998), ch. 1.
6. Timothy W. Church, *Italo-Turkish Diplomacy and the War over Libya, 1911–12* (New York, 1990).
7. Alan Palmer, *The Decline and Fall of the Ottoman Empire* (London, 1995).
8. A.P. Wavell, *The Palestine Campaigns* (London, 1928), p. 19.
9. David Nicholle, *The Ottoman Army, 1914–18* (London, 1994), p. 9.

## CHAPTER 2    THE DEFENCE OF THE SUEZ CANAL

1. Farnie, op. cit.
2. Harry Hopwood papers, 7403–29 (National Army Museum: NAM).
3. Sheffy, pp. 39–47.
4. George MacMunn and Cyril Falls, *Military Operations Egypt and Palestine. From the Outbreak of War with Germany to June 1917* (London, 1928), p. 22.
5. Ibid., p. 21.
6. Ibid., p. 38.

7. Ibid., p. 40.
8. Friedrich Kress von Kressenstein, *Zwischen Kaukasus und Sinai* (Berlin, 1921), vol. I, pp. 2–18.
9. Sheffy, p. 56.
10. Wavell, *Palestine Campaigns*, p. 43.
11. Sheffy, p. 106.
12. T.E. Lawrence, *The Letters of T.E. Lawrence*, selected and edited by Malcolm Brown (London, 1988), p. 75. All references to the Lawrence *Letters* are to this edition unless otherwise indicated.
13. Quoted in MacMunn and Falls, p. 54.
14. Sheffy, p. 62.
15. Friedrich Kress von Kressenstein, 'The Campaign in Palestine from the Enemy's Side', *Journal of the Royal United Service Institution*, LXVII (1922), 47–59.
16. MacMunn and Falls, p. 77.
17. Ibid.
18. Harold F.M. Clark papers, 9403–74 (NAM).
19. MacMunn and Falls, p. 78.
20. Ibid., p. 85.
21. Ibid., p. 96.
22. Wavell, *Palestine Campaigns*, p. 41.
23. Sir William Robertson, *The Military Correspondence of Field Marshal Sir William Robertson December 1915–February 1918*, edited by David R. Woodward (London, 1989).
24. William Barron, Diary, 7408–63 (NAM).
25. Ibid.
26. Lieutenant J.W. McPherson, letters, 80/25/1 (Imperial War Museum: IWM).
27. MacMunn and Falls, p. 162.
28. Robertson, *Military Correspondence*, p. 71.
29. Ibid.
30. McPherson, letters (IWM).
31. MacMunn and Falls, p. 179.
32. Otto Liman von Sanders, *Fünf Jahre Türkei* (Berlin, [1922]), p. 183: *Five Years in Turkey*, translated by C. Reichmann (Annapolis, Md, 1927).
33. Quoted in MacMunn and Falls, p. 203.
34. Dawnay papers, 69/21/2 (IWM).
35. MacMunn and Falls, p. 185.
36. Ibid., p. 189.
37. Ibid., p. 195.
38. Ibid.
39. Robert Wilson, *Palestine 1917. Robert Henry Wilson*, edited by Helen Millgate (Tunbridge Wells, 1987), p. 49.
40. MacMunn and Falls, p. 201.
41. Robertson, *Military Correspondence*, pp. 73–4.

CHAPTER 3    THE ARAB REVOLT

1. Edouard Brémond, *Le Hedjaz dans la guerre mondiale* (Paris, 1931).
2. Sir Henry McMahon, *Correspondence between Sir Henry McMahon and the Sherif Hussein of Mecca* (London, HMSO, 1939).
3. MacMunn and Falls, p. 217.
4. T.E. Lawrence, 'The Evolution of a Revolt', *Army Quarterly* 1 (1920), 59.
5. The most detailed biography to date, which is based on extensive archival research, is by Jeremy M. Wilson, *Lawrence of Arabia. The Authorised Biography of T.E. Lawrence* (London, 1989). Another recent study, *The Golden Warrior. The Life and Legend of Lawrence of Arabia* (London, 1990), was produced by Lawrence James.
6. Lawrence, *Letters*, p. 84.
7. J. Wilson, p. 295.
8. MacMunn and Falls, p. 232.
9. Brian Gardner, *Allenby* (London, 1956), p. 134.
10. T.E. Lawrence, *Seven Pillars of Wisdom. A Triumph* (London, 1939), vol. I, p. 98.
11. Quoted in J. Wilson, p. 325.
12. Ibid., p. 326.
13. Lawrence, *Letters*, p. 91.
14. MacMunn and Falls, p. 233.
15. Lawrence, *Seven Pillars of Wisdom*, vol. I, p. 134.
16. Quoted in J. Wilson, p. 344.
17. Ibid., pp. 346–7.
18. Ibid.
19. Lawrence, *Seven Pillars of Wisdom*, vol. I, pp. 144–5.
20. J. Wilson, p. 350.
21. Lawrence, *Seven Pillars of Wisdom*, vol. I, p. 169.
22. Ibid., p. 141.
23. Ibid., p. 179.
24. Quoted in J. Wilson, p. 380.
25. Lawrence, *Seven Pillars of Wisdom*, vol. I, p. 232.
26. Ibid., p. 200.
27. J. Wilson, p. 387.
28. Lawrence, *Letters*, pp. 109–10.
29. Quoted in J. Wilson, p. 393.
30. Ibid., p. 397.
31. Lawrence, *Seven Pillars of Wisdom*, vol. I, p. 230.
32. Ibid., vol. I, p. 233.
33. Ibid., vol. I, p. 254.
34. Quoted in J. Wilson, p. 408.
35. Ibid., p. 410.
36. Gardner, p. 138.

CHAPTER 4      ADVANCE THROUGH SINAI

1. Robertson, *Military Correspondence*, p. 96.
2. Noel Drury papers, 7607–69 (NAM).
3. McGrigor papers (IWM).
4. Kress von Kressenstein, 'The Campaign in Palestine', 51.
5. Dawnay papers, 69/21/2 (IWM).
6. MacMunn and Falls, pp. 257–8.
7. Dawnay papers (IWM).
8. Hopwood papers, 7403–29, (NAM).
9. MacMunn and Falls, p. 265; S.H. Kershaw, 'Sidelights on the Battle of Rafa 9th of January, 1917', *Army Quarterly* 20 (1930), 78–85.
10. MacMunn and Falls, p. 267.
11. Ibid.
12. Quoted in ibid., p. 268.
13. R. Wilson, p. 73.
14. Robertson, *Military Correspondence*, p. 138.
15. Ibid.
16. Kress von Kressenstein, quoted in MacMunn and Falls, p. 276.
17. Kress von Kressenstein, 'The Campaign in Palestine', 51.
18. MacMunn and Falls, p. 321.
19. Ibid., p. 289.
20. Ibid., p. 284. A detailed account of the Gaza battles from an Australian perspective may be found in Henry S. Gullett, *The A.I.F. in Sinai and Palestine. The Official History of Australia in the War of 1914–1918*, vol. VII (Sydney, 1944), pp. 262ff.
21. MacMunn and Falls, p. 293.
22. Ibid., p. 311.
23. Ibid., p. 312.
24. Ibid., p. 317.
25. Ibid., p. 318; see also Robertson, *Military Correspondence*, p. 165.
26. MacMunn and Falls, p. 318.
27. Ibid., p. 320.
28. A.J. Hill, *Chauvel of the Light Horse. A Biography of General Sir Harry Chauvel* (Melbourne, 1978), p. 105.
29. MacMunn and Falls, p. 319.
30. Ibid., p. 326.
31. Ibid., p. 327.
32. Ibid., p. 330.
33. Kress von Kressenstein, 'The Campaign in Palestine', 53.
34. MacMunn and Falls, p. 343.
35. Ibid., pp. 348–9.
36. Ibid., p. 347.
37. Kress von Kressenstein, 'The Campaign in Palestine', 53.

38. Marquess of Anglesey, *A History of the British Cavalry 1816 to 1919*, vol. 5: *Egypt, Palestine and Syria, 1914–1919* (London, 1994), p. 105.
39. Clark papers (NAM).
40. Edmund H.H. Allenby, *A Brief Record of the Advance of the Egyptian Expeditionary Force under the Command of General Sir Edmund H.H. Allenby. July 1917 to October 1918*, compiled from official sources (London, HMSO, 1919), p. 1.
41. Sheffy, p. 266.
42. Wilson, p. 81.
43. MacMunn and Falls, p. 355.
44. Arthur Fletcher papers (IWM).
45. MacMunn and Falls, p. 368.
46. Gardner, p. 110.
47. Archibald Wavell, *Allenby. Soldier and Statesman* (London, 1946), p. 153.
48. Wavell, *Allenby*, p. 154.
49. David Lloyd George, *War Memoirs* (London, 1938), vol. I, pp. 1089–90; see also Matthew D. Hughes, *Allenby and British Strategy in the Middle East, 1917–1919* (London, 1999).

CHAPTER 5    VICTORY AT GAZA

1. Cyril Falls, *Military Operations Egypt and Palestine. From June 1917 to the End of the War* (London, HMSO, 1930), part I, pp. 63–5.
2. Fletcher papers, 78/9/1 (IWM).
3. Wavell, *Allenby*, p. 254.
4. Gardner, p. 125.
5. Wavell, *Allenby*, p. 157.
6. Gullett, p. 357.
7. Gardner, p. 117.
8. Drury papers, 7007/69 (IWM).
9. Wavell, *Allenby*, p. 165.
10. Quoted in Gardner, p. 127.
11. Dawnay papers, 69/21/2 (IWM).
12. Falls, *Military Operations*, part I, p. 33.
13. Ibid., p. 11.
14. Allenby, p. 10.
15. Falls, *Military Operations*, part I, p. 15.
16. Ibid.
17. Robertson, *Military Correspondence*, p. 214.
18. Ibid., p. 262.
19. Dawnay papers (IWM).
20. A.W. Lawrence (ed.), *T.E. Lawrence by his Friends* (London, 1937), p. 145.
21. Richard Meinertzhagen, *Army Diary, 1899–1926* (Edinburgh, [1960]), entry for 10 October 1917.

22. Dawnay papers (IWM).

23. Allenby, p. 2.

24. Falls, *Military Operations*, part I, p. 27.

25. Kress von Kressenstein, 'The Campaign in Palestine', 54–5.

26. Ibid., 55.

27. Dawnay papers (IWM).

28. Ibid.

29. Falls, *Military Operations*, part I, p. 36.

30. F.V. Blunt diary, 94/5/1 (IWM).

31. Falls, *Military Operations*, part I, p. 39.

32. Ibid., p. 41.

33. Wavell, *Allenby*, p. 173.

34. F.V. Blunt diary (IWM).

35. Falls, *Military Operations*, part I, p. 36.

36. Quoted in ibid., p. 47.

37. F.V. Blunt diary (IWM).

38. Turkish reports quoted in Falls, *Military Operations*, part I, p. 62.

39. Ibid., p. 51.

40. Blunt papers (IWM).

41. Hubert Earney papers (IWM).

42. Falls, *Military Operations*, part I, p. 65.

43. Harry Milson papers (IWM).

44. Falls, *Military Operations*, part I, p. 68.

45. Wavell, *Palestine Campaigns*, p. 129.

46. Dawnay papers (IWM).

47. Allenby, p. 4.

48. Falls, *Military Operations*, part I, p. 92.

49. Ibid.

50. Blunt papers (IWM).

51. Dawnay papers (IWM).

52. Falls, *Military Operations*, part I, p. 94.

53. Drury papers (NAM).

54. Falls, *Military Operations*, part I, p. 116.

55. Milson papers (IWM), p. 55.

56. Kress von Kressentein, quoted in Falls, *Military Operations*, part I, p. 77.

57. Falls, *Military Operations*, part I, p. 75.

58. Dawnay papers (IWM).

59. Gardner, p. 153.

60. Quoted in Falls, *Military Operations*, part I, p. 123.

61. Alan Williams scrapbooks, 84/55/1A (IWM).

62. Falls, *Military Operations*, part I, p. 122.

63. Ibid., p. 123.

64. Alan Williams papers (IWM).

65. Falls, *Military Operations*, part I, p. 129.

66. Gardner, p. 154.

67. Falls, *Military Operations*, part I, p. 140.
68. Ibid., p. 180.
69. Dawnay papers (IWM).
70. Ibid.

### CHAPTER 6    THE FALL OF JERUSALEM

1. Blunt papers, 94/5/1 (IWM).
2. C.W. Battine papers, 90/37/1 (IWM).
3. Ibid.
4. Dawnay papers, 69/21/2 (IWM).
5. Falls, *Military Operations*, part I, p. 197.
6. Allenby, p. 8.
7. J. Wilson papers, 84/52/1 (IWM).
8. Wavell, *Allenby*, p. 193.
9. Wilson papers (IWM).
10. Kress von Kressenstein, 'The Campaign in Palestine', 59.
11. Bayley papers (IWM).
12. Ibid.
13. Wilson papers (IWM).
14. Lawrence, *Letters*, p. 131.
15. Dawnay papers (IWM).
16. Edmund Allenby papers (Centre for Military Archives, King's College, London).
17. Quoted in Gardner, p. 160.
18. Wavell, *Palestine Campaigns*, p. 167.
19. Battine papers (IWM).
20. Allenby, p. 11.
21. Ibid.
22. Falls, *Military Operations*, part I, pp. 273–4.
23. Ibid., p. 259.

### CHAPTER 7    THE ARAB ADVANCE

1. Gardner, p. 139.
2. Ibid.
3. Quoted in J. Wilson, pp. 423–4.
4. Falls, *Military Operations*, part II, p. 396.
5. Basil H. Liddell Hart, *T.E. Lawrence. In Arabia and After* (London, 1945), p. 59.
6. Falls, *Military Operations*, part II, p. 406.
7. J. Wilson, p. 439.
8. Lawrence, *Letters*, pp. 125–6.

9. Lawrence, *Seven Pillars of Wisdom*, vol. II, p. 394.
10. Lawrence, *Letters*, p. 129.
11. Lawrence, *Seven Pillars of Wisdom*, vol. II, p. 433.
12. Lawrence, *Letters*, p. 129.
13. Falls, *Military Operations*, part II, p. 409.
14. Liddell Hart, *T.E. Lawrence*, p. 113.
15. Quoted in J. Wilson, p. 481.
16. Robertson, *Military Correspondence*, p. 267.
17. Dawnay papers (IWM).
18. Falls, *Military Operations*, part I, p. 295.
19. Ibid., p. 297.
20. Ibid.
21. Robertson, *Military Correspondence*, p. 274.
22. Quoted in Falls, *Military Operations*, part I, p. 298.
23. Ibid., p. 299.
24. Robertson, *Military Correspondence*, p. 280.
25. Wavell, *Allenby*, p. 204.
26. Quoted in Falls, *Military Operations*, part I, p. 305.
27. Ibid., p. 310.
28. Battine papers (IWM).
29. Wavell, *Allenby*, p. 205.
30. Battine papers (IWM).
31. C.T. Atkinson, 'General Liman von Sanders on his Experiences in Palestine', *Army Quarterly* 3 (1921–2), 260.
32. Quoted in J. Wilson, p. 491.
33. Lawrence, *Letters*, p. 142.
34. Dawnay papers (IWM).
35. Allenby, p. 18.
36. Falls, *Military Operations*, part I, p. 335.
37. Atkinson, 263.
38. Quoted in J. Wilson, p. 499.
39. Allenby, p. 20.
40. Quoted in Atkinson, 265.
41. Ibid., 266.
42. Falls, *Military Operations*, part I, p. 392.

### CHAPTER 8    TIME TO RECOUP

1. Wavell, *Allenby*, p. 223.
2. Atkinson, 269.
3. Wavell, *Palestine Campaigns*, p. 183.
4. Quoted in J. Wilson, p. 501.
5. Falls, *Military Operations*, part II, p. 420.

6.  Ibid., p. 423.
7.  Wavell, *Allenby*, pp. 216–17.
8.  R. Wilson, p. 108.
9.  Battine papers (IWM).
10. Quoted in J. Wilson, p. 502.
11. Atkinson, 267.
12. Ibid., 268.
13. Falls, *Military Operations*, part II, p. 444.
14. Ibid., p. 454.
15. Dawnay papers (IWM).
16. Ibid.
17. Atkinson, 263.
18. Ibid.
19. Falls, *Military Operations*, part II, p. 445.
20. Quoted in Atkinson, 261.
21. Ibid., 262.
22. Ibid., 269.
23. Allenby, p. 25.
24. Wavell, *Allenby*, pp. 224–5.
25. Quoted in J. Wilson, p. 542.
26. Charles Harvey, 'Gallop to Aleppo', *Journal of the Royal United Service Institution* 113 (1968), 155.
27. Allenby, p. 27.
28. Falls, *Military Operations*, part II, p. 467.
29. J. Wilson, p. 546.
30. Quoted in Liddell Hart, *T.E. Lawrence*, pp. 336–7.
31. Ibid., p. 337.
32. Quoted in Falls, *Military Operations*, part II, p. 468.
33. Ibid., p. 469.
34. Quoted in Gardner, p. 196.

### CHAPTER 9     THE BATTLE OF MEGIDDO

1.  Harvey, 155.
2.  Falls, *Military Operations*, part II, pp. 472–3; see also Cyril Falls, *Armageddon* (London, 1964).
3.  Allenby, p. 28.
4.  Harvey, 155.
5.  Wilson papers (IWM).
6.  Harvey, 155.
7.  Falls, *Military Operations*, part II, p. 487.
8.  Atkinson, 269–70.
9.  Falls, Military Operations, part II, p. 488.

10. Allenby, p. 28.
11. Harvey, 153.
12. Falls, *Military Operations*, part II, p. 526.
13. Atkinson, 272–3.
14. Harvey, 155.
15. Ibid.
16. Falls, *Military Operations*, part II, p. 502.
17. Harvey, 153.
18. Ibid., 155.
19. Ibid., 153.
20. Ibid., 155–6.
21. Allenby papers (Centre for Military Archives, King's College, London).
22. Quoted in J. Wilson, p. 549.
23. Ibid.
24. Wavell, *Palestine Campaigns*, p. 224.
25. Quoted in J. Wilson, p. 554.
26. Ibid., p. 555.
27. Ibid., pp. 556–7.
28. Ibid., p. 557.
29. Ibid.
30. Lawrence, *Seven Pillars of Wisdom*, vol. II, p. 656.
31. Quoted in J. Wilson, p. 560.
32. Harvey, 154.
33. Atkinson, 274.
34. Allenby papers (Centre for Military Archives, King's College, London).
35. Quoted in Gardner, p. 191.

CHAPTER 10    PURSUIT TO ALEPPO

1. Falls, *Military Operations*, part II, p. 598.
2. Ibid.
3. R. Wilson, pp. 145–6.
4. Harvey, 154.
5. Falls, *Military Operations*, part II, p. 604.
6. Ibid., p. 610.
7. Gardner, p. 193.
8. Falls, *Military Operations*, part II, p. 611.
9. Quoted in ibid., pp. 611–12.
10. Quoted in ibid., p. 613.
11. Ibid., p. 616.
12. Ibid.
13. Harvey, 156.
14. Falls, *Military Operations*, part II, p. 624.

15. Ibid., p. 619.
16. Gwynne Dyer, 'The Turkish Armistice of 1918', *Middle Eastern Studies* 8 (1972), 336.
17. Falls, *Military Operations*, part II, p. 624; S. Tanvir Wasti, 'The Defence of Medina, 1916–19', *Middle Eastern Studies* 27 (1991), 642–53.
18. Falls, *Military Operations*, part II, p. 645.

# *Bibliography*

MANUSCRIPTS

*Imperial War Museum (IWM)*

H.V. Bailey papers
C.W. Battine papers
H. Bayley papers
F.V. Blunt papers
Guy Dawnay papers
Hubert Earney papers
Arthur Fletcher papers
F.S. Hammond papers
A.M. McGrigor papers
J.W. McPherson letters
Harry Milson papers
Alan Williams papers
J. Wilson papers

*Liddell Hart Centre for Military Archives, King's College, London*

Edmund Allenby papers
William Bartholomew papers

*National Army Museum (NAM)*

William Barron diary
Harold Clark papers
Noel Drury papers
Harry Hopwood papers

BOOKS

Abdullah, *Memoirs* (London, 1950)

Aldington, Richard, *Lawrence of Arabia. A Biographical Enquiry* (London, 1955)

Allenby, Edmund H.H., *A Brief Record of the Advance of the Egyptian Expeditionary Force under the Command of General Sir Edmund H.H. Allenby. July 1917 to October 1918*, compiled from official sources (London, HMSO, 1919)

Anglesey, Marquess of, *A History of the British Cavalry 1816 to 1919*, vol. 5: *Egypt, Palestine and Syria, 1914–1919* (London, 1994)

Arthur, Sir George, *Sir John Maxwell* (London, 1932)

Badcock, G.E., *A History of the Transport Services of the Egyptian Expeditionary Force, 1916–1918* (London, 1925)

Barker, A.J., *The Mesopotamian Campaign of 1914–1918* (London, 1967)

Barrett, J.W., and Deane, P.E., *The Australian Army Medical Corps in Egypt* (London, 1918)

Barrow, George de S., *Two Cavalry Episodes from the Palestine Campaign, 1917–1918* (London, 1937)

——*The Fire of Life* (London, 1943)

Bell, Gertrude, *The Arab War. Confidential Information for GHQ Cairo from Gertrude L. Bell. Dispatches for the Arab Bulletin* (London, 1940)

Berrie, G.L., *Under Furred Hats (6th Australian Light Horse Regiment)* (Sydney, 1919)

Blackwell, F., and Douglas, D.R., *The Story of the 3rd Australian Light Horse Regiment* (Adelaide, [1950])

Blaser, Bernard, *Kilts across the Jordan: being experiences and impressions with the Second Battalion 'London Scottish' in Palestine* (London, 1926)

Blenkinsop, Sir L.J., and Rainey, J.W., *History of the Great War based on Official Documents. Veterinary Series* (London, 1925)

Bonham-Carter, Victor, *Soldier True. The Life and Times of Field Marshal Sir William Robertson* (London, 1963)

Bostock, Henry P., *The Great Ride. The Diary of a Light Horse Brigade Scout: World War I* (London, 1982)

Bourne, G.H., *The History of the 2nd Light Horse Regiment, Australian Force: August 1914–April 1919* [n.d.]

Brémond, Edouard, *Le Hedjaz dans la guerre mondiale* (Paris, 1931)

Brown, Malcolm, and Cave, Julia, *A Touch of Genius. The Life of T.E. Lawrence* (London, 1988)

Brown, W. Sorley, *My War Diary (1914–1919). Recollections of Gallipoli, Lemnos, Egypt and Palestine* (Galashiels, [1941])

Brugger, S., *The Australians in Egypt, 1914–1919* (Melbourne, 1980)

Buchan, John, *A History of the Great War*, 4 vols (London, 1921–2)

Bullock, David, *Allenby's War. The Palestine-Arabian Campaigns, 1916–1918* (London, 1988)

Callwell, Charles E., *Field-Marshal Sir Henry Wilson. His Life and Diaries*, 2 vols. (London, 1927)

Charmley, John, *Lord Lloyd and the Decline of the British Empire* (London, 1987)

Church, Timothy W., *Italo-Turkish Diplomacy and the War over Libya, 1911–12* (New York, 1990)

Connell, John, *Wavell. Scholar and Soldier* (London, 1964)

Djemal Pasha, *Memories of a Turkish Statesman, 1913–1919* (London, 1922)

Falls, Cyril, *Military Operations Egypt and Palestine. From June 1917 to the End of the War*, 2 parts (London, 1930)

——*Armageddon* (London, 1964)

Farnie, Douglas A., *East and West of Suez. The Suez Canal in History, 1854–1956* (Oxford, 1969)

Fox, Frank, *The History of the Royal Gloucestershire Hussars Yeomanry, 1898–1922; the great cavalry campaign in Palestine* (London, 1923)

Gardner, Brian, *Allenby* (London, 1965)

Gilbert, Martin, *Jerusalem. Rebirth of a City* (London, 1985)

——*First World War* (London, 1994)

Graves, Philip, *The Life of Sir Percy Cox* (London, 1941)

Graves, Robert, *Lawrence and the Arabs* (London, 1927)

Gullett, Henry S., *The A.I.F. in Sinai and Palestine. The Official History of Australia in the War of 1914–1918*, vol. VII (Sydney, 1944)

Gullett, Henry S., Barrett, C., and Barker, D., *Australia in Palestine* (Sydney, 1919)

Hickey, Michael, *Gallipoli* (London, 1995)

Hill, A.J., *Chauvel of the Light Horse. A Biography of General Sir Harry Chauvel* (Melbourne, 1978)

Hughes, Matthew D., *Allenby and British Strategy in the Middle East, 1917–1919* (London, 1999)

James, Lawrence, *The Golden Warrior. The Life and Legend of Lawrence of Arabia* (London, 1990)

——*Imperial Warrior. The Life and Times of Field Marshal Viscount Allenby, 1861–1936* (London, 1993)

James, Robert Rhodes, *Gallipoli* (London, 1965)

Jones, H.A., *The War in the Air*, vol. V (Oxford, 1935)

Kearsey, A., *The Operations in Egypt and Palestine August, 1914, to June, 1917*, 3rd edition (Aldershot, [1937])

Kedourie, E., *England and the Middle East. The Destruction of the Ottoman Empire 1914–1921* (London, 1956)

——*In the Anglo-Arab Labyrinth. The McMahon Correspondence and its Interpretation, 1914–39* (Cambridge, 1976)

Keegan, John, *The First World War*, new edition (London, 1999)

Kent, M.S. (ed.), *The Great Powers and the Ottoman Empire* (London, 1984)

Kinross, Patrick, *Atatürk. The Rebirth of a Nation* (London, 1964)

Knightley, Phillip, and Simpson, Colin, *The Secret Lives of Lawrence of Arabia* (London, 1969)

Kress von Kressenstein, Friedrich, *Zwischen Kaukasus und Sinai*, vol. I (Berlin, 1921)

Lawrence, A.W. (ed.), *T.E. Lawrence by his Friends* (London, 1937)

Lawrence, T.E., *Revolt in the Desert* (London, 1927)

——*Seven Pillars of Wisdom. A Triumph*, 2 vols. (London, 1939)

——*The Letters of T.E. Lawrence*, edited by David Garnett (London, 1938)

——*Secret Despatches from Arabia*, edited by A.W. Lawrence (London, 1939)

——*The Home Letters of T.E. Lawrence and his Brothers*, edited by M.R. Lawrence (London, 1954)

——*The Letters of T.E. Lawrence*, selected and edited by Malcolm Brown (London, 1988)

Leslie, Shane, *Mark Sykes. His Life and Letters* (London, 1923)

Liddell Hart, Basil H., *T.E. Lawrence. In Arabia and After* (London, 1945)

——*A History of the First World War* (London, 1970)

Liman von Sanders, Otto, *Funf Jahre Turkei* (Berlin, [1922]); *Five Years in Turkey*, translated by C. Reichmann (Annapolis, Md, 1927)

Livesey, Anthony, *Great Battles of World War I* (London, 1989)

Lloyd George, David, *War Memoirs*, 6 vols. (London, 1938)

McMahon, Sir Henry, *Correspondence between Sir Henry McMahon and the Sherif Hussein of Mecca* (London, HMSO, 1939)

MacMunn, George, and Falls, Cyril, *Military Operations Egypt and Palestine. From the Outbreak of War with Germany to June 1917* (London, 1928)

Mallett, Ross, 'The Interplay between Technology, Tactics and Organisation in the first AIF', MA thesis (Australian Defence Force Academy, 1999)

Mansfield, Peter, *The Ottoman Empire and its Successors* (London, 1973)

——*The Arabs*, 2nd edition (London, 1985)

Massey, W.T., *The Desert Campaigns* (London, 1918)

——*How Jerusalem was won, being the record of Allenby's campaign in Palestine* (London, 1919)

——*Allenby's Final Triumph* (London, 1920)

May, Ernest, *Signal Corporal. The Story of the 2nd Battalion London Irish Rifles in the First World War* (London, 1972)

Meinertzhagen, Richard, *Army Diary, 1899–1926* (Edinburgh, [1960])

——*Middle East Diary, 1917–56* (London, 1959)

Mills, Fred, *Great Uncle Fred's War. An Illustrated Diary, 1917–20*, edited by Alan Pryor and Jennifer K. Woods (Whitstable, Kent, 1985)

Moberley, F.J., *The Campaign in Mesopotamia*, 3 vols. (London, 1923)

Monroe, Elizabeth, *Britain's Moment in the Middle East, 1914–56* (London, 1963)

Murray, Sir Archibald, *Sir Archibald Murray's Despatches. June 1916 to June 1917* (London, 1920)

Nicolle, David, *The Ottoman Army, 1914–18* (London, 1994)

Palmer, Alan, *The Decline and Fall of the Ottoman Empire* (London, 1995)

Powles, C. Guy, *The New Zealanders in Sinai and Palestine* (London, 1922)

Preston, R.M.P., *The Desert Mounted Corps. An Account of the Cavalry Operations in Palestine and Syria, 1917–18* (London, 1921)

Robertson, Sir William, *Soldiers and Statesmen*, 2 vols. (London, 1926)

——*The Military Correspondence of Field Marshal Sir William Robertson December 1915–February 1918*, edited by David R. Woodward (London, 1989)

Savage, R., *Allenby of Armageddon* (London, 1925)

Sheffy, Yigal, *British Military Intelligence in the Palestine Campaign, 1914–1918* (London, 1998)

Shepherd, Naomi, *Ploughing Sand. British Rule in Palestine, 1917–1948* (London, 1999)

Slater, Guy, *My Warrior Sons. The Borton Family Diary 1914–1918* (London, 1973)

Smuts, Jan C., *Selections from the Smuts Papers*, edited by W.K. Hancock and Jan van der Poel, vol. III: *June 1910 to November 1918* (Cambridge, 1966)

Stein, L., *The Balfour Declaration* (London, 1961)

Storrs, Ronald, *Orientations* (London, 1944)

Tauber, Eliezer, *The Arab Movements in World War I* (London, 1993)

Thomas, L., *With Lawrence in Arabia* (London, 1962)

Thompson, R.R., *The Fifty-Second (Lowland) Division 1914–1918* (Glasgow, 1923)

Townshend, A.P., *My Campaign in Mesopotamia* (London, 1920)

Travers, Tim, *Gallipoli 1915* (London, 2001)

Trumpener, U., *Germany and the Ottoman Empire 1914–1918* (Princeton, Md, 1968)

Vatikiotis, P.J., *The History of Modern Egypt* (London, 1991)

Verrier, Anthony (ed.), *Agents of Empire. Anglo-Zionist Intelligence Operations 1915–1919. Brigadier Walter Gribbon, Aaron Aaronsohn and the NILI ring* (London, 1995)

Wallach, Janet, *Desert Queen. The Extraordinary Life of Gertrude Bell* (London, 1997)

Wasserstein, Bernard, *The British in Palestine. The Mandatory Government and the Arab-Jewish Conflict, 1917–29* (London, 1978)

Wavell, Archibald, *The Palestine Campaigns* (London, 1928)

——*Allenby. Soldier and Statesman* (London, 1946)

Wilson, Sir Henry, *The Military Correspondence of Field Marshal Sir Henry Wilson, 1918–1922*, edited by Keith Jeffery (Army Records Society, London, 1985)

Wilson, Jeremy, *Lawrence of Arabia. The Authorised Biography of T.E. Lawrence* (London, 1989)

——*T.E. Lawrence* (exhibition catalogue, National Portrait Gallery, London, 1968)

Wilson, Robert, *Palestine 1917. Robert Henry Wilson*, edited by Helen Millgate (Tunbridge Wells, 1987)

Wingate, Ronald, *Wingate of the Sudan* (London, 1955)

Winstone, H.V.F., *The Illicit Adventure. The Story of Political and Military Intelligence in the Middle East from 1898 to 1926* (London, 1982)

Wintringham, J.W., *With the Lincolnshire Yeomanry in Egypt and Palestine 1914–1918* (Grimsby, 1979)

Yardley, Michael, *T.E. Lawrence. A Biography* (London, 2000)

## ARTICLES

Atkinson, C.T., 'General Liman von Sanders on his Experiences in Palestine', *Army Quarterly* 3 (1921–2), 257–75

Chipperfield, Stanley, 'I was there. When they all took Jerusalem', *The Observer*, 16 January 1977

Croft, John, 'Palestine 1918', *Journal of the Society for Army Historical Research* 70 (1992), 33–45

Dyer, Gwynne, 'The Turkish Armistice of 1918', *Middle Eastern Studies* 8 (1972), 143–78, 313–48

Green, Howard, 'Jerusalem – 1917', *Army Quarterly* 92 (1966), 204–11

Harvey, Charles, 'Gallop to Aleppo', *Journal of the Royal United Service Institution* 113 (1968), 153–7

Kershaw, S.H., 'Sidelights on the Battle of Rafa 9th of January, 1917', *Army Quarterly* 20 (1930), 78–85

——'The Battle of Romani, 4th of August, 1916', *Army Quarterly* 37 (1938), 84–95

Kress von Kressenstein, Friedrich, 'The Campaign in Palestine from the Enemy's Side', *Journal of the Royal United Service Institution* 67 (1922), 503–13

Lawrence, T.E., 'The Evolution of a Revolt', *Army Quarterly* 1 (1920), 55–69

Liman von Sanders, Otto, 'The Turkish Operations in Palestine, 19th–23rd September, 1918', *Journal of the Royal United Service Institution* 66 (1921), 326–36

Newall, Jonathan, 'Allenby and the Palestine Campaign', in Brian J. Bond, *The First World War and British Military History* (Oxford, 1991), 189–226

Reid, Brian Holden, 'T.E. Lawrence and his Biographers', in Brian J. Bond, *The First World War and British Military History* (Oxford, 1991), 227–59

Sheffy, Yigal, 'Institutionalised Deception and Perception Reinforcement. Allenby's Campaigns in Palestine', *Intelligence and National Security* 5 (1990), 173–236

Wasti, S. Tanvir, 'The Defence of Medina, 1916–19', *Middle Eastern Studies* 27 (1991), 642–53

Wavell, A.P., 'The Strategy of the Campaigns of the Egyptian Expeditionary Force', *Army Quarterly* 3 (1921–2), 235–49

# Index

Ranks and titles are generally the most senior mentioned in the text